The Brief English Handbook

Second Edition

Edward A. Dornan
Orange Coast College

Charles W. Dawe
Orange Coast College

 Little, Brown and Company
Boston   Toronto

Library of Congress Cataloging-in-Publication Data

Dornan, Edward A.
  The brief English handbook.

  Includes index.
  1. English language—Grammar—1950–   . 2. English
language—Rhetoric. I. Dawe, Charles W. II. Title.
PE1112.D67   1986   428.2   86-10524
ISBN 0-316-19017-9

Library of Congress Catalog Card No. 86–10524

ISBN 0-316-19017-9 Student Edition

ISBN 0-316-19018-7 Instructor's Annotated Edition

9 8 7 6 5 4 3 2 1

FG

Published simultaneously in Canada
by Little, Brown & Company (Canada) Limited

Printed in the United States of America

Acknowledgments

We would like to thank the following authors and publishers for permission to
quote from their works.

Joan Baez, from *Daybreak*, 1968. Reprinted by permission.

Jan Harold Brunvand, from *The Vanishing Hitchhiker, American Urban Legends
and Their Meanings* by Jan Harold Brunvand. W. W. Norton & Company, Inc. ©
1981 by Jan Harold Brunvand. Reprinted by permission of the publisher.

William G. Carleton from "Take Your College in Stride," *Vital Speeches of the
Day*, March 1947.

(*continued on page 425*)

CONTENTS

Grammar *gr* 1

1 Parts of Speech 2
a. Nouns
b. Pronouns
c. Verbs
d. Adjectives
e. Adverbs
f. Prepositions
g. Conjunctions
h. Interjections

2 Parts of Sentences 14
a. Simple subject
b. Simple predicate
c. Complete subject
d. Complete predicate
e. Compound subject
f. Compound predicate
g. Direct object
h. Indirect object
i. Predicate adjective
j. Predicate nominative

3 Phrases 19
a. Prepositional
b. Appositive
c. Infinitive
d. Participial
e. Gerund
f. Absolute

4 Clauses 25
a. Main clauses
b. Dependent clauses

5 Kinds of Sentences 28
a. Simple
b. Compound
c. Complex
d. Compound-complex
e. Declarative
f. Imperative
g. Interrogative
h. Exclamatory

Sentence Errors 33

6 Sentence Fragments *frag* 34
a. Dependent clause
b. Phrase fragments
c. Compound predicate
d. Acceptable uses

7 Comma Splices and Fused Sentences *cs/fs* 39
a. Run-on sentences

8 Subject and Verb Agreement *agr* 44
a. Subject and verb
b. Subjects joined by *and*
c. Subjects joined by *or* or *nor*
d. Singular and plural subjects joined by *or* or *nor*
e. Indefinite pronouns
f. Collective nouns
g. Plural nouns
h. Inverted word order
i. Linking verbs
j. Relative pronouns
k. *Every* and *many a*
l. Time, etc.
m. Titles, words as words

9 Pronoun and Antecedent Agreement *agr* 53
a. Compound antecedents
b. Singular antecedents
c. Singular and plural antecedents
d. Collective nouns
e. Indefinite pronouns
f. Relative pronouns

10 Case *ca* 58
a. Subjective
b. Objective
c. *We* or *us* before nouns
d. Pronouns as appositives
e. Elliptical comparisons
f. Objects of infinitives
g. Nouns preceding gerunds
h. *Who* and *whom*

11 Verb Forms *vb* 65

12 Tense *t* 69
a. Present
b. Past
c. Future
d. Present perfect
e. Past perfect
f. Future perfect
g. Sequence of tenses

13 Subjunctive Mood *mood* 76
a. Wishes, contrary-to-fact clauses
b. *That* clauses
c. Idioms

14 Active and Passive Voice *pass* 78

15 Adjectives and Adverbs *adj/adv* 82
a. Modifying nouns and pronouns
b. After linking verbs
c. After direct objects
d. *Bad, badly, well, good*
e. Comparisons
f. Double comparatives and superlatives
g. Illogical comparatives and superlatives

Sentence Clarity and Variety 89

16 Coordination and Subordination *coord/sub* 90
a. Coordination
b. Excessive coordination
c. Subordination
d. Excessive subordination

17 Placement of Modifiers *mm/dm* 97
a. Phrases and clauses
b. Squinting modifiers
c. Limiting modifiers
d. Between subjects and predicates
e. Between verbs and complements
f. Within verb phrases
g. Split infinitives
h. Dangling modifiers

18 Pronoun Reference *ref* 104
a. Broad reference
b. Indefinite use of *it, they,* and *you*
c. Clear reference
d. Reflexive pronouns

19 Consistency *shift* 107
a. Person and number

Contents continued inside the back cover

Preface

The second edition of *The Brief English Handbook* has maintained the high standard of the first edition. The text is still an easy-to-use guide to standard American English and college writing. The organization is still straightforward, the design clear, the rules prominent and carefully indexed, and the coverage as thorough as a brief format will allow.

We added an eighth part titled "Manuscript Form, Business Letters, and Resume" and updated "Writing a Research Paper" (chapter 48) in order to conform to the current documentation style of the Modern Language Association. In "Writing a Research Paper," we also added examples of the American Psychological Association documentation style. We revised "Writing the Essay" (chapter 46) by concentrating on selecting a subject, narrowing a subject, and choosing a suitable tone. Finally, we expanded "Spelling" (chapter 40) by adding common spelling rules and a list of spelling demons. The rest of the revision comes under the title "polishing." We polished definitions, examples, and exercises. During revision, we never lost sight of our intent in the first edition: to simplify the task of looking for help in writing and revising.

The handbook still begins with a review of the essentials of grammar before presenting sentence structure and punctuation. We also list grammar terms alphabetically in a glossary at the back of the book and meticulously cross-reference terms to their definitions throughout the book. Following the grammar review, we present several chapters on sentence errors, sentence clarity, and sentence variety, where we emphasize the common faults that plague so many students' essays. Our approach is necessarily prescriptive in matters of standard English but more relaxed in matters of style. In the chapters on punctuation and mechanics, we have added more detail and more examples than other handbooks of comparable length. We saw no good reason to take short cuts here; students should refer to punctuation rules, especially those on comma usage, with the assurance that the text can answer their queries succinctly and directly. In the chapters on diction and logic, we cover a wide range of topics, including guidelines for avoiding sexist language and a concise list of common logical fallacies. Common usage problems, especially matters of diction, are also listed alphabetically in a glossary.

The next four chapters concentrate on composition. In the chapter on paragraphs, we offer more than twenty models of professional and student writing to illustrate unity, coherence, and methods of paragraph development. In the essay chapter we integrate current research on composing and trace the development of a model essay from conception to proofreading. The chapter on writing about literature defines literary analysis and offers brief models for composing an analytical essay. The chapter on the research paper, like the essay chapter, follows one student's research process from concept to final paper and offers a full menu of reference aids. Bibliographical and note formats are based on current MLA style. In this chapter we also present and answer twenty questions students typically ask about research papers. The last three chapters present format guidelines for manuscript form, business letters, and résumés.

Other features of *The Brief English Handbook* deserve special mention. Throughout the book, rules and advice are indexed by tabs in the corners of the pages and by a thorough system of cross-referencing; in addition, of course, there is a complete subject index. The comments addressed to the student, which follow, explain how these reference aids will make the student's job of composing and correcting papers much easier. Exercises reinforce rules and examples in every part of the book. Many of the exercises focus on a single theme or topic rather than on five or ten unrelated ideas. There are many types of exercises. For the sentence variety chapter, for instance, we rely on sentence combining and controlled composition.

When revising *The Brief English Handbook,* we committed ourselves to keeping the tone of the book lively. In our exercises, examples, and advice to students, we have tried to invigorate the book with some personality. We hope you and your students will find this tone refreshing.

Many reviewers helped us to shape and refine our manuscript. We are grateful to Jennifer Bradley, U.C.L.A.; Barbara Carson, University of Georgia; Norma Engberg, University of Nevada at Las Vegas; Michael Grimwood, North Carolina State University; Joyce Lipkis, Santa Monica College; Michael Meyer, University of Connecticut; Elizabeth Mitchell, Ocean County College; Jeannette Morgan, University of Houston; Janice Neulieb, Illinois State University; Jack Oruch, University of Kansas; William Reynolds, Hope College; Shirley Saint-Leon, Santa Monica College; Alan Schwartz, Queensborough Community College; William Zehringer, Bloomsburg State College.

For the second edition of *The Brief English Handbook* we had the good fortune to receive suggestions from many students and instructors throughout the country. We owe a special thanks to several diligent and perceptive reviewers: Terence A. Dalrymple, Angelo State University; Rosanna Grassi, Syracuse University; Melinda G. Kramer, Purdue University; Robert Mueller, Illinois Valley Community College; Charles Reinhardt, Vincennes University; Maureen Ryan, University of Southern Mississippi; Robert A. Schwegler, University of Rhode Island; and Anne B. Slater, Frederick Community College.

We wish to express our deepest gratitude to all the professionals at Little, Brown and Company, but especially to sponsoring editor Joe Opiela for his spirited encouragement; to developmental editor Greg Tobin for his astute suggestions, diplomatic criticisms, and patient endurance; and to Lauren Green and her editorial assistant Pascha Gerlinger for guiding the manuscript through production. We thank copy editors Barbara Flanagan and Susan M. S. Brown, and designers George McLean and Virginia Mason, whose skills brought the final manuscript to life. We also thank Robert Dees of Orange Coast Community College for his contribution to the research paper and Jane Aaron for her assistance with the essay chapter. Gabriele

Rico is acknowledged for the clustering diagram on page 281. Finally, we owe a special debt to Richard S. Beal for helping launch *The Brief English Handbook* and for his wise counsel at critical stages in its creation.

To the Student:

We wrote *The Brief English Handbook* as a concise guide to grammatical accuracy, effective sentences, correct punctuation, word selection, and sound development of paragraphs, essays, and research papers. *The Brief English Handbook's* primary use will probably be in a composition class, where the teacher might assign chapters and exercises for class discussion or refer you to the book to correct your written work. We hope you will also see its value as a companion to any course that requires writing.

We have kept the structure of *The Brief English Handbook* simple and direct. We begin with the essentials of grammar. The first part presents parts of speech, parts of sentences, phrases, clauses, and kinds of sentences. Your instructor might ask you to review these first five chapters; indeed, if you feel apprehensive about such terms as *noun, verb, subject, predicate, clause,* and *phrase,* we also recommend that you do so.

In the second part, "Sentence Errors," we cover common mistakes writers make when expressing their thoughts in writing — fragments, comma splices and fused sentences, failure to establish the correct relations between subjects and verbs as well as between pronouns and antecedents — the kinds of errors that hinder clear communication. In the third part, "Clarity and Variety," we continue the discussion of sentences, but we emphasize ways to write clear and accurate sentences while keeping a reader interested in what you have to say. Some of the techniques we explain are varying sentence patterns, using modifiers, arranging words for emphasis, organizing sentences through subordination and coordination, and enhancing the impact of sentences through parallel structure.

In the fourth and fifth parts, "Punctuation" and "Mechanics," we give rules for using commas, semicolons, colons, dashes, capitalization, abbreviations, and the like. In the sixth part, "Diction and Logic," we concentrate on words and urge you to select words that are appropriate, exact, and concise. We also show you how to avoid committing logical fallacies in your writtern work.

In the seventh part, "Writing Paragraphs, Essays, and Research Papers," we present the kinds of writing you will be required to do in college and in your professional life. We begin with paragraphs, stressing the importance of clear topic sentences, paragraph unity, and paragraph coherence. We then discuss the whole essay and guide you through the process of selecting a topic, generating ideas, organizing a paper, completing a rough draft, revising the draft, and writing a final draft. The last chapter of that part traces the process of writing and documenting a research paper, perhaps the most important learning activity you will undertake in freshman writing.

Finally, in the eighth part we offer guidelines for manuscript form, business letters, and résumés. At the end of the book we have included two glossaries. The glossary of usage explains many of the words and phrases writers find troublesome and confusing. The glossary of grammatical terms defines the specialized words we use throughout the text.

REVISING YOUR PAPERS

Sometimes your instructor might write comments in the margins of your paper suggesting that you refer to *The Brief English Handbook* for certain information. You can best find the information first by deciphering the key terms in the teacher's comments and then by looking them up in the index, which lists every important term we have used, or by scanning the table of contents, which lists the book's main parts, chapters, and chapter sections.

At other times your instructor might write numbers or symbols in the margins of your paper. Numbers refer to chapters, and if a letter is used with a number, the letter refers to a chapter section (for instance, 19g refers to section g in Chapter 19). For easy reference, you can check the contents guide printed on the book's endpapers. The guide shows all the parts, chapters, and chapter sections of *The Brief English Handbook* along with the numbers and letters that identify them. The numbers and letters are also printed before each rule or guideline and in the colored tabs on the pages where you can find the information they refer to. You can find out what symbols such as *frag* or / / indicate — *frag* indicates fragment and / / indicates parallelism — by referring to the endpapers, where the symbols are listed by chapter, or by referring to the inside front cover, where the words the symbols represent are listed alphabetically. They also appear next to the appropriate colored tabs on each page and at the beginning of each chapter.

If your instructor uses numbers to indicate needed corrections and to suggest revisions, your returned papers might look like the following example, which is the introductory paragraph of the student essay that begins on page 273.

28b   "Time to Slow Down"

      When I first returned to the city after ten months in a for-

38g estry camp, I was not ready to reenter the pace of daily life. For a

few uncomfortable days, I had the feeling I was living within the

11 frenetic action of an old silent movie. People around me rushing as

though they were late for an appointment. At first this activity

7a made me nervous, my experience in the forestry camp had given me a

more leisurely approach to daily activities.

If instead of numbers your instructor uses symbols, your returned papers might look like the following, which is the continuation of the paragraph in the student essay.

In the months that followed, I began to understand that the speed
of daily living which had upset me when I returned was only the
most obvious part of a deeper attitude. We are so busy when rushed
from one experience to another, developing new interests and dropping old ones, that we seldom take the time to do anything well.
This shows in our responses to public affairs, in our educational
programs, and in our relationships with each other.

After your instructor returns your paper, use the text to look up
the notations; in a different color ink, make the necessary corrections
in your paper before beginning the revised draft. With corrections
the sample paragraph looks like the one on page 273.

Your instructor's notations can be a valuable aid in learning the
rules and guidelines for clear writing. We suggest you use the notations
as a study guide, carefully reading the information they refer to and
completing the exercises that accompany the information. We also
suggest you keep a record of the notations so that you can return to
The Brief English Handbook before each new assignment to review
the rules and guidelines that have given you trouble. By following
these two procedures, you will gain as much as possible from the
experience of having your instructor, who is a professionally trained
reader, evaluate your written work.

E.A.D.

C.W.D.

Contents

Grammar   1

1.   Parts of Speech   2

    a. Nouns   2
    b. Pronouns   3
    c. Verbs   5
    d. Adjectives   8
    e. Adverbs   9
    f. Prepositions   10
    g. Conjunctions   11
    h. Interjections   13

2.   Parts of Sentences   14

    a. Simple Subject   14
    b. Simple Predicate   15
    c. Complete Subject   15
    d. Complete Predicate   15
    e. Compound Subject   15
    f. Compound Predicate   16
    g. Direct Object   17
    h. Indirect Object   17
    i. Predicate Adjective   18
    j. Predicate Nominative   18

3.   Phrases   19

    a. Prepositional Phrases   19
    b. Appositives   19

    c. Infinitives and Infinitive Phrases   *21*
    d. Participles and Participial Phrases   *21*
    e. Gerunds and Gerund Phrases   *23*
    f. Absolute Phrases   *24*

4. Clauses   25
    a. Main Clauses   *25*
    b. Dependent Clauses   *26*

5. Kinds of Sentences   28
    a. Simple Sentences   *29*
    b. Compound Sentences   *29*
    c. Complex Sentences   *29*
    d. Compound-Complex Sentences   *29*
    e. Declarative Sentences   *30*
    f. Imperative Sentences   *30*
    g. Interrogative Sentences   *30*
    h. Exclamatory Sentences   *30*

Sentence Errors   33

6. Sentence Fragments   34
    a. Dependent Clause   *34*
    b. Phrase Fragments   *36*
    c. Compound Predicate   *37*
    d. Acceptable Uses   *38*

7. Comma Splices and Fused Sentences   39
    a. Run-on Sentences   *40*

8. Subject and Verb Agreement   44
    a. Subject and Verb   *44*
    b. Subjects Joined by *and*   *45*
    c. Singular Subjects Joined by *or* or *nor*   *45*
    d. Singular and Plural Subjects Joined by *or* or *nor*   *46*
    e. Indefinite Pronouns   *46*

f. Collective Nouns   47

g. Plural Nouns   47

h. Inverted Word Order   48

i. Linking Verbs   48

j. Relative Pronouns   48

k. *Every* and *many a* Preceding a Subject   49

l. Time, Money, Measurement, Weight, Volume, and Fractions   49

m. Titles and Words as Words   50

9. Pronoun and Antecedent Agreement   53

a. Compound Antecedents Joined by *and*   53

b. Singular Antecedents Joined by *or* or *nor*   53

c. Singular and Plural Antecedents Joined by *or* or *nor*   54

d. Collective Nouns   55

e. Indefinite Pronouns   55

f. Relative Pronouns   56

10. Case   58

a. Subjective   59

b. Objective   60

c. *We* or *us* Before a Noun   60

d. Pronouns as Appositives   61

e. Elliptical Comparisons   61

f. Objects of Infinitives   62

g. Nouns Preceding Gerunds   62

h. *Who* and *whom*   63

11. Verb Forms   65

12. Tense   69

a. Present   69

b. Past   70

c. Future   70

d. Present Perfect   71

e. Past Perfect   71

f. Future Perfect *71*

g. Sequence of Tenses *71*

13. Subjunctive Mood 76

a. Expressing a Wish, Contrary-to-Fact Clauses *77*

b. *That* Clauses Following Verbs *78*

c. Standard Phrases and Idioms *78*

14. Active and Passive Voice 78

15. Adjectives and Adverbs 82

a. Modifying Nouns and Pronouns *82*

b. After Linking Verbs *82*

c. After Direct Objects *83*

d. Using *bad, badly, well, good* *83*

e. Making Comparisons *85*

f. Double Comparatives and Superlatives *86*

g. Illogical Comparatives and Superlatives *86*

Sentence Clarity and Variety 89

16. Coordination and Subordination 90

a. Coordination for Equal Emphasis *90*

b. Excessive Coordination *91*

c. Subordination to Emphasize Main Clause *93*

d. Excessive Subordination *94*

17. Placement of Modifiers 97

a. Prepositional Phrases and Dependent Clauses *98*

b. Squinting Modifiers *98*

c. Limiting Modifiers *99*

d. Lengthy Modifiers Between Subjects and Predicates *100*

e. Lengthy Modifiers Between Verbs and Complements *100*

f. Lengthy Modifiers Within Verb Phrases *101*

g. Split Infinitives   *101*
h. Dangling Modifiers   *102*

18. Pronoun Reference   104

a. Broad Reference   *104*
b. Indefinite Use of *it*, *they*, and *you*   *105*
c. Clear Reference to One Antecedent   *105*
d. Reflexive Pronouns   *106*

19. Consistency   107

a. Person and Number   *107*
b. Tense   *108*
c. Mood   *109*
d. Subject and Voice   *109*
e. Direct and Indirect Discourse   *110*
f. Grammatical Plan   *112*
g. Faulty Predication   *112*

20. Sentence Completeness   113

a. Complete Comparisons   *114*
b. Omitted Words   *114*

21. Parallelism   115

a. Coordinate Elements   *116*
b. Compared and Contrasted Ideas   *117*
c. Correlative Constructions   *117*

22. Sentence Variety   118

a. Sentence Beginnings   *119*
b. Sentence Structures   *120*
c. Sentence Forms   *121*

Punctuation   125

23. The Comma   126

a. Main Clauses Linked by Coordinating
Conjunctions   *126*

b. Introductory Phrases and Clauses   *127*
c. Nonrestrictive Elements   *129*
d. Parenthetical Expressions   *135*
e. Interjections, Direct Address, *yes, no*   *136*
f. Words, Phrases, and Clauses in a Series   *137*
g. Coordinate Adjectives   *138*
h. Absolute Phrases   *140*
i. Contrasting Phrases, Interrogative Elements   *140*
j. Expressions such as *he said*   *140*
k. Numbers, Addresses, Place Names, Dates, and Friendly Letters   *142*
l. To Avoid Misreading   *143*

24. Unnecessary Commas   144

a. Between Subject and Verb   *144*
b. Between Verb and Object   *144*
c. Between Preposition and Its Object   *145*
d. Between Adjective and the Word It Modifies   *145*
e. With Compound Elements Joined by a Coordinating Conjunction   *145*
f. With Restrictive Elements   *146*
g. After *such as* and *like*   *146*
h. Before and after a series   *147*
i. Indirect Quotations   *147*
j. Before *than*   *147*
k. With Periods, Question Marks, Exclamation Points, or Dashes   *148*

25. The Semicolon   151

a. With Main Clauses Not Joined by Coordinating Conjunctions   *151*
b. With Main Clauses Joined by Conjunctive Adverbs   *152*
c. With Long Main Clauses   *152*
d. With Phrases and Clauses in a Series   *152*
e. Misuses   *153*

26. The Colon   155

- a. Introducing a Series   *155*
- b. With *the following* and *as follows*   *156*
- c. Separating Main Clauses   *156*
- d. Preceding Final Appositives   *156*
- e. Introducing Long Quotations   *156*
- f. With Subtitles, Subdivisions of Time, Parts of the Bible, Bibliographical Entries   *157*
- g. With Formal Salutations   *157*
- h. Misuses   *157*

27. The Dash   158

- a. For Parenthetical Elements   *158*
- b. Preceding a Series   *158*
- c. For Emphasis and Clarity   *158*
- d. For Breaks in Tone   *159*
- e. Preceding an Author's Name   *159*

28. Quotation Marks   159

- a. Direct Quotations   *159*
- b. Titles   *162*
- c. Words Used in a Special Sense   *162*
- d. With Other Punctuation Marks   *162*
- e. Single Quotation Marks   *163*

29. The Ellipsis Mark   166

- a. Omissions in Quotations   *166*
- b. Omissions of Prose Paragraphs and Lines of Poetry   *167*
- c. Unfinished Statements   *168*

30. Parentheses   168

- a. Enclosing Parenthetical Elements   *169*
- b. Labeling Items in a Series   *169*

31. Brackets   170

32. The Slash   170

33. End Punctuation   171
    a. Periods in Statements, Mild Commands, and Indirect Questions   *171*
    b. Periods With Abbreviations   *171*
    c. Question Marks After Direct Questions   *172*
    d. Question Marks Within Parentheses   *172*
    e. Exclamation Points After Interjections, Strong Commands, Emphatic Statements   *172*

Mechanics   175

34. Capitals   176
    a. First Word of a Sentence   *176*
    b. *O*, *I*, *I've*, and *I'm*   *177*
    c. Titles of Works   *177*
    d. Direct Quotations and Dialogue   *178*
    e. Poetry   *178*
    f. Proper Nouns, Proper Adjectives, and Essential Parts of Proper Names   *179*
    g. Titles and Degrees   *181*
    h. Abbreviations   *181*
    i. Common Mistakes   *181*

35. The Apostrophe   184
    a. Possessive Case   *184*
    b. Possessive Pronouns   *186*
    c. Contractions   *186*
    d. Plurals of Letters, Numbers, and Words   *186*

36. Abbreviations   187
    a. Titles Before Proper Names   *187*
    b. Titles Following Proper Names   *188*
    c. Corporations, Organizations, and Countries   *188*
    d. Common Abbreviations   *189*

    e. Footnotes, Bibliographies, Parenthetical
      Comments   *189*
    f. Common Mistakes   *189*

37. Italics   **190**

    a. Titles of Works   *190*
    b. Spacecraft, Aircraft, Ships, and Trains   *192*
    c. Foreign Words and Phrases   *192*
    d. Words, Letters, Numbers, Phrases, and Symbols   *193*
    e. Emphasis   *193*
    f. Titles of Papers   *193*

38. The Hyphen   **194**

    a. Broken Words at the Margin   *194*
    b. Compound Words   *194*
    c. Joining Descriptive Words   *194*
    d. Numbers   *195*
    e. Prefixes, Suffixes, and Letters   *195*
    f. Suspended Hyphen   *196*
    g. To Avoid Confusion   *196*

39. Numbers   **196**

    a. Spelling Out Numbers   *196*
    b. Using Figures   *197*
    c. Combining Figures and Words   *197*
    d. Uses of Figures   *197*
    e. Beginning a Sentence   *198*

40. Spelling   **199**

    a. Visualization   *200*
    b. Practice Writing   *200*
    c. Pronunciation   *200*
    d. Proofreading   *200*
    e. Distinguishing *ie* and *ei*   *201*
    f. Adding Suffixes Beginning With Vowels   *202*
    g. Adding Suffixes Beginning With Consonants   *202*

h. Changing *y* to *i*   *202*
i. Doubling Consonants Before Suffixes   *203*
j. Plurals of Nouns   *204*
k. Commonly Confused Words   *206*
l. Frequently Misspelled Words   *209*

Diction and Logic   211

41. Appropriate Language   212
a. Standard English   *213*
b. Slang   *214*
c. Regional Expressions   *215*
d. Obsolete Words   *216*
e. Technical Terms or Jargon   *216*
f. Pretentious Language   *218*
g. Sexist Language   *219*

42. Exactness   220
a. Denotation and Connotation   *220*
b. Abstract, General, Concrete, and Specific Words   *222*
c. Idioms   *224*
d. Figurative Language   *226*
e. Trite Expressions   *228*

43. Conciseness   229
a. Empty Phrases   *230*
b. Needless Repetition   *232*
c. Redundancy   *232*
d. Euphemism   *233*

44. Logical Fallacies in Writing   236
a. Overgeneralization   *236*
b. Oversimplification   *237*
c. *Either/Or* Fallacy   *238*
d. *Post hoc* Argument   *238*

e. *Non sequitur* 239
f. False Analogy 239
g. *Ad hominem* Argument 240
h. Association Fallacy 240

Paragraphs, Essays, and Research Papers 243

45. Writing Paragraphs 244

a. Topic Sentence 246
b. Unity 251
c. Coherence Through Structure 253
d. Coherence Through Transitions 257
e. Coherence Through Repetition 259
f. Coherence Through Parallelism 260
g. Development 261

46. Writing the Essay 268

a. Selecting a Subject 278
b. Narrowing the Subject 278
c. Prewriting for Ideas 280
d. Planning for an Audience 282
e. Making a Preliminary Plan 283
f. Phrasing the Thesis Statement 285
g. Developing the Final Plan 287
h. Choosing a Suitable Tone 290
i. Writing the Introduction 291
j. Writing the Discussion 291
k. Writing the Conclusion 293
l. Creating the Title 293
m. Revising the First Draft 294

47. Writing an Analytical Essay About Literature 296

a. Selecting a Subject for Analysis 296

b. Reviewing the Text for Evidence   *298*
c. Formulating a Thesis and Plan   *298*
d. Anticipating the Reader   *299*
e. Writing the Introduction   *299*
f. Writing the Discussion   *300*
g. Writing the Conclusion   *302*
h. Creating the Title   *303*
i. Identifying Quotations and References   *303*
j. Using the Present Tense   *304*
k. Avoiding Common Mistakes   *304*

48. Writing a Research Paper   305
a. Finding and Limiting a Topic   *306*
b. Using Library Sources   *308*
c. Preparing a Bibliography   *315*
d. Reading for a Tentative Thesis and Outline   *323*
e. Taking Detailed Notes   *325*
f. Revising the Thesis and Outline   *331*
g. Writing the First Draft   *333*
h. Acknowledging Sources   *333*
i. Finishing the Final Draft   *343*
j. Common Questions and Answers   *345*
k. Sample Research Paper: "Credit Cards: A Popular Blessing or Curse?"   *351*

Manuscript Form, Business Letter, and Résumé   389

49. Manuscript Form   390

50. Business Letter Forms   393

51. Résumé Form   397

Glossaries   401

Glossary of Usage   402
Glossary of Grammatical Terms   414

Index   427

Grammar

1 Parts of Speech

2 Parts of Sentences

3 Phrases

4 Clauses

5 Kinds of Sentences

Why study grammar? Unless you know the rules and terminology of grammar, you may be unable to identify faults or embarrassing mistakes in your writing. A knowledge of grammar may not prevent these errors, but it will at least help you keep close watch over your sentences.

You have probably studied grammar before, and many of its terms may already be familiar to you. This section of the handbook offers a review that will refresh your understanding of grammar and increase your confidence when writing.

1 Parts of Speech

There are eight parts of speech in English: nouns, pronouns, verbs, adjectives, adverbs, prepositions, conjunctions, and interjections. The same word can function as more than one part of speech. To identify a word's part of speech, you must determine how the word is used in a sentence. The word *coach*, for instance, may function as a noun in one sentence and as a verb in another.

> The coach has a gentle way with players. [Noun.]
> She coached my daughter. [Verb.]

1a Nouns name persons, places, things, or ideas.

Nouns may be classified as proper, common, abstract, concrete, and collective.

Proper nouns name particular persons, places, things, or events and are capitalized: *Charles Dickens, London, Christmas.*

Common nouns do not name particular persons, places, things, or events; therefore they are not capitalized: *writer, city, holiday.*

Abstract nouns name intangible qualities, ideas, or characteristics: *love, democracy, courage.*

Concrete nouns name tangible things that can be perceived through the senses: *wind, rain, pencil, nose, knife, needle.*

Collective nouns name groups of individuals: *audience, family,* *army, herd, jury, squad.* (See agreement of collective nouns and verbs, p. 47; of collective nouns and pronouns, p. 55.)

NOTE: A **compound noun,** which may be a common or proper noun, is composed of more than one word: *high school, crosswalk, sister-in-law, Labor Day.* (See hyphen, p. 194; forming the possessive case, p. 184; forming plurals, p. 186). A good dictionary will list a compound noun as a single entry. Referring to a dictionary is especially important for determining capitalization of compound nouns. (See capitals, p. 176.)

1b Pronouns take the place of nouns.

In the following sentence, the pronoun *him* substitutes for *John Franklin*, and the pronoun *them* substitutes for *fans.*

> John Franklin ran eighty yards for a touchdown. Six fans ran onto the field to greet *him* before officials chased *them* back to the stands.

The word that a pronoun replaces is called the **antecedent** of the pronoun. *John Franklin* is the antecedent of *him,* and *fans* is the antecedent of *them.*

Pronouns are classified as personal, possessive, reflexive, relative, interrogative, demonstrative, and indefinite.

Personal pronouns refer to a person or a thing. They have plural and singular forms.

	SINGULAR	PLURAL
FIRST PERSON	I, me	we, us
SECOND PERSON	you	you
THIRD PERSON	he, she, him, her, it	they, them

Possessive pronouns are forms of personal pronouns that show ownership or relation. (See case, p. 58.)

my, mine	his	its	their, theirs
your, yours	her, hers	our, ours	

Reflexive pronouns are formed by combining personal pronouns with *-self* and *-selves.*

myself	ourselves
yourself	yourselves
himself, herself, itself	themselves

A reflexive pronoun indicates that someone or something named in a sentence acts upon itself.

Leo treated *himself* to shrimp scampi.

A reflexive pronoun can also be used to emphasize a noun or pronoun.

Leo *himself* will eat the shrimp scampi.

Relative pronouns introduce adjective clauses. (See dependent clauses, p. 26.)

who	whom	whose	that	which

The couple *who performed the tango* won first prize.

Interrogative pronouns are used in questions.

who	whom	whose	which	what

Whom did you call?

Demonstrative pronouns are used to point to or identify a noun.

this	that	these	those

That is your problem.
This is the question: How will we raise the money?

Indefinite pronouns function as nouns in a sentence but do not take the place of a specific person or thing. Following are some common indefinite pronouns.

all	anybody	each	everyone
another	anyone	either	many
any	anything	everybody	most

| one | nobody | several | somebody |
| neither | none | some | something |

Somebody will reap the benefits.

Exercise 1

Underline the nouns and circle the pronouns in the following sentences. (The sentences contain nineteen nouns and six pronouns.)

1. New York City is under attack by gangs with cans of paint.

2. Its walls and subways are smeared with layers of painted names and obscenities.

3. What is to be done?

4. Some believe the city should create an area in which young people may paint buildings at no risk.

5. Many want stronger laws and harsher punishment that will discourage the messy criminals from the practice.

1c Verbs express action or a state of being.

A **verb** may express physical action *(dance, walk, jump)* or mental action *(dream, guess, trust)*. A group of words must have a verb to form a complete sentence. (See sentence, p. 14; sentence fragments, p. 34.)

Action Verbs

Action verbs are classified by whether they must be followed by an object — a noun or pronoun that completes the action of the verb by showing who or what is acted upon.

A **transitive verb** expresses action that has an object. (See direct object, p. 17; indirect object, p. 17.)

> The pitcher *tossed* the ball. [Tossed what? The *ball*, the object of *tossed*.]
>
> The voters *believed* the politician. [Believed whom? The *politician*, the object of *believed*.]

An **intransitive verb** expresses action that has no object.

> The pitcher *smiled*.
> The stream *runs* through the canyon.

Although some verbs are transitive only *(destroy, send, forbid)* and others are intransitive only *(tremble, chuckle, happen)*, most verbs can function as either transitive or intransitive.

> The guide *explained* the danger. [Transitive.]
> The guide never *explained*. [Intransitive.]

Linking Verbs

Linking verbs express a state of being or a condition rather than an action. The most common linking verbs are forms of *be,* such as *am, is, are, was,* and *were.* Words such as *appear, become, feel, grow, look, seem, smell,* and *taste* function as both linking verbs and action verbs. These verbs link the subject of a sentence with a predicate nominative or predicate adjective — a noun, pronoun, or adjective that identifies or modifies the subject. (See subject, p. 14; predicate nominative, p. 18; predicate adjective, p. 18.)

> The butler *is* the killer. [The predicate nominative *killer* identifies the subject *butler.*]
>
> The silence *became* frightening. [The predicate adjective *frightening* modifies the subject *silence.*]

Many linking verbs also function as transitive as well as intransitive verbs.

The butler *looked* gloomy. [Linking verb.]
The butler *looked* for an escape. [Intransitive verb.]
Harold's hair *grew* gray from shock. [Linking verb.]
Mr. Higgins *grew* plums. [Transitive verb.]

Helping Verbs and Verb Phrases

A verb often includes one or more **helping verbs,** sometimes called **auxiliary verbs.**

COMMON HELPING VERBS

am	has	can (may) have
are	had	could (would, should) be
is	can	could (would, should) have
was	may	will (shall) have been
were	will (shall) be	might have
do	will (shall) have	might have been
did	has (had) been	must
have	can (may) be	must have
		must have been

The verb and its helping verb form a **verb phrase.**

The comet *has been approaching* earth for two years. [*Has* and *been* are helping verbs for the verb *approaching*.]

In some sentences the verb and its helping verb are separated.

The day *has* finally *arrived.*
Did they *reach* Georgia?

(See tense, p. 69; passive voice, p. 78.)

Exercise 2

In the following sentences underline the verbs, including helping verbs, and identify them as transitive (T), intransitive (I), linking (L), or helping (H). Be sure to mark all the verbs in verb phrases.

1. Diaries are popular with people of all ages.

2. Creative people have kept diaries throughout history.

3. Diarist Anaïs Nin wrote thousands of pages in several volumes.

4. Could you record your thoughts every day?

5. Some diarists have accumulated over a thousand pages in a single

   year, and they have written for only thirty minutes a day.

1d Adjectives modify nouns and pronouns.

To modify a word means to limit — that is, to make its meaning more definite. **Adjectives** limit in three ways.
  By describing:

> A *tall* boy stepped from the *curious* crowd.
> The *white* and *black* car won the race.

By pointing out which one:

> *That* man is my brother.

By telling how many:

> *Twelve* children and *several* parents attended.

Adjectives normally come directly before the words they modify, but sometimes a writer places descriptive adjectives after the words they modify.

> The stallion, *long* and *lean*, galloped past us.

Predicate adjectives generally follow linking verbs and modify the subject of a sentence. (See predicate adjective, p. 18.)

> The runners were *tired* and *thirsty*. [*Tired* and *thirsty* modify the subject *runners*.]

Adjectives or Pronouns?

A word may be used as more than one part of speech. This is especially true of the words listed below, which may serve as adjectives or pronouns depending on how they function in a sentence.

all	either	one	these
another	few	other	this
any	many	several	those
both	more	some	what
each	neither	that	which

This book is overdue. *Those* books are on reserve. [Adjectives.]

This is the overdue book. *Those* are the books on reserve. [Pronouns.]

The definite article *the* and the indefinite articles *a* (used before words beginning with a consonant sound) and *an* (used before words beginning with a vowel sound) are also classified as adjectives.

1e Adverbs modify verbs, adjectives, other adverbs, and groups of words.

Adverbs most commonly modify verbs by telling how, when, where, or to what extent.

He reads *carefully*. [How.]
He reads *late*. [When.]
He reads *everywhere*. [Where.]
He reads *widely*. [To what extent.]

Adverbs sometimes modify adjectives and other adverbs.

He is *truly* dedicated. [Modifies the adjective *dedicated*.]
He studies *terribly* hard. [Modifies the adverb *hard*.]

Adverbs sometimes modify groups of words.

Unfortunately, I cannot attend the wedding. [Modifies the whole sentence.]

Many adverbs end in *-ly*, but not all words that end in *-ly* are adverbs.

> The day was *chilly*, but the group jogged *briskly* through the park. [*Chilly* is an adjective; *briskly* is an adverb.]

Exercise 3

In the following paragraph, fill in the blanks with adjectives or adverbs. Be sure the words you select fit the meaning of the sentences. Identify each new word with the label ADJ or ADV.

The _____ pilot _____ missed a _____ collision with a

skyscraper. _____, on the street a _____ crowd screamed

_____. A _____ man raised a _____ hand to his throat and

then fainted when he saw the _____ plane dive from the _____,

_____ clouds to within inches of the _____ building. A police

officer, _____ and _____, dashed to a phone and _____

dialed the station. _____, the pilot, who must have been _____

insane, swooped toward the crowd, skyscrapers looming _____ on

both sides like _____ canyon walls, and saluted as he passed

_____.

1f A preposition shows the relation of a noun or pronoun to some other word in a sentence.

Prepositions usually introduce a word group called a **prepositional phrase,** which always consists of the preposition and an **object of the**

preposition — a noun or pronoun that relates to another word in the sentence.

The effect *of pesticides* threatens wildlife *in marshes*.

Pesticides is related to *effect* because it indicates which effect. *Marshes* is related to *wildlife* because it indicates where wildlife is threatened. The prepositions *of* and *in* indicate the relations between these words. (See prepositional phrases, p. 19.)

Prepositions usually show direction or position. The following words are among the most common prepositions:

above	at	beyond	into	under
across	before	by	of	up
after	behind	down	on	upon
against	below	during	out	with
along	beneath	for	over	within
among	beside	from	through	without
around	between	in	to	

Around the corner and *beyond* the tracks the road turns.

Groups of words, such as *along with, according to,* and *in spite of,* sometimes serve as prepositions. (See idioms, p. 224.)

According to the latest report, the company is nearly bankrupt.

Exercise 4

Write five sentences about a recent experience, each sentence containing two prepositions from the list above. Underline each prepositional phrase and place an *O* above the object of the preposition.

1g Conjunctions join words, phrases, or clauses.

Conjunctions are usually classified into three categories: coordinating conjunctions, correlative conjunctions, and subordinating conjunctions.

There are seven **coordinating conjunctions:** *and, but, or, yet, for,* *nor,* and *so.* (See subject and predicate, p. 14; main clauses, p. 25; compound sentences, p. 29.)

> Oranges, lemons, *and* limes are citrus fruits. [Joining words.]
>
> The fish bite in the morning *or* after sundown. [Joining prepositional phrases.]
>
> The comet hit, *but* no one saw it. [Joining the clauses of a compound sentence.]

Correlative conjunctions are always used in pairs: *both . . . and; not only . . . but also; either . . . or;* and *neither . . . nor.*

> *Both* the California condor *and* the Maryland darter are struggling to survive.
>
> *Neither* animal *nor* plant species are safe from human encroachment.

Subordinating conjunctions begin dependent clauses. Some common subordinating conjunctions, several of which also function as prepositions, are *after, although, because, before, if, since, so that, though, unless, until, when, where,* and *while.* (See dependent clauses, p. 26.)

> Humans must uncover their fears *before* they can uncover their courage.
>
> *When* psychology develops a model of human nature, it will not be solely based on neuroses and character disorders.

NOTE: **Conjunctive adverbs** join main, or independent, clauses. Words such as *consequently, furthermore, hence, however, indeed, moreover, nevertheless, subsequently, therefore, thus,* and *yet* are conjunctive adverbs. (See main clauses, p. 25; semicolon, p. 152.)

> Paralysis was President Franklin Delano Roosevelt's only psychological experience with defeat; *consequently,* he never revealed the true extent of his handicap.
>
> Statistics show that advertising generates sales; manufacturers, *therefore,* will continue to support Madison Avenue copywriters.

Exercise 5

Underline the conjunctions in the following paragraph and indicate whether they are coordinating (COOR), correlative (COR), or subordinating conjunctions (SUB) or conjunctive adverbs (CONJ ADV).

Garden owners enjoy fresh vegetables and fruits, but most people have neither a home garden nor access to a community garden. Most people must depend on mass-harvested produce or canned goods. Although the transportation of vegetables and fruits to supermarkets has improved, bad weather often causes delay; moreover, supermarket produce is often harvested too early. This early picking sometimes means the produce has not developed all the nutrients it can; consumers, consequently, do not always receive full value in vitamins and minerals.

1h **Interjections express surprise or strong emotion and have no grammatical relation to sentences.**

Examples of interjections are: *Oh! Wow! Ah! Ouch! Hey! My goodness! Ouch!* It bit my finger.

Exercise 6: Review

Name the part of speech of each italicized word in the following paragraph, using the abbreviations N for noun, PRO for pronoun, V for verb, ADJ for adjective, ADV for adverb, PREP for preposition, C for conjunction, and I for interjection.

Television and *cinema* are able to use the camera to create *artistic* experiences. The cinematographer *carefully points* the lens. The *director* says, *"OK!* Roll 'em." The *action* moving *before* the lens is recorded *on* film as the scene unfolds. *Although this* sounds like a simple process, *it* requires an artist's sense of craft to make the *photographic* experience meaningful. *Neither* the camera *nor* unlimited rolls of film *will* guarantee that the result will have any value; each day's shooting, *therefore, offers* the thrill associated *with* creating art.

2   Parts of Sentences

Good writing starts with clear, grammatical sentences. You can take a step toward writing good sentences by understanding their structure.

A **sentence** is a group of words that contains a **subject** and a **predicate** and is not dependent on another group of words to complete its meaning. (See subordinating conjunctions, p. 12; main clauses, p. 25; dependent clauses, p. 26). *Although the celebration ended with a fireworks display* is not a sentence because its meaning is not complete, but *The celebration ended with a fireworks display* and *How did the celebration end?* are sentences.

Subject and Predicate

2a   The simple subject is the essential word or words that act, are acted upon, or are described.

> *Quail Hill* rises at the end of University Drive.
> *Birds* have been nesting among the rocks and shrubs.
> Bundled in coats, *students* stroll to the peak each evening.

NOTE: Sometimes the subject *you* is implied.

Speak to us! [Meaning *You speak to us.*]

2b The simple predicate, sometimes referred to as the *verb*, is the essential word or words that tell what the subject did or how it was acted upon.

Quail Hill *rises* at the end of University Drive.
Birds *have been nesting* among the rocks and shrubs.
Bundled in coats, students *stroll* to the peak each evening.

2c The complete subject is the group of words that includes the simple subject and its modifiers.

The student rally began at noon. [*Rally* is the simple subject. *The student rally* is the complete subject.]

The candidate from Benton Hall will speak at two o'clock. [*Candidate* is the simple subject. *The candidate from Benton Hall* is the complete subject.]

2d The complete predicate is the group of words that includes the simple predicate and its modifiers.

The student rally *began at noon.* [*Began* is the simple predicate. *Began at noon* is the complete predicate.]

The candidate from Benton Hall *will speak at two o'clock.* [*Will speak* is the simple predicate (note that it includes the helping verb *will*). *Will speak at two o'clock* is the complete predicate.]

2e A compound subject consists of two or more subjects that are joined by a conjunction and that have the same predicate.

Samuel King and *William Black* took the first aerial photographs.
Either *he* or *she* will fly the balloon.

2f A compound predicate consists of two or more verbs that are joined by a conjunction and that have the same subject.

> The rumble of the train *echoes* through the valley and *rolls* over the hills.
>
> Space shuttles *will fly* to the moon and *return* with payloads of minerals.

Exercise 7

Underline the complete subject and circle the simple subject in each sentence.

1. A variety of cookbooks are best sellers at stores around the country.

2. Cookbooks have become more than lists of recipes.

3. The best cookbooks include bits of history, a pinch of geography, and dollops of philosophy and legend.

4. Regional recipes mix these ingredients well.

5. Many home chefs appreciate cultural information about recipes.

Exercise 8

Underline the complete predicate and circle the simple predicate in each sentence.

1. Suspense novels climb to the top of the best-seller lists also.

2. A good suspense writer usually sets the action in exotic locations.

3. The hero often combines grace and ruthless drive.

4. The plot will move quickly but will seldom cover more than a week's

   time.

5. The suspense hinges on the hero's chances for survival.

Complements

Some sentences express the writer's thought by means of a subject and verb only: *He worked. She arrived.* Most sentences, however, have within the complete predicate one or more words that add to the meaning of the subject and simple predicate:

> He is *an engineer.*
> They appointed *a new president.*

These elements are called **complements,** and they function as direct and indirect objects and as predicate adjectives and predicate nominatives. (See verbs, p. 5.)

2g A direct object is a word or word group that receives the action of a transitive verb.

A **direct object** answers the question What? or Whom?

> The Civic League invited *John* to speak. [*John* is the direct object of the transitive verb *invited.*]
>
> She teaches *fifth grade.* [*Fifth grade* is the direct object of the transitive verb *teaches.*]

2h An indirect object of a verb precedes the direct object and usually indicates to whom or for whom the action is done.

> The caretaker gave *Ralph* the key. [*Ralph* is the indirect object (*key* is the direct object) of the transitive verb *gave.*]

To identify an indirect object, reconstruct the sentence by using the preposition *to* or *for:*

> The caretaker gave the key *to Ralph.* [Now *Ralph* no longer functions as the indirect object but as the object of the preposition *to.*]

2i   A predicate adjective is an adjective that follows a linking verb and modifies the subject of the verb.

> The animals seem *restless.* [The predicate adjective *restless* follows the linking verb *seem* and modifies the subject *animals.*]

2j   A predicate nominative is a noun or pronoun that follows a linking verb and renames or identifies the subject of the verb.

(See subjective case, p. 59.)

> The man with gray hair is *Mr. Reed.* [The predicate nominative *Mr. Reed* follows the linking verb *is* and identifies the subject *man.*]

Exercise 9

Underline and identify the direct objects (DO), indirect objects (IO), predicate adjectives (PA), and predicate nominatives (PN) in the following sentences.

1. Metaphors create vivid images in people's minds.

2. Highly charged images can become trademarks or handicaps for politicians.

3. Lincoln's "a house divided" won him success, but Hoover's "a chicken in every pot" brought him scorn.

4. In fear of vivid language, many politicians give us empty phrases.

5. This vague use of expression often sounds dull.

3 Phrases

Words in sentences function not only individually but also in groups. The most common word group is the **phrase.** A phrase may be used as a noun, verb, adjective, or adverb.

Prepositional Phrases

3a Prepositional phrases begin with a preposition and end with a noun or pronoun.

Prepositional phrases function as adjectives or adverbs. (See prepositions, p. 10.)

> The fibula *of the left leg* is broken. [Adjective.]
> As she turned, her mask fell *to the floor.* [Adverb.]

Appositives

3b An appositive is a noun or pronoun — often with modifiers — placed near another noun or pronoun to explain, describe, or identify it.

> The Wolves' Den, *a hangout for college intellectuals,* caught fire. [*A hangout for college intellectuals* describes *Wolves' Den.*]
> My brother *David* works nights. [*David* identifies *brother.*]

Usually an appositive follows the word it refers to, but it may also precede the word. (See comma, p. 126.)

> A *thrilling love story*, John and Marsha's romance would make a wonderful film. [*A thrilling love story* describes *romance*.]

Exercise 10

Combine each group of sentences into one sentence by using prepositional phrases and appositives. For example:

> John and Paul are my older brothers. They argued constantly. They argued during the entire trip. They sat in the back seat.
>
> John and Paul, *my older brothers*, argued *in the back seat* during the entire trip.

1. The 1957 Chevrolet is still popular. It came with large tail fins. It is popular among rare car collectors.

2. Belle Starr was shot to death. She was a notorious outlaw. She died in Oklahoma. She was forty-one years old.

3. Once again the tango is becoming popular. The tango is a dance that began a century ago in Buenos Aires bordellos. It is becoming popular in New York nightspots.

4. Logic bombs are exploding every week. Logic bombs are bits of destructive software coding designed to confuse a computer system. They are exploding in the country's leading business firms.

5. Mary Harris organized labor unions. She was a native of Cork,

Ireland. She organized unions in West Virginia, Pennsylvania, and

Colorado.

Verbals and Verbal Phrases

A **verbal** is a verb that does not function as the verb of a clause. Instead, verbals, which include infinitives, present participles, and past participles, function as nouns, adjectives, and adverbs.

3c Infinitives and infinitive phrases function as nouns, adjectives, and adverbs.

An **infinitive phrase** includes the **infinitive,** the plain form of a verb preceded by *to,* as well as its complements or modifiers. (See verb forms, p. 65.)

> His favorite pastime is *to dance.* [Noun: predicate nominative.]
> I have three choices *to offer you.* [Adjective: modifies *choices.*]
> He seems eager *to gain knowledge.* [Adverb: modifies *eager.*]

3d Participles and participial phrases are verb forms that function as adjectives.

Present participles end in *-ing (running, laughing, flying).* **Past participles** usually end in *-ed (flopped, jumped, dangled),* but a few end in *-en (beaten),* and some change entirely *(begun, swum, brought).* (See note on gerunds, p. 23; verb forms, p. 65.)

> *Tired,* the runner slumped to the ground. [Past participle: modifies *runner.*]
>
> The *developing* crisis dominated the news. [Present participle: modifies *crisis.*]

Participial phrases consist of a participle and its complements or modifiers.

> The cat *howling through the night* belongs to Jim.
>
> *Glutted with inexpensive imports*, the automobile market has declined.
>
> *Beaten by Lady Luck*, the gambler quit the game.

Exercise 11

Underline and identify the infinitive (INF) phrases and participial (PART) phrases in the following sentences.

1. I wanted to attend the auction to bid on the yacht.

2. Concerned about the cost, Phil has decided to learn to play the flute instead of the piano.

3. Covered with ice, the tree limb cracked loose, tumbling to the ground.

4. The Canadian inventor of A Question of Scruples hopes to market her game as successfully as Trivial Pursuit was marketed.

5. To change established rules merely for the sake of change is a mistake. Would baseball be improved by ending the game after six innings?

Exercise 12

Combine each group of sentences by using participial phrases. For example:

> I lost six pounds this month. I swim four times a week.
> *Swimming four times a week*, I lost six pounds this month.

1. The professor was frustrated by the puzzle. The puzzle was spread before him.

2. Pilgrims visit the shrine each year. They thirst for divine benediction.

3. African dogs feed on wildebeest calves. They often chase them for a mile before bringing them down.

4. Alexander the Great was a powerful warrior who pillaged much of the world. He enslaved whole populations and exacted tribute from those he ruled.

5. Fans were stunned by the strike. They were disappointed the season would start late.

3e Gerunds and gerund phrases function as nouns.

A **gerund** is the present participle of a verb — formed by adding *-ing* to the infinitive — and is used as a noun.

> *Dreaming* leads to creation. [Gerund as subject.]

A **gerund phrase** consists of a gerund and its complements or modifiers. Like the gerund, the gerund phrase is used as a noun.

> I love *dancing until dawn.* [Gerund phrase as direct object.]
> *Flying to Rome* is costly. [Gerund phrase as subject.]

NOTE: Since both gerunds and present participles end in *-ing*, they are sometimes confused. You can avoid confusing them by determining their function in a sentence. Gerunds function as nouns. Present participles, when not serving as part of the predicate, function as adjectives.

> *Running* keeps me fit for tennis. [*Running* is the subject of the sentence; therefore, it is a gerund.]

> The water *running* in the kitchen is a nuisance. [*Running* modifies *water*; therefore, it is a participle.]

Absolute Phrases

3f An absolute phrase consists of a noun and usually a participle, plus modifiers, that add to the meaning of a sentence but have no grammatical relation to it.

An absolute phrase differs from other phrases because it does not modify a particular word but instead modifies an entire sentence. An absolute phrase may appear almost anywhere in a sentence.

> The palm tree swayed, *its slick leaves shimmering with light.*

> *A magnifying glass raised to his eye,* Sherlock Holmes examined the weapon.

> The two of us worked the entire night — *Barbara at the computer and I at the tape recorder* — transcribing our field notes.

Exercise 13

Underline and identify the gerund (GER) and absolute (ABS) phrases in the following sentences.

1. Jerry feared living alone.

2. By saving every extra cent and working overtime, he acquired enough money for a car.

3. Living in times like these puts pressure on philosophers to create concepts that help readers understand their dilemmas.

4. She spent years, her nose buried in ancient books, seeking the secrets

of the alchemists.

5. A guitar slung over his shoulder, his eyes bulging but eager, his lips

thin as a razor slash, Frog Williams stared at the audience a moment

before he tapped his foot to signal the music to begin.

Exercise 14

Write two sentences for each of the following words, using the word in a gerund phrase and a present participial phrase. For example:

> *diving*
> *Diving from the ten-meter board* is thrilling. [Gerund phrase.]
> *Diving beneath the surface*, he saw a world of splendid color. [Participial phrase.]

1. swimming

4. studying

2. bragging

5. camping

3. crusading

4 Clauses

A **clause** is a group of words that has a subject and a predicate. There are two kinds of clauses: main clauses (sometimes called *independent clauses*) and dependent clauses (sometimes called *subordinate clauses*).

4a Main clauses form grammatically complete sentences.

Main clauses may stand alone or be joined by coordinating conjunctions (see p. 11), conjunctive adverbs (see p. 12), or semicolons (see p. 151). (Also see comma, p. 126.)

> The cobra is a poisonous snake. Its bite is often fatal. [Two main clauses standing alone, separated by a period.]

> The cobra is a poisonous snake, and its bite is often fatal. [Two main clauses joined by the coordinating conjunction *and*.]

> The cobra is a poisonous snake; indeed, its bite is often fatal. [Two main clauses joined by the conjunctive adverb *indeed*.]

> The cobra is a poisonous snake; its bite is often fatal. [Two main clauses joined by a semicolon.]

4b Dependent clauses do not form grammatically complete sentences.

Dependent clauses are usually introduced by a subordinating conjunction (see p. 12) or a relative pronoun (see p. 4). Dependent clauses function as nouns, adjectives, or adverbs within a sentence. The exact relation between the thought expressed in a dependent clause and the main clause is indicated by the subordinating conjunction or relative pronoun that joins them.

Adjective Clauses

An **adjective clause** modifies a noun or pronoun. It often begins with a relative pronoun — *who, whom, whose, that, which* — that refers to or is related to a noun or pronoun that precedes it. (See comma, p. 126.)

> The trumpet player *who left the stage* fell asleep in the lounge. [Modifies the noun *player*.]

> Anything *that stands on the seafront* will be leveled by the storm. [Modifies the pronoun *anything*.]

> Karla is the spy *Smiley seeks*. [Modifies the noun *spy*, with the relative pronoun *that* or *whom* understood.]

Adverb Clauses

An **adverb clause** modifies a verb, an adjective, or an adverb. It begins with a subordinating conjunction, such as *when, although, whenever, since, after, while, because, where, if, that,* or *than.*

> *Whenever he is asked,* he plays the banjo. [Modifies the verb *plays.*]
>
> I am happy *because it is Saturday.* [Modifies the adjective *happy.*]
>
> She studies more effectively *than I do.* [Modifies the adverb *effectively.*]

Noun Clauses

A **noun clause** is a dependent clause that functions as a noun. It may serve as subject, predicate nominative, direct object, indirect object, or object of a preposition. The dependent clause is likely to begin with a relative pronoun. (See complements, p. 17.)

> *That life is difficult for some* means little to insensitive bureaucrats. [Subject.]
>
> He described *what he wanted.* [Direct object.]

Exercise 15

Combine each group of sentences by using dependent clauses as indicated in the instructions in brackets. You may need to change some words to avoid needless repetition. For example:

> Few people have heard of hydrocephalus. Hydrocephalus affects at least a million families. [Use *although* to form an adverb clause.]
>
> Although few people have heard of the disease, hydrocephalus affects at least a million families.

1. Hydrocephalus is caused by a build-up of fluid in the brain cavity.

   Hydrocephalus is often called "water on the brain." [Use *which* to

   form an adjective clause.]

2. As many as eight thousand babies are born with the defect every year. This number does not relieve the mark of shame attached to the disease. [Use *that* to form a noun clause.]

3. Some doctors have attempted to educate the public about the defect. These doctors are prominent in the medical profession. Many people still believe that any child suffering from it always develops a head perhaps twice the normal size. [Use *although* to form an adverb clause and use *who* to form an adjective clause.]

4. Enlarged heads can be avoided. Doctors have developed an operation for hydrocephalics. The operation drains the fluid to avoid retardation in the patient. [Use *because* to form an adverb clause and use *that* to form an adjective clause.]

5. The surgical procedure has brought new hope to the parents of children suffering from the disease. They still worry about the future of their children. [Use *although* to form an adverb clause.]

5   Kinds of Sentences

Sentences can be classified according to their structure — simple, compound, complex, and compound-complex — and their purpose — declarative, imperative, interrogative, and exclamatory.

Sentence Structures

5a Simple sentences have only one main clause and no dependent clauses, although they may have several phrases.

> Years ago the family of a bride would supply the groom with a dowry. [One main clause.]
>
> The bride and the groom were not consulted about the choice of a mate and sometimes met each other for the first time on the day of their wedding. [One main clause with a compound subject and a compound predicate.]

5b Compound sentences have two or more main clauses but no dependent clauses.

> Chauvinism has fueled many political skirmishes, but jingoism has ignited wars. [Two main clauses joined by the coordinating conjunction *but*.]
>
> Some people are flattered into virtue; other people are bullied out of vice. [Two main clauses joined by a semicolon.]

5c Complex sentences have one main clause and at least one dependent clause.

> Although he was a cunning investor, Bennett went bankrupt. [One main clause and one dependent clause beginning with the subordinating conjunction *although*.]

5d Compound-complex sentences have at least two main clauses and at least one dependent clause.

> If they wish to live fully, most people need amusement to relax, and many people need intellectual challenges to develop their

minds. [Two main clauses joined by the coordinating conjunction *and* and one dependent clause beginning with the subordinating conjunction *if.*]

Sentence Purposes

5e   **A declarative sentence makes a statement.**

Spelunking requires the skill of a mountain climber and the courage of a coal miner.

5f   **An imperative sentence gives a command or makes a request.**

Don't walk on the grass.
Please stay off the grass.

(See note, implied subject, p. 15.)

5g   **An interrogative sentence asks a question.**

Which point of view is most valid?

5h   **An exclamatory sentence expresses strong feeling.**

The mountains are glorious!

Exercise 16

Write sentences according to the following directions.

1. Write a simple, declarative sentence that states a fact about your campus.
2. Using the coordinating conjunction *or,* write a compound sentence about a friend.

3. Write an interrogative sentence directed to a politician.
4. Write a declarative compound-complex sentence directed to a parent.
5. Write an imperative sentence that gently directs a child.
6. Write a complex sentence that deals with a foreign country.
7. Using a semicolon, write a compound sentence that deals with a sports event.
8. Using *who*, write a compound-complex sentence describing a friend.
9. Write a series of three simple sentences followed by a complex sentence that deals with a subject you read about in a newspaper.
10. Using a variety of sentence structures, describe a place that is important to you. Identify each sentence as simple, compound, complex, or compound-complex.

Sentence Errors

6 Sentence Fragments

7 Comma Splice and Fused Sentences

8 Subject and Verb Agreement

9 Pronoun and Antecedent Agreement

10 Case

11 Verb Forms

12 Tense

13 Subjunctive Mood

14 Active and Passive Voice

15 Adjectives and Adverbs

In some situations a noise or gesture will communicate. For instance, if you hear a shriek and glance out the window to see your neighbor holding a hammer in one hand while waving the other as if it were aflame, you would probably conclude that he had smashed a finger. Individual words also can communicate effectively. When you hear someone shout "stop," "run," or "fire," you react, for not to react might be foolhardy. But in more complex situations, only sentences can effectively communicate. Like all languages, English has developed sentence conventions that help writers and speakers convey meaning correctly and accurately. While you will never be evaluated on how well you express the pain of a smashed finger or shout a warning, you will be evaluated as a college student, and later as a college graduate, on how correctly and accurately you shape sentences. This section concentrates on common sentence errors and on ways to avoid those errors so that you can use sentences effectively.

6 Sentence Fragments *frag*

To stand as a main clause, a complete sentence must have a subject and a predicate and not be introduced by a subordinating conjunction or a relative pronoun. (See parts of sentences, p. 14.)

A **sentence fragment** is a portion of a sentence punctuated as though it were a complete sentence. Sentence fragments are usually serious errors in writing. Except for a few situations, which are noted below, their use indicates that the writer lacks an understanding of the basic principles of sentence structure and is not fully in control of his or her writing. You can learn to avoid most sentence fragments by heeding the following guidelines.

6a Do not punctuate a dependent clause as a main clause.

A group of words introduced by a subordinating conjunction (such as *when, while, although, because, if, until*) or by a relative pronoun (such as *who, which, that*) functions as a dependent clause. Although dependent clauses have subjects and verbs, they cannot stand alone as main clauses. You can correct such fragments by attaching the dependent clause to a main clause or by rewriting the dependent clause as a complete sentence. (See subordinating conjunctions, p. 12; relative pronouns, p. 4.)

> Ingrid won one thousand dollars on a quiz show. *Because she knew that shoelaces had not been invented until the eighteenth century.* [Fragment.]
>
> Ingrid won one thousand dollars on a quiz show because she knew that shoelaces had not been invented until the eighteenth century. [Corrected as one sentence with a main clause and a dependent clause.]
>
> John Steinbeck was a Nobel Prize–winning novelist. *Who wrote about the difficult life of migrant farm workers in California.* [Fragment.]
>
> John Steinbeck was a Nobel Prize–winning novelist who wrote about the difficult life of migrant farm workers in California. [Corrected as one sentence with a main clause and a dependent clause.]
>
> John Steinbeck was a Nobel Prize-winning novelist. He wrote about the difficult life of migrant farm workers in California. [Corrected as two complete sentences.]

Exercise 1

Correct each fragment, either by attaching it to a main clause or by rewriting the fragment as a complete sentence.

1. Although a grizzly bear weighs less than one pound at birth. An

   average adult grizzly weighs over five hundred pounds.

2. Because the grizzly bear population of the United States has shrunk

   to fewer than eight hundred.

3. Grizzlies have caused only nine human deaths in our national parks

in over one hundred years. Even though millions of tourists visit those parks every year.

4. Humans in the wilderness are usually not bothered by grizzlies. Who seem indifferent to everything but their own affairs.

5. Since a grizzly can run a hundred yards in about 6.7 seconds. It would be foolish to try to outrace one.

6b Do not punctuate a phrase as a main clause.

Like a dependent clause, a phrase is only part of a sentence and cannot stand alone. Phrase fragments can be corrected by joining them to main clauses or by rewriting them as complete sentences. (See phrases, p. 19.)

> The society sponsors an annual fair to commemorate the statehood of Nebraska. *And to raise money for famine relief.*

> The society sponsors an annual fair to commemorate the statehood of Nebraska and to raise money for famine relief.

> The group traveled by bus for three days. *Finally arriving on Friday.* [Participial phrase fragment.]

> The group traveled by bus for three days, finally arriving on Friday. [Corrected as one sentence.]

> The group traveled by bus for three days. They finally arrived on Friday. [Corrected as two sentences.]

> Geoffrey worked on his novel. *In a tiny cabin on the far corner of his property.* [Prepositional phrase fragment.]

> Geoffrey worked on his novel in a tiny cabin on the far corner of his property. [Corrected as one sentence.]

> One of the century's great medical discoveries is penicillin. *A miracle drug that has saved millions of lives.* [Appositive phrase fragment.]

One of the century's great medical discoveries is penicillin, a miracle drug that has saved millions of lives. [Corrected as one sentence.]

6c **Do not punctuate a part of a compound predicate as a main clause.**

(See compound predicate, p. 16; unnecessary commas, p. 145.)

The campaign committee wrote several hundred letters. *And made countless phone calls.* [Fragment: part of compound predicate.]

The campaign committee wrote several hundred letters, *and made countless phone calls.* [Still incorrect: compound predicate punctuated as two main clauses.]

The campaign committee wrote several hundred letters and made countless phone calls. [Corrected.]

Exercise 2

Correct each fragment either by attaching it to a main clause or by rewriting the fragment as a complete sentence.

1. Grandmother Rosa is the last member of a Chilean Indian tribe. About to become extinct.

2. When Grandmother Rosa dies, there will be no more Yaghans. Bringing to a close the twelve-thousand-year history of her people.

3. One famous Yaghan, Jemmy Button, was taken to England aboard the British survey ship *Beagle* in 1830. To be taught English and to meet the king.

4. The melodic Yaghan language seems to be heading for extinction, too. Once spoken by over three thousand people.

5. Missionaries who arrived in 1870 taught the Indians destructive eating habits. And brought new diseases.

Exercise 3

Write a main clause to be attached before or after each prepositional phrase. For example: *inside the small box*

> A huge pearl rested on a tiny velvet pillow inside the small box.

1. along the path that leads to the old mill

2. within the next three hundred years

3. except for a few complainers and doubters

4. despite the ever-increasing cost of education

5. after the long winter

6d Fragments are sometimes acceptable in special situations.

Use fragments such as the following sparingly and only when your purpose is clear.

ADVERTISING	Improved mileage!
HEADLINES	Two on Trial for Robbery
QUESTIONS AND ANSWERS	What next? Another term paper.
EXCLAMATIONS IN DIALOGUE	Holy cow! "Of course." "Wonderful."

FOR EMPHASIS   I've been patient, understanding, attentive, and
gentle. Now it's over. No more Mr. Nice Guy!

AS TRANSITIONS   My final point.

Exercise 4

Revise the following paragraph to eliminate sentence fragments.

Ernest Hemingway's first major work, *The Sun Also Rises*, takes place
in France and Spain. A few years after World War I. It has been called
the best expression of the disillusionment felt by young people of that
period. The characters live one day at a time, drifting from place to place,
engaging in small talk and petty quarrels. Always seeking new sensations
To ease their anguish. Jake Barnes, the narrator and principal character,
has a stoical approach to life. Which stems from his physical impotence,
the result of a wound he received while fighting in the war. Despite its
bleakness, or perhaps because of it, the novel spoke clearly and intimately
to post–World War I youth. The so-called lost generation.

7 Comma Splices and Fused Sentences *cs/fs*

Like unintentional sentence fragments, comma splices and fused or
run-on sentences are serious errors in writing. In speaking, you quite
naturally run clauses together, linking or separating them with
breaths and pauses. In writing, you must use coordinating conjunctions and punctuation marks to link or separate clauses. If you are

not careful, your speech habits will influence your writing habits, and your work will be marred by comma splices and fused or run-on sentences. The key to avoiding comma splices and fused or run-on sentences is the ability to recognize main clauses, dependent clauses, coordinating conjunctions, subordinating conjunctions, and conjunctive adverbs.

7a Do not write comma splices and fused or run-on sentences.

A **comma splice** occurs when main clauses are joined by a comma alone. (See main clauses, p. 25.)

> Once Stewart was a small mountain town of only a few dozen households, today it is a busy city of sixty thousand people.

A **fused** or **run-on sentence** occurs when main clauses are joined without a coordinating conjunction or any punctuation mark.

> Women jockeys have had great success they work hard to achieve their goals.

Comma splices and fused or run-on sentences can be corrected in four ways.

1. Use a period to make two separate sentences.

> Once Stewart was a small mountain town of only a few dozen households. Today it is a busy city of sixty thousand people.

> Women jockeys have had great success. They work hard to achieve their goals.

2. Use a semicolon to show a close relation between the main clauses.

> Once Stewart was a small mountain town of only a few dozen households; today it is a busy city of sixty thousand people.

> Women jockeys have had great success; they work hard to achieve their goals.

NOTE: When two main clauses are joined by a conjunctive adverb, such as *nevertheless, consequently, however,* or *therefore,* a semicolon must come before the clause containing the conjunctive adverb. (See conjunctive adverbs, p. 12.)

> Women jockeys work hard to achieve their goals; *therefore,* they have had great success.

3. Use a comma and a coordinating conjunction to show the appropriate relation between the main clauses. (See coordinating conjunctions, p. 11.)

> Once Stewart was a small mountain town of only a few dozen households, *but* today it is a busy city of sixty thousand people.
>
> Women jockeys work hard to achieve their goals, *and* they have had great success.

4. Use a subordinating conjunction to introduce the less important clause. (See subordinating conjunctions, p. 12.)

> *Although Stewart was once a small mountain town of only a few dozen households,* today it is a busy city of sixty thousand people.
>
> Women jockeys have had great success *because they work hard to achieve their goals.*

Exercise 5

Label each sentence as correct (C), fused (FS), or containing a comma splice (CS). Correct the fused sentences and comma splices in any of the four ways listed in the text.

1. Although Morton is an independent, he has earned the respect of

   Democrats and Republicans.

2. The grocery store is on the right the drugstore is on the left.

3. The flood waters ruined the carpet, many pieces of furniture were

   damaged beyond repair.

4. I didn't expect to be late however, I wasn't counting on such a slow bus ride.

5. Sea horse eggs are tended by the male, he carries them in a belly pouch until they hatch.

6. Morocco's earthquake registered 9.5 on the Richter scale, it killed one thousand people.

7. The ski team had expected to win another championship this year, but injuries plagued them all season.

8. The new tenants were pleased with the offices, they rented the entire tenth floor.

9. The ability of a human to recall specific information rises for a brief period after study, then it falls rapidly in the next few hours.

10. Besides working in the shoe factory, Hank caddies at the golf course on weekends.

Exercise 6

Correct the ten comma splices or fused sentences in the following paragraph, using the four methods of correction given in the text.

Diego Rivera, Mexico's famous revolutionary artist, created controversy throughout his life, his giant murals celebrating the cause of the working class were too radical for many people. A portrait of Lenin appeared in a mural he was painting at Rockefeller Center in New York City in spite of a public outcry, he refused to remove it he did offer to add a portrait of Abraham Lincoln. That wasn't enough. His commission was canceled. The unfinished mural was destroyed. He had lost this battle, however, he later challenged all the artistic *isms* of the early twentieth century. He disdained ordinary canvas-sized pictures he believed that they inevitably end up in stuffy museums or the homes of the rich. Instead, he looked for huge walls on buildings where art could be used as a weapon in the class struggle. A typical Rivera mural is ablaze with color and full of people; it condemns exploitation of the masses or symbolizes the strength of purpose of awakened workers. Out of his sympathy for the poor, Rivera joined the Communist Party he denounced the party in 1929 then he was attacked by both leftists and rightists he often carried a pistol for protection. When he died in 1957, controversy surrounded his funeral, too. The Communist Party covered his coffin with a red flag, others opposed this gesture fights erupted on the streets even as his body was lowered into the grave.

8 Subject and Verb Agreement *agr*

The subject of any sentence you write will determine whether you use a singular or plural verb. If you wish to describe how a boy dresses, your subject is *boy* and you might write *The boy dresses sloppily*. If your subject is *boys*, your sentence might read *The boys dress sloppily*. In either case the verb must agree in number with the subject.

8a A verb should agree with its subject even when words come between them.

Many agreement problems arise because words often come between a subject and a verb, thus obscuring their relation.

> The *intricacy* of the overlapping, brightly colored patterns *makes* a viewer slightly dizzy at first.

In this sentence the singular noun *intricacy* is the subject, and the singular verb *makes* agrees with it. The plural noun *patterns* is the object of the preposition *of*, not the subject of the sentence. Some writers, however, might mistakenly believe *patterns* to be the subject and commit an agreement error by writing *The intricacy of the overlapping, brightly colored patterns make a viewer slightly dizzy at first*.

To determine which form of a verb agrees with the subject in sentences like this one, read the sentence omitting all prepositional phrases.

> The *intricacy* ~~of the overlapping, brightly colored patterns~~ *makes* a viewer slightly dizzy at first.

NOTE: Expressions such as *together with*, *as well as*, *in addition to*, and *along with* function as prepositions, not coordinating conjunctions. They do not, therefore, change the number of the subject.

> The *candidate* as well as her relatives *was* pleased with the results. [The singular subject, *candidate*, takes a singular verb, *was*.]

The *neighbors* together with the inspector *were* concerned about the hazard. [The plural subject, *neighbors*, takes a plural verb, *were*.]

8b Two or more subjects joined by *and* usually take a plural verb.

The *chairman and* the *president battle* over the budget together.
Tom, Bill, and Beth are correct.

NOTE: When the parts of a compound subject function as a single idea or refer to a single person or thing, they take a singular verb.

Apple pie and ice cream is my favorite dessert.
The *star and host* of the show *is* backstage.

When a compound subject is preceded by *each* or *every*, the verb is usually singular. Although these words refer to more than one, they imply consideration of one at a time.

Under the border guard's keen eye, *every pedestrian, cyclist*, and *motorist suffers* a close scrutiny.

When a compound subject is followed by *each*, the verb is singular.

Speaking and writing *each requires* a mastery of words. [The writer is referring to speaking and writing separately.]

8c Singular subjects joined by *or* or *nor* take singular verbs, and plural subjects joined by *or* or *nor* take plural verbs.

A painted *seascape or landscape is* not my idea of art.
Neither *strawberry shortcake nor pecan pie attracts* their attention.
Either the *dogs or* the *rabbits have become* exhausted.

Singular and Plural Subjects **45**

8d When a singular subject and a plural subject are joined by *or* or *nor*, the verb must agree with the subject nearer to it.

> *Field testing or surveys determine* their marketing strategies.
> *Surveys or field testing determines* their marketing strategies.

Since following this convention often leads to writing that sounds awkward, try to avoid the awkwardness problem by reworking such sentences.

> **AWKWARD**   Neither *they nor I am* happy with the results.
>
> **REVISED**   They are not happy with the results, and neither am I.

8e Generally, use singular verbs with indefinite pronouns.

Most indefinite pronouns — such as *anybody, anyone, anything, each, either, everybody, everyone, everything, neither, nobody, none, no one, one, some, somebody, someone,* and *something* — are singular and refer to a single unspecified person or thing; consequently, they take singular verbs.

> *Everyone* on the team *was* excited about the game.
> *Neither* of the twins *was* helpful.

A few indefinite pronouns, such as *all, any, none,* and *some,* may be singular or plural. Whether you use a singular or a plural verb depends on the noun or pronoun to which the indefinite pronoun refers.

> The chairperson announced that *all* of the members *were* present. [*All* refers to *members,* so the verb is plural.]
>
> The committee found that *all* of the report *was* helpful. [*All* refers to *report,* so the verb is singular.]

8f Collective nouns take singular or plural verbs depending on how they are used.

Collective nouns, such as *army, audience, class, committee, faculty, group, herd, public,* and *team,* are singular in form, but they name groups of individuals. When referring to a group as a single unit, a collective noun takes a singular verb.

> Given time, the *public* always *sees* through political deception.
>
> Some cynics claim that the American *family is* no longer functioning.

When referring to a group's members as individuals, a collective noun takes a plural verb. (See agreement of collective nouns and pronouns, p. 55.)

> The *faculty argue* among themselves about the value of general education courses.
>
> The Rogers *family have been parking* their cars on our lawn.

8g Most nouns plural in form but singular in meaning take singular verbs.

Nouns such as *athletics, civics, economics, mathematics, measles, mumps, news, physics, politics, species,* and *statistics* are singular and take singular verbs.

> *Mumps is* no longer a threat to Americans.
> The *news* about the economy *is* bleak.

Words such as *trousers* and *scissors* are regarded as plural and take plural verbs, except when used after *pair.*

> *Scissors are* in the drawer.
>
> A *pair* of scissors *functions* as a tantalizing symbol in Kafka's "Jackals and Arabs."

8h The verb must agree with the subject even when the subject follows the verb and when the sentence begins with *there* or *here*.

> Where *is* the *truth?*
>
> Out of the pages of that best-selling novel *appear* eerie *characters*, mysterious *situations*, and philosophical *riddles*.

Don't mistake the expletives *there* and *here* for subjects. They merely signal that the subject follows the verb.

> There *are* several *answers* to the problem. [The actual subject is *answers*.]
>
> Here *is* a *bit* of advice. [The actual subject is *bit*.]

When a compound subject follows the verb in a sentence beginning with *there* or *here*, a singular verb is sometimes used, especially if the first item of the compound subject is singular. Such sentences are best rewritten.

> There *is* [*are*] a *can* of fruit and six *jars* of peanut butter in the cupboard.
>
> A can of fruit and six jars of peanut butter are in the cupboard. [Rewritten.]

8i A linking verb must agree with its subject, not with the predicate nominative or predicate adjective.

> The best *hope* for the future *is* our children.
> Our *children are* the best hope for the future.

8j After the relative pronouns *who*, *which*, and *that*, use a singular verb when the antecedent is singular and a plural verb when the antecedent is plural.

The antecedent is the word to which the pronoun refers. (See antecedent, pp. 3, 53.)

Our elected officials obviously listen to *people* who *give* them campaign contributions. [*Who* refers to *people*, so the verb is plural.]

The boss likes a *worker* who always *arrives* on time. [*Who* refers to *worker*, so the verb is singular.]

NOTE: Agreement errors involving relative pronouns often occur in sentences that include a phrase beginning with *one of the*. You must look carefully at the sense of such sentences to determine whether the verb should be singular or plural.

He is one of the *members* who *are* quarrelsome. [The antecedent of *who* is *members* because the sentence says that some members are quarrelsome. Therefore, the verb is plural.]

She is *the only one* of the members who *has paid* the dues. [This sentence says that only one member paid the dues. The antecedent of *who* is *one*, so the verb is singular.]

She is only one of the *members* who *have paid* the dues. [This sentence says that more than one member paid the dues, so the antecedent of *who* is *members*, and the verb is plural.]

8k Use a singular verb when *every* or *many a* precedes a subject, even a compound subject.

Although these words refer to more than one, they imply consideration of one at a time.

Every cave, gorge, and *grove was* searched for the missing campers.

Many a motorist breathes a sigh of relief when exiting from the freeway.

8l Expressions of time, money, measurement, weight, volume, and fractions are singular when the amount is considered as a single unit.

Twenty dollars is a small price to pay.

Two hundred and twenty yards is a long way to sprint.
Three-fourths of the day *is* gone.

When the amount is considered as separate units, use a plural verb.

The last *six miles were* grueling in different ways.

8m Titles and words named as words take singular verbs.

Carl Jung's <u>Memories, Dreams, Reflections</u> *is* a fine work of autobiography.

<u>Chitlins</u> *is* a variation of <u>chitterlings,</u> which refers to the part of the small intestines of pigs used for food.

Exercise 7

In the following sentences, correct any errors in subject and verb agreement. If you find a correct sentence, mark it with a *C.*

1. The preschool's giggling gang of three- and four-year-olds love to chase the rabbits through the field.

2. At least once a week liver and onions are the main dish for an evening meal.

3. The gallery as well as the interior halls were redecorated before the tourist season.

4. A committee of students are meeting to discuss the library budget.

5. Neither the Department of State nor the visiting diplomats understand the reasons for the attack.

6. The creature prowling the moors makes loud noises at night.

7. Both a school of piranhas and a great white shark is deadly to swimmers.

8. All but three of the projects has been completed on time.

9. Cycling in the park or hiking in the woods relax a person.

10. Everybody at the Smiths' were wearing a costume.

Exercise 8

In the following sentences, correct any errors in subject and verb agreement. If you find a correct sentence, mark it with a *C*.

1. Do not merely study English; study linguistics, which are connected to anthropology, psychology, and sociology as well as English.

2. From Robert Brytan's pen comes images of mysterious journeys, questioning visitors, and relentless endurance tests.

3. *The Pickwick Papers*, first published as a serial, are a good example of Charles Dickens' genius as a caricaturist.

4. Randy is one of those people who dreams of a future filled with fast cars and speed boats.

5. *Quizzes* are not as commonly misspelled as *existence*.

6. Every detective, desk sergeant, and traffic cop know the suspect has flaming red hair and a scarred cheek.

7. Porcupines exist around the world in numerous sizes and various shapes, but only one species exist in the United States.

8. There is a couple of wrong paths to the left.

9. Four pounds of beans are more than they can carry.

10. The battle of the sexes are composed of minute-to-minute encounters at home, on the streets, and in work places.

Exercise 9

In the following paragraph, correct the errors in subject and verb agreement.

Computerized psychological testing services around the country is gaining widespread use. A report published in recent months indicate that almost everybody taking the tests are pleased by the method. The automated testing proceeds in the following fashion: Sitting before a TV-like screen, a patient answers a group of questions that demands true/false responses or offers multiple-choice answers. Either a psychiatrist or a clinician who has been trained in psychiatry sit in another room and score the data and analyze the results. Immediately following the test, doctor and patient meets to discuss the outcome and plans an initial treatment. Some critics of computerized testing claim the testing dehumanizes the doctor-patient relationship, but neither doctors using the method nor patients undergoing the process seem to agree with the critics.

9 Pronoun and Antecedent Agreement *agr*

A pronoun must agree in person and number with its **antecedent,** the word to which the pronoun refers, and the reference must be clear. Singular pronouns are used to refer to singular antecedents and plural pronouns are used to refer to plural antecedents. (See pronouns, p. 3.)

> *Carl* rigged *his* yawl with new sails.
>
> Since the *students* requested the *test,* the instructor gave *it* to *them.*

9a Use a plural pronoun to refer to a compound antecedent joined by *and*.

The coordinating conjunction *and* joins items together, creating a compound subject, so a plural pronoun is required.

> *Hugh and Aaron* practiced jujitsu until *they* collapsed on the mats.

9b Use a singular pronoun to refer to two or more singular antecedents joined by *or* or *nor*. Use a plural pronoun to refer to two or more plural antecedents joined by *or* or *nor*.

The coordinating conjunctions *or* and *nor* keep items separate for individual consideration. If the antecedents are singular and considered separately, a singular pronoun is required.

> *Jan or Pam* will give *her* flute rendition of Pachelbel's Kanon in D.

Of course, if the separately considered antecedents are plural, a plural pronoun is required.

> Neither the *students nor* the *teachers* are presenting *their* position at the meeting.

NOTE: Confusion can arise when the pronoun refers to only one of the antecedents.

> Neither *Ann nor Sarah* could find *her* notebook. [Whose notebook?]

The meaning can be made clear simply by substituting the correct noun for the pronoun.

> Neither *Ann nor Sarah* could find *Ann's* notebook.

(See 18c, p. 105.)

9c When a singular antecedent and a plural antecedent are joined by *or* or *nor*, use a pronoun that agrees with the nearer antecedent.

> The council *members* or the *mayor* will lose *her* supporters over this disagreement.

Since sentences that follow this convention, such as the preceding example, often sound awkward, writers usually rework them.

> The *mayor* or the council *members* will lose supporters over this disagreement.

Or:

> The *mayor* or the council *members* will lose supporters over this disagreement.

9d Generally use a singular pronoun to refer to a collective noun.

Words such as *army, audience, class, committee, group, herd, public,* and *team* are singular in form, but they name groups of individuals. When a collective noun refers to a group as a single unit, use a singular pronoun.

> The *committee* announced that *it* will vote on Friday.

When a collective noun refers to a group's members as individuals, use a plural pronoun. (See agreement of collective nouns and verbs, p. 47.)

> The *committee* remained in *their* chairs.

NOTE: Take special care to avoid mistakenly treating a collective noun as both singular and plural in the same sentence.

> The hiring *committee arrives* at a decision only after *they have discussed* all the applicants. [Singular verb, plural pronoun, plural verb.]
>
> The hiring *committee arrives* at a decision only after *it has discussed* all the applicants. [Corrected.]

9e Use singular pronouns to refer to indefinite pronouns used as antecedents.

Most indefinite pronouns — such as *anybody, anyone, each, everybody, everyone, nobody, one, none, somebody, someone,* and *something* — are singular and refer to a single unspecified person or thing; consequently, they call for singular pronouns.

> *Each* of the women had *her* book published.
> *Everyone* on the men's cross-country team ran *his* best race.
> *Something* ominous made *its* presence felt in the woods.

In the preceding examples the gender of the antecedents is clear from the context, but often the gender of the antecedent of an indefinite pronoun is unknown or mixed. Traditionally in such cases, a masculine pronoun has been used to refer to the indefinite pronoun.

> *Everyone* living in the apartment building did *his* best to clean the halls.

Although men and women are probably living in the apartment building, grammatical convention calls for the masculine pronoun *his* to refer to the indefinite pronoun *everyone*. This practice, however, is changing because using *he* or *his* to refer to indefinite pronouns in the sentence ignores the presence of women. As an alternative you can recast such a sentence by making the antecedent plural; by using *he or she, his or her;* or by avoiding pronouns to refer to indefinite pronouns.

> *People* living in the apartment building did *their* best to clean the halls. [Making the antecedent plural.]
>
> *Everyone* living in the apartment building did *his or her* best to clean the halls. [Using *his or her*.]
>
> Everyone living in the apartment building kept the halls as clean as possible. [Avoiding pronouns referring to the indefinite pronoun.]

NOTE: Avoid overusing *he or she, his or her.* Repeating those constructions excessively will make your writing unwieldy and monotonous. (See sexist language, p. 219).

9f Use the relative pronouns *who, whom, which,* and *that* with the appropriate antecedents.

Who refers to persons and sometimes to animals that have names.

> Jenkins is the dentist *who* pulled my wisdom teeth.
>
> Their dog Flash, *who* seems harmless, bit a burglar on the heel last week.

Which refers to animals and things.

> Their cat, *which* is pure-bred Siamese, cost a week's wages.
>
> Andorra, *which* is located in the Pyrenees between Spain and France, is also called Andorra la Vella.

That refers to animals, things, and sometimes to persons. (See nonrestrictive and restrictive elements, p. 129.)

> The creek *that* flows into the pasture has gone dry.
>
> Do you believe the old saying "Dogs *that* bark will never bite"?

NOTE: *Whose*, the possessive form of *who*, is often used to refer to animals and things to avoid awkward constructions using *of which*.

> This is a riddle the answer *of which* no longer interests me.
> This is a riddle *whose* answer no longer interests me.

Exercise 10

Rewrite the following sentences according to the directions in brackets. Be sure to make all the changes necessary to keep the agreement of pronouns and antecedents correct.

1. Jane and her sister asked to bring their skis. [Change *and* to *or*.]

2. The judges differ in their interpretations of proper courtroom behavior. [Change *The judges* to *Each judge*.]

3. The dancer or the magician will perform his routine. [Change *or* to *and*.]

4. The army withdrew its support of the junta leaders. [Change *The army* to *Some members of the army*.]

5. Someone attending the mother-and-daughter banquet forgot her coat. [Change *mother-and-daughter* to *father-and-son*.]

6. Either the kitten or her mother purr until she goes to sleep. [Change *Either . . . or* to *and*.]

7. The class, which usually meets on Wednesday, forgot that it had agreed to meet on Saturday. [Change *The class* to *Some class members*.]

8. By taking a moral stand, the governor or the chief justice can enhance his reputation. [Change *chief justice* to *members of the Supreme Court*.]

9. The cat, which appears daily in the cartoon section, cherishes the good life. [Change *The cat* to *Garfield*.]

10. Runners who stretch each morning have fewer injuries during workouts. [Change *Runners* to *Anyone*.]

10 Case *ca*

The **case** of nouns and pronouns indicates how the words function in a sentence. Nouns and most pronouns have only two case forms (that is, the spelling the word has when it is used in a particular case): the plain form *(day, someone)* and the possessive form *(day's, someone's)*.

The pronouns *I, we, he, she, they,* and *who* have three different case forms: the subjective form, the objective form, and the possessive form. The pronouns *you* and *it* have one form for both the subjective and the objective case and a different form for the possessive case. (See possessive case, p. 62; possessive pronouns, p. 3.)

PERSONAL PRONOUNS	SUBJECTIVE CASE	OBJECTIVE CASE	POSSESSIVE CASE
Singular			
First person	I	me	my, mine
Second person	you	you	your, yours
Third person	he, she, it	him, her, it	his, her, hers, its
Plural			
First person	we	us	our, ours
Second person	you	you	your, yours
Third person	they	them	their, theirs
RELATIVE OR INTERROGATIVE PRONOUNS			
Singular	who	whom	whose
Plural	who	whom	whose

10a Use the subjective case of pronouns for subjects and for predicate nominatives.

Ross and *I* flew to Reno. [Subject.]

After Hammond and *she* joined the party, a storm blew in from the mountains. [Subject.]

The ones who took the blame were Harold and *she*. [Predicate nominative.]

NOTE: When the subject is compound, as in the first two examples, many beginning writers make a mistake in the selection of a pronoun. Whereas they would not write *Me flew to Reno*, they might write *Ross and me flew to Reno*. To avoid this error with compound subjects that include pronouns, try reading each subject separately with the verb.

In speech it is common practice to use the objective forms of personal pronouns as predicate nominatives in expressions beginning with *it is* or *it's: It's me, It is him, It's us, It's them.* Such use of the objective form is unacceptable in writing.

10b Use the objective case when pronouns are direct objects, indirect objects, and objects of the preposition.

> Garret met *her* while ice skating. [Direct object.]
>
> Molly bought *him* and *me* some roasted chestnuts. [Indirect objects.]
>
> The victory belonged to the Cougars and *us*. [Object of the preposition.]

Exercise 11

From the pairs of words in parentheses, select the correct form of the pronoun for each sentence.

1. Standing on the cliff overlooking the swamp, Robert and *(I, me)* heard the wind howling through the trees.

2. The children reached the hilltop, but Martha wasn't sure it was *(they, them)*.

3. Bruce gave *(she, her)* and *(I, me)* the map.

4. I enjoy the company of Ralph and *(she, her)* more than they know.

5. Seldom have Richard and *(I, me)* argued so violently.

10c Use the appropriate case when the pronoun *we* or *us* comes before a noun.

If the pronoun functions as a subject, use *we*.

> *We* linguists meet once a year at a major university.

If the pronoun functions as an object, use *us*.

A number of *us* mycologists regularly collect mushrooms in the foothills.

10d   When a pronoun is used as an appositive, its case depends on the function of the word it refers to.

(See appositives, p. 19.)

Our two best players, Bob and *she*, were beaten in the first match. [The pronoun refers to *players*, the subject of the sentence, so it is in the subjective case.]

Poor judgment beat our two best players, Bob and *her*, in the first match. [*Players* is the object of the verb *beat*, so the pronoun is in the objective case.]

Exercise 12

From the pair of words in parentheses, select the correct form of the pronoun for each sentence.

1. The country is divided into two camps, the government and *(we, us)*.

2. Beth has chosen to create cave paintings, an art form that tests the endurance of *(we, us)* admirers of her work.

3. The two silhouettes, Ford and *(she, her)*, crept through the fog.

4. A bolt of lightning startled the group, *(we, us)* inexperienced hikers.

5. "The future is grim," *(we, us)* prophets claim.

10e   In elliptical, or incomplete, comparisons following *than* or *as*, the case of the pronoun depends on the meaning of the sentence.

In comparisons, *than* and *as* often introduce incomplete constructions.

The case of the pronoun in such constructions depends on how the incomplete clause would be completed. Use the subjective case if the pronoun functions as the subject of the omitted clause.

> I have lived in this city longer than *they* [have lived here].
> I trust John just as much as *she* [trusts John].

Use the objective case if the pronoun functions as the object in the omitted clause. (See sentence completeness, p. 113.)

> I visit my grandmother more than [I visit] *them*.
> I trust John just as much as [I trust] *her*.

10f Use the objective case for pronouns that are subjects or objects of infinitives.

> The attorney considered *him* to be a prime suspect. [Subject of infinitive.]
>
> He tried to trap *him* with tough questions. [Object of infinitive.]

10g Usually use the possessive case of a pronoun or noun preceding a gerund.

A gerund is the present participle of a verb used as a noun. (See gerunds and gerund phrases, p. 23.)

> What was the reason for *his* appearing tonight? [*His* modifies the gerund *appearing*.]
>
> *Dr. Kidd's* running for office shocked us all. [*Dr. Kidd's* modifies the gerund *running*.]

The possessive is not used when the present participle serves as an adjective. (See present participles, p. 21.)

> The crowd watched *him* tottering on the tightrope. [*Tottering* is a present participle used as an adjective modifying *him*.]
>
> I often hear *Tom* talking in his sleep. [*Talking* is a present participle used as an adjective modifying *Tom*.]

Avoid using the possessive with a gerund when doing so creates an awkward construction.

> **AWKWARD**   I am pleased about Harold's cooking dinner.
>
> **REVISED**   I am pleased about Harold cooking dinner.
>
> **BETTER**   I am pleased that Harold is cooking dinner.

Exercise 13

From the pair of words in parentheses, select the correct pronoun form for each sentence.

1. The librarian wanted *(she, her)* to do the research alone.

2. Can the computer calculate this problem as well as *(he, him)?*

3. *(Our, Us)* tugging on the branch did not break it.

4. Have you lived in the neighborhood as long as *(they, them)?*

5. Marge flies a plane better than *(he, him).*

6. After hours of tests they thought *(he, him)* to be insane.

7. I dislike *(his, him)* singing in the shower.

8. The Bergers have traveled to Paris more often than *(we, us).*

9. The schoolchildren watch *(us, our)* running each morning.

10. She respects Tom's intelligence more than *(they, them).*

10h   The case of the pronoun *who* is determined by its function in its own clause.

You can usually determine which case to use in interrogative sentences by answering the question the sentence poses.

Who led England to victory? [*The prime minister* led England to victory: subject.]

Whom shall we hold responsible? [We shall hold *her* responsible: direct object.]

Whom is the letter addressed to? [The letter is addressed to *her:* object of the preposition *to.*]

In dependent clauses use *who* or *whoever* for all subjects; use *whom* or *whomever* for all objects. The case of the pronoun depends only on its function within the clause, not on the function of the clause in the sentence.

The Sisters of Mercy give help to *whoever* requests it. [*Whoever* is the subject of the clause *whoever requests it.* The entire clause is the object of the preposition *to.*]

I do not remember *whom* I met at the party. [*Whom* is the direct object of *met.* The entire clause *whom I met at the party* is the direct object of the verb *do remember.*]

To determine whether to use *who, whom, whoever,* or *whomever,* substitute a personal pronoun for the relative pronoun. The case of the personal pronoun is the correct case for the relative pronoun. If necessary, change the word order of the clause.

I do not recall to *(who, whom)* I lent the book.
I lent the book to *him* (or *her*). [Objective case.]

Therefore, *whom* is the correct relative pronoun.

I do not recall to *whom* I lent the book.

Sometimes a dependent clause includes an expression such as *I think* or *he said.*

She is the woman *(who, whom)* he said called last night.

To decide between *who* or *whom* in such a construction, repeat the sentence without the intervening expression.

She is the woman *who* called last night.

Exercise 14

From the pair of words in parentheses, select the correct relative pronoun in each sentence.

1. Many women *(who, whom)* have raised their children would like to start a career.

2. The club is open to *(whoever, whomever)* can pay the dues.

3. The reporter is looking for a witness from *(who, whom)* she can get answers.

4. He is the man *(who, whom)* some claim is the power behind the mayor.

5. To *(who, whom)* do we owe the honor?

11 Verb Forms *vb*

Every verb has three principal forms: the infinitive (the form of the verb listed in the dictionary), the past, and the past participle.

INFINITIVE	PAST	PAST PARTICIPLE
dance	danced	danced

The **infinitive** form of the verb usually appears in combination with *to* to form a verbal that functions as a noun, an adjective, or an adverb. (See 3c, p. 21.) A **participle** is a verbal that functions as an adjective, an adverb, or a part of a verb phrase. (See 3d, p. 21.)

All verbs form the **present participle** by the addition of *-ing* to the infinitive form. Neither a present participle nor a past participle can function as the verb in a sentence unless it is combined with one or more helping verbs.

Any verb may be combined with helping (or auxiliary) verbs to express time relations and other meanings. *Shall* and *will; have, has,* and *had; do, does,* and *did;* and forms of the verb *be (am, are, is, was, were, been, being)* are helping verbs used to indicate time and voice. (See tense, p. 69; voice, p. 78.) *Can, could, may, might, must, ought, shall, should, will,* and *would* are helping verbs used to indicate necessity, obligation, permission, or possibility.

> You *could* learn to ski.
> You *must* attend.
> She *should* know better.

Verbs have either regular or irregular forms. A **regular verb** forms its past and past participle by adding *-d* or *-ed* to the infinitive.

INFINITIVE	PAST	PAST PARTICIPLE
live	lived	lived
jump	jumped	jumped

An **irregular verb** forms its past and past participle in a different way from regular verbs. This difference may be a change in spelling or no change at all from the infinitive form. Spelling changes usually involve a change in vowels or the addition of an *-n* or *-en* ending.

INFINITIVE	PAST	PAST PARTICIPLE
swim	swam	swum
throw	threw	thrown
hit	hit	hit

The major difficulty you will confront in the use of irregular verbs is in selecting the correct past or past participle form. When in doubt, consult a dictionary. If a verb is regular, the dictionary does not include the past and past participle. If the verb is irregular, the dictionary includes the irregular forms. You can also learn the correct forms of some common irregular verbs by studying the following list.

INFINITIVE	PAST	PAST PARTICIPLE
begin	began	begun
bite	bit	bitten
blow	blew	blown
break	broke	broken
bring	brought	brought
catch	caught	caught
choose	chose	chosen
come	came	come
creep	crept	crept
dig	dug	dug
dive	dived or dove	dived
do	did	done
draw	drew	drawn
dream	dreamed or dreamt	dreamed or dreamt
drink	drank	drunk
eat	ate	eaten
fall	fell	fallen
find	found	found
fit	fit or fitted	fit or fitted
fling	flung	flung
fly	flew	flown
fly (baseball)	flied	flied
forbid	forbade or forbad	forbidden
forget	forgot	forgotten or forgot
get	got	got or gotten
go	went	gone
know	knew	known
lay (place or put)	laid	laid
lead	led	led
lend	lent	lent
lie (recline)	lay	lain
lose	lost	lost
ride	rode	ridden
rise	rose	risen
run	ran	run
say	said	said

INFINITIVE	PAST	PAST PARTICIPLE
see	saw	seen
set (place or put)	set	set
shine	shone or shined	shone or shined
sing	sang or sung	sung
sink	sank or sunk	sunk
sit (take a seat)	sat	sat
steal	stole	stolen
sting	stung	stung
swim	swam	swum
tear	tore	torn
throw	threw	thrown
wear	wore	worn
write	wrote	written

Exercise 15

With another student, test yourself on the principal forms of the irregular verbs in the list.

Exercise 16

Use a dictionary to determine the correct form of the irregular verb necessary to complete each sentence.

1. I _____ my book on the table, and someone _____ it. *(put, take)*

2. Because the dog has _____ on bones for years, its teeth have been _____ to nubs. *(feed, grind)*

3. I had already _____ to work when the pipe _____. *(begin, burst)*

4. They have _____ all the milk, but they have not _____ all the

cookies. *(drink, eat)*

5. No matter which road we _____, we would have _____ lost.

(choose, become)

12 Tense *t*

Verb forms change to show the time of the action they express. The change in time (past, present, or future) is called **tense.**

12a The present tense expresses action about something occurring now, at the present time.

> Marcie *attends* Kettler College.
> Who *goes* there?

The present tense also serves some special functions in writing.
Use the present tense to state a general truth or fact.

> Water *freezes* at 0° C.

Use the present tense to state what a writer does in his or her written work or to describe a character's activities in a written work.

> In *A Distant Mirror*, a history of the fourteenth century, Barbara W. Tuchman skillfully *combines* discussion of great events and the lives of common people.

> In the first chapter of *Great Expectations*, Pip *meets* an escaped convict.

Use the present tense to describe elements in artistic works.

> The closing scene of *Casablanca appeals* to our sentimentality.

Use the present tense to state habitual action.

He *sleeps* until noon every day.

Use the infinitive form with *do* to create an **emphatic form.**

I *do study* hard.

NOTE: In all tenses you can show continuing action by using the **progressive form,** which is the present participle of the verb together with a form of the helping verb *be.*

Marcie *is attending* Kettler College.

12b The past tense expresses action that occurred in the past but did not continue into the present.

I *slipped* on the icy street several times.
I *was slipping* on the ice when he grabbed my arm.

Use the infinitive form with *did* to create an emphatic form.

I *did slip* on the ice.

NOTE: Past action may be shown in other ways.

I *used to slip* on the icy streets.

12c The future tense expresses action about something happening in the future.

The visitors from Oxford *will debate* four of our pre-law students next week.

The visitors from Oxford *will be debating* four of our pre-law students next week.

NOTE: Future action may be shown in other ways.

The visitors from Oxford *are going to debate* four of our pre-law students next week.

The visitors from Oxford and four of our pre-law students *are about to debate.*

12d   The present perfect tense expresses action occurring at no definite time in the past or action occurring in the past and continuing into the present.

Environmentalists *have enlisted* the help of sensitive business people. [The action has not occurred at a specific time in the past.]

Environmentalists *have been enlisting* the help of sensitive business people. [The progressive form indicates that the past action continues into the present.]

12e   The past perfect tense expresses action completed in the past before another past action occurred.

I *had flown* in a glider before I flew in a single-engine Cessna. [Flying in the glider preceded flying in the Cessna.]

After I *had been flying* for three months, I gave it up. [Flying for three months preceded giving it up.]

12f   The future perfect tense expresses action that will be completed in the future before another action occurs.

By the end of 1995, the Galaxy Probe *will have traveled* through space for five years.

By the end of 1995, the Galaxy Probe *will have been traveling* through space for five years.

12g   Use an appropriate sequence of verb tenses.

Sequence of verb tenses refers to the time relation expressed by verbs in main clauses and verbs in dependent clauses, infinitives, or participles. In the sentence *The crowd cheered when he served an ace*, the past tense of the verb *cheer (cheered)* is in sequence with the past tense of the verb *serve (served)*. (See dependent clauses, p. 26; verbals and verbal phrases, p. 21.)

Dependent Clauses

When the verb in the main clause of a complex sentence is in any tense other than the past or past perfect, you may use any verb tense in the dependent clause that is consistent with the meaning of the sentence.

> Naturalists *predict* that the whooping crane *will be extinct* by the century's end. [The prediction takes place in the present, and the extinction will take place in the future. The sequence moves from the present tense, *predict*, in the main clause to the future tense, *will be extinct*, in the dependent clause.]

> The plane *will arrive* after the buses *have stopped* for the night. [The sequence moves from the future tense in the main clause to the present perfect tense in the dependent clause.]

> Ralph *will leave* Detroit because he *believes* that the automobile industry *will* never *recover* from its losses. [The sequence moves from the future tense in the main clause to the present tense and the future tense in the two dependent clauses.]

When the verb in the main clause is in the past tense or past perfect tense, use the past tense or past perfect tense in the dependent clause, except when the dependent clause expresses a general truth.

> The creature *growled* when the children *peeked* into the shed. [Past tense in both the main clause and the dependent clause.]

> The children *had escaped* before the sheriff *arrived*. [Past perfect tense in the main clause and past tense in the dependent clause.]

> The children *discovered* that wild dogs *bite*. [Although the verb in the main clause is in the past tense, the verb in the dependent clause is in the present tense because *wild dogs bite* is a general truth.]

Infinitives

Use the **present infinitive,** which is composed of the plain form of the verb preceded by *to*, as in *to dance, to sing, to grow,* to express action that takes place at the same time as or later than that of the verb in the main clause. Use the **present perfect infinitive,** which is composed of *to have* followed by a past participle, as in *to have danced, to have sung, to have grown,* to express action that takes place before that of the verb in the main clause. (See infinitives, p. 21.)

> Last July I wanted *to attend* summer school. [Present infinitive: Action takes place at the same time as that of the main verb, *wanted.*]

> They hoped *to go.* They hope *to go.* [Present infinitive: Action takes place at a time later than the main verbs, *hoped* and *hope.*]

> Ralph would like *to have entered* last week's race. [Present perfect infinitive: Action takes place before that of the main verb, *would like.* Note that *to enter,* the present infinitive, is not the correct form.]

> Ralph would have liked *to enter* last week's race. [Present infinitive: Action takes place at the same time as that of the main verb, *would have liked.*]

Participles

Use the **present participle** to express action that takes place at the same time as that of the main verb. Use the **past participle** or **present perfect participle** to express action that takes place earlier than that of the main verb. (See present participle, pp. 21, 65.)

> *Running* in the woods, he felt free of worries. [Present participle: The running occurs at the same time as the feeling.]

> *Encouraged* by friends, Pat decided to attend college. [Past participle: The encouragement took place before the decision.]

Having danced all night, Martha slept past noon. [Present perfect participle: The dancing took place before the sleeping.]

Exercise 17

Choose the verb form in parentheses that is in sequence with the other verb or verbs in each sentence.

1. Water *(has been, had been)* scarce until the rains came.

2. After weeks of digging in the hills, the scout troop discovered that all that glitters *(is, was)* not gold.

3. The housing development will begin after the woods *(are, were)* cleared.

4. Kim had not expected *(to receive, to have received)* the award.

5. *(Finishing, Having finished)* the investigation, Gail called the *Daily Pilot*.

6. Hours earlier, the Christensens tried *(to reserve, to have reserved)* opera tickets.

7. *(Running, Having run)* for Congress, Dr. Rourke developed a forceful speaking style.

8. The former secretary of the interior will testify before the subcommittee because he *(believes, believed)* that wildlife protection *(is, was)* important.

9. Jenkins *(has been, had been)* a computer technician for two years

before he finished college.

10. The Glee Club decided not to sing because they *(believe, believed)* that

their budget *(is, was)* unfairly reduced.

Exercise 18

Rewrite the following passage as if you were living in the twenty-first century and the events happened in the past. Change verb tenses wherever necessary. Your opening sentence will read as follows:

> Years ago throughout Orange County, visitors *seemed* unable to tell where fantasy *ended* and real life *began.*

Throughout Orange County, visitors seem unable to tell where fantasy

ends and real life begins. One reason is *theme architecture,* which accounts

for perhaps as much as 60 percent of the county's buildings. Within the

county you can find triplex homes that look like English Tudor mansions,

restaurants that look like a French chateau or a Mississippi riverboat,

and a motel that resembles a Persian mosque. Theme architecture adds

a dash of Disneyland to most neighborhoods. Visitors can travel from

one exotic land to another within a few blocks. The variety bewilders

visitors, but local residents take it in stride. The themes divide into

several categories. Some homeowners prefer a Spanish mission style.

Others choose the Mediterranean look. Still others want Tudor, Cape Cod, or plantation designs. One aspect of all this diversity is tragically real: As developers hack down the orange groves, they replace the foliage with glittering fantasy structures.

Exercise 19

Rewrite the following passage as if the events were going to take place at some time in the future. Change verb tenses wherever necessary. Your opening sentence will begin as follows:

> Tomorrow's female writer will face. . .

Today's female writer faces a peculiar confusion because she is susceptible to the images of women in literature. She goes to poetry or fiction looking for her role in the world, but she is disappointed. She is looking for guides, models, possibilities. But what she finds are many images of women in works by men. She discovers a terror and a dream. She encounters a *Belle Dame sans Merci* and a Daisy Buchanan. She does not find an image of herself, the struggling female writer.

13 Subjunctive Mood *mood*

The three **moods** of a verb indicate a writer's intent. The **indicative mood,** the one most frequently used, states a fact or an opinion or asks a question. The **imperative mood** gives a command or direction (usually with the subject *you* implied: *Be here at ten sharp*). The **subjunctive mood** expresses doubt or uncertainty, a condition contrary to fact, or a wish.

You will rarely have a problem with mood. In fact, the subjunctive mood, which can be problematic, has almost disappeared from current English. Nevertheless, you should master the remaining forms and the three uses of the subjunctive mood.

Forms of the Subjunctive

In the present tense the subjunctive mood consists of only the infinitive form of the verb no matter what the subject is. (See infinitive, p. 65.)

> The choreographer urged that he *consider* a ballet career. [Present subjunctive.]

> The guidelines demand that procedures *be* in effect tomorrow. [Present subjunctive.]

In the past tense the only commonly used subjunctive verb form is *were*.

> If I *were* retired, I would live a carefree life. [Past subjunctive.]

Uses of the Subjunctive

13a Use the subjunctive form *were* in sentences expressing a wish and in contrary-to-fact clauses beginning with *if*.

> I wish she *were* my teacher. [But she is not my teacher: expresses a wish.]

> I would be able to finish all my work if the day *were* thirty hours long. [But the day is twenty-four hours long: contrary-to-fact clause.]

13b Use the subjunctive form in *that* clauses following verbs that demand, request, or recommend.

> Jane's aunt urged that Brian *save* the money.
> The attorney asked that the witness *be* ready to testify.

NOTE: Often writers find substitute constructions for the subjunctive in sentences such as those above.

> Jane's aunt urged Brian to save the money.

13c Use the subjunctive form in some standard phrases and idioms.

> Peace *be* with you.
> Heaven *forbid!*
> *Come* rain or *come* shine

Exercise 20

Revise the following sentences by using appropriate subjunctive verb forms.

1. If I was rich, I would move to the country.

2. Since her classes are boring, I wish I was not her student.

3. The judge demands that he completes the defense.

4. People laugh when I suggest changes, as if I was a comedian.

5. Heaven helps us!

14 Active and Passive Voice *pass*

Voice is the quality in verbs that shows whether a subject is the actor or is acted upon.

The fire destroyed the building. [The subject, *fire*, is the actor.]

The building was destroyed by the fire. [The subject, *building*, is being acted upon.]

Good writing is vigorous and direct. In nearly all circumstances, the active voice achieves vigor and directness better than the passive voice. Consequently, you should use the active voice except when you do not know the doer of an action or when you want to emphasize the receiver of an action or the action itself.

Demonstrators from the New Earth Alliance *closed* the nuclear plant. [Active voice.]

The nuclear plant *was closed* by demonstrators from the New Earth Alliance. [Passive voice.]

These sentences contain the same information, but each emphasizes a different point. The active construction emphasizes the demonstrators because *demonstrators* is the subject. The passive construction emphasizes the nuclear plant because *nuclear plant* is the subject.

Transitive verbs have both active and passive voice. When a verb is in the **active voice,** the subject performs the action and the object receives the action. When a verb is in the **passive voice,** the subject receives the action. (See transitive verb, p. 6.)

To form a passive construction, move the direct object of the sentence ahead of the verb; it becomes the subject. Use a form of *be* as a helping verb; the actual subject may be contained in a prepositional phrase. (See direct object, p. 17.)

William Faulkner *won* a Pulitzer Prize in 1963. [Active voice.]

A Pulitzer Prize *was won* by William Faulkner in 1963. [Passive voice: The direct object from the previous sentence, *Pulitzer Prize*, becomes the subject; *was* is added to the verb *won;* and the subject of the previous sentence, *William Faulkner*, becomes the object of the preposition *by.*]

Active sentences that have direct objects often have indirect objects also. When rewritten in a passive construction, either the direct object or the indirect object can become the subject, and the actual subject can be dropped. (See indirect object, p. 17.)

The committee awarded Tom a scholarship. [Active voice.]

Tom was awarded a scholarship. [Passive voice: Indirect object, *Tom*, becomes the subject; the original subject, *committee*, is dropped.]

A scholarship was awarded to Tom. [Passive voice: Direct object, *scholarship*, becomes the subject; the original subject, *committee*, is dropped.]

Although the meaning of each of the above sentences is the same, as the subject changes so does the emphasis: from *the committee* to *Tom* to *a scholarship*. The choice depends on the writer's intention.

In most situations, you should use the active voice for several reasons.

The active voice is more concise.

An ancient soothsayer predicts the end of the world. [Active voice: nine words.]

The end of the world is predicted by an ancient soothsayer. [Passive voice: eleven words.]

The active voice emphasizes the actual subject and is, therefore, more direct.

The astronauts who circled the earth and walked on the moon captured America's imagination. [Active voice.]

America's imagination was captured by the astronauts who circled the earth and walked on the moon. [Passive voice.]

The active voice is more forceful.

Lee slammed the softball into right field. [Active voice.]

The softball was slammed into right field by Lee. [Passive voice.]

The passive voice is appropriate in several situations.
When you do not know the doer of the action:

The clubhouse was left a shambles, and the parking lot was littered with cans and garbage.

When you want to emphasize the receiver of the action:

Tom Clark was wounded by falling rocks.

When you want to emphasize the action itself:

A curved incision was made behind the hairline so the scar would be concealed when the hair grew back.

Exercise 21

Rewrite the following passage, changing the passive constructions into active constructions.

A poison ivy infection is considered by some to be humorous. But it is not funny at all. A rash that has the intensity of a fresh mosquito bite and lasts for several days is caused by contact with the plant. Poison ivy infection has been studied by scientists for centuries, but no preventive pill or inoculation has been found. The poisonous substance in the plant is called urushiol. After the skin has been touched by urushiol, the exposed area will soon be covered by blisters and weeping sores.

What can you do after coming into contact with poison ivy?

First, the urushiol should be washed off as soon as possible. Any available hand soap and plenty of scrubbing should be used. Then take a cold shower and soap yourself all over. The course of the infection seems to be shortened by cold water. Finally, see a doctor.

15 Adjectives and Adverbs *adj/adv*

The misuse of adjectives and adverbs occurs frequently in writing. You will find that errors involving adjectives and adverbs are easy to correct once you understand how the words function in a sentence.

Adjectives modify nouns and pronouns. Adverbs can modify verbs, adjectives, and other adverbs. You can form adverbs by adding -*ly* to adjectives *(rapid, rapidly; complete, completely; happy, happily; desperate, desperately)*. But not all words ending in -*ly* are adverbs; some are adjectives *(womanly, lonely, saintly)*. Some adverbs and adjectives have the same form *(well, late, early)*, and some adverbs have two forms *(slow, slowly; quick, quickly; cheap, cheaply)*.

15a Use adjectives to modify nouns and pronouns. Use adverbs to modify verbs, adjectives, and other adverbs.

An adjective modifies a noun or a pronoun.

> Jose is a *swift* runner.
> I prefer the *checkered* one.

An adverb, not an adjective, modifies a verb.

> Jose ran *swiftly*.

An adverb, not an adjective, modifies an adjective.

> Jose is *terribly* swift.

An adverb, not an adjective, modifies an adverb.

> Jose ran *very* swiftly.

15b Use an adjective after a linking verb to refer to the subject. Use an adverb to refer to the verb.

The most common linking verb is *be* and its forms — *am, are, is, was, were,* and *been.* Other common linking verbs include *seem, appear, become, grow, remain, prove,* and *turn,* along with verbs of the senses — *feel, look, smell, sound, taste.* When these verbs link the subject with a modifier, use an adjective as the modifier. When the modifier describes the verb, use an adverb.

> The climber felt *uneasy* about the darkening sky. [Adjective: *Uneasy* describes the climber.]
>
> The climber felt *uneasily* for a firm handhold. [Adverb: *Uneasily* describes how the climber used a hand to find a firm place to grip.]

15c   After a direct object, use an adjective to modify the object. Use an adverb to modify the verb.

> The investigator considered the pilot's performance *diligent.* [Adjective: *Diligent* describes *performance.*]
>
> The investigator considered the pilot's performance *diligently* before leaving the test site. [Adverb: *Diligently* describes *considered.*]

15d   Use the words *bad* and *badly* and *good* and *well* correctly.

Bad is an adjective; *badly* is an adverb. Since verbs of the senses — *feel, look, smell, sound, taste* — require adjectives to modify the subjects, use *bad,* not *badly,* after them.

> The diners felt *bad* after the third course.
>
> The rendering plant smells *bad* each evening.

Good is always an adjective, never an adverb.

> **INCORRECT**   The band played *good* last night.
>
> **CORRECT**   The band played *well* last night.

Well may be used as either an adjective or an adverb. As an adjective, *well* has three meanings.

To be in good health:

> He seems *well* after a bout with the flu.

To appear well dressed or groomed:

> They look *well* in the new uniforms.

To be satisfactory:

> All is *well.*

Exercise 22

Select the correct word from the pair in parentheses to complete each sentence.

1. Tom did not feel (*well, good*) after the trip.

2. The winners stood *(silent, silently)* while the crowd cheered.

3. Aunt Ruth likes bacon fried *(crisp, crisply).*

4. The chances of success are (*well, good*).

5. The leader declared the situation *(hopeless, hopelessly)* because no

   one knew the location of the children.

6. Bowman chose to dress *(well, good)* rather than to eat *(well, good).*

7. The birds appeared *(nervous, nervously)* as the cat came into the room.

8. No matter how hard he scrimped, John's monthly expenses grew

   (disproportionate, disproportionately) to his income.

9. Burned kidney usually smells *(bad, badly)* enough to drive me from

the house.

10. The batter must be beaten *(thorough, thoroughly)* for the pancakes to

cook properly.

15e Use the correct forms of adjectives and adverbs when making comparisons.

Adjectives and adverbs have three forms or degrees: the **positive**, or dictionary, form, which only describes; the **comparative**, which is used to compare two things; and the **superlative**, which is used to compare three or more things.

The comparative and superlative of most adjectives and adverbs are formed either by adding *-er* and *-est*, respectively, to the positive form or by placing *more* and *most* (or *less* and *least*), respectively, before the positive form.

Using *more* and *most* (or *less* and *least*) is the only way to form the comparative and superlative for most adverbs of two or more syllables and for adjectives of three or more syllables. Some adjectives of two syllables can add either *-er* and *-est* or *more* and *most*.

	POSITIVE	COMPARATIVE	SUPERLATIVE
ADJECTIVES	thick	thicker	thickest
	happy	happier	happiest
	beautiful	more beautiful	most beautiful
		less beautiful	least beautiful
ADVERBS	fast	faster	fastest
	often	more often	most often
	sadly	more sadly	most sadly

A few adjectives and adverbs change their spelling to form the comparative and superlative.

POSITIVE	COMPARATIVE	SUPERLATIVE
bad, badly	worse	worst
good, well	better	best
many, much	more	most
little	littler, less	littlest, least

Use the comparative form to compare two things.

> In August the sea seems *bluer* than the sky.
>
> Although the two tours cost the same, the one to Paris will be the *more exciting*.
>
> Her client was *less anxious* today than yesterday.

Use the superlative form to compare three or more things.

> Of the three agents, Bozarth has the *deadliest* charm.
>
> Apparently the *most* skilled of all the drivers, Randolph wins nearly every race.
>
> This novel is the *least interesting* in the series.

15f   Do not use double comparatives or double superlatives.

INCORRECT	They are the *most happiest* couple I know.
CORRECT	They are the *happiest* couple I know.

15g   Do not use comparative or superlative forms with words that cannot logically be compared.

Words such as *unique, perfect, dead, empty, infinite,* and *impossible* are absolute. That is, their positive form describes their only state. They cannot, therefore, be compared.

ILLOGICAL	Dr. Bernard is the *most unique* surgeon.
CORRECT	Dr. Bernard is a *unique* surgeon.

Exercise 23

Identify any errors in the use of adjective and adverb forms in the following sentences and correct the errors.

1. When the four horses turned into the stretch, My Game had the greater stamina.

2. Although he was the same height as Bridesmaid, his strides seemed the longest by a yard as Perez rose in the saddle and swung the crop to drive the thoroughbred toward the finish.

3. My Game won in record time, proving to be the most fastest three-year-old to win the cup.

4. After the race, Perez said, "My Game is perhaps the most perfect horse I've ever ridden."

5. Whether Perez is right or wrong, today this marvelous animal was the better horse.

Sentence
Clarity
and Variety

16 Coordination and Subordination

17 Placement of Modifiers

18 Pronoun Reference

19 Consistency

20 Sentence Completeness

21 Parallelism

22 Sentence Variety

In writing, you must hold a reader's attention. Shaping accurate sentences and maintaining the relation between words and ideas help to keep a reader moving from sentence to sentence but are not always enough in themselves. Too often, writing that may be correct is monotonous. You must, therefore, shape your thoughts in interesting ways. This section not only illustrates ways to write clear and accurate sentences but also illustrates ways to keep a reader interested in your paper's content.

16 Coordination and Subordination *coord/sub*

When a single sentence contains more than one clause, the clauses may be given equal or unequal emphasis. Clauses given equal emphasis in one sentence are **coordinate** and should be connected by a coordinating word or punctuation. Clauses given less emphasis in a sentence are **dependent,** or subordinate, and should be introduced by a subordinating word. (See clauses, p. 25.)

> In recent years many Tibetans have moved to Switzerland, and now there is a famous Tibetan Institute at Rikon. [Two main clauses given equal emphasis and connected by the coordinating conjunction *and.*]
>
> Because Switzerland is politically neutral, the country has become the headquarters for many international organizations. [Dependent clause introduced by the subordinating conjunction *because;* main clause begins with *the country.*]

16a Use coordination to give main clauses equal emphasis.

To indicate the relation between coordinate ideas, select the proper coordinator.

COORDINATING CONJUNCTIONS
and   but   for   nor   or   so   yet

CORRELATIVE CONJUNCTIONS

both . . . and   either . . . or   neither . . . nor
not only . . . but also   whether . . . or

CONJUNCTIVE ADVERBS

accordingly	finally	instead	nonetheless
also	furthermore	likewise	otherwise
anyhow	hence	meanwhile	still
anyway	however	moreover	then
besides	incidentally	nevertheless	therefore
consequently	indeed	next	thus

Different coordinators may be used to express different relations. The common kinds of relation between coordinate clauses are addition, contrast, choice, and result.

I majored in physics, *and* he majored in astronomy. [Addition.]

The concertina is similar to an accordion, *but* its musical range is narrower. [Contrast.]

Either humans will learn to live together in peace, *or* they will die together in war. [Choice.]

He felt he had been deceived; *therefore*, he withdrew his support. [Result.]

(For correct punctuation marks to use with these coordinators see 23a, p. 126, and 25a, b, and c, pp. 151–52.)

16b   Avoid faulty or excessive coordination.

Faulty coordination gives emphasis to unequal or unrelated clauses.

Alice Adams has published four novels, and she lives in San Francisco.

The clause *she lives in San Francisco* has little or no connection to *Alice Adams has published four novels.* Therefore, the two clauses should not be coordinated. But the writer may want to include this information in the paragraph because it is interesting and perhaps important, even though it does not pertain directly to the main idea of the paragraph. Placing *she lives in San Francisco* in a separate sentence might detract from the paragraph's unity.

Revise faulty coordination by putting part of the sentence in a dependent clause, modifying phrase, or appositive phrase.

> Alice Adams, *who lives in San Francisco*, has published four novels. [Dependent clause.]
>
> Alice Adams, *from San Francisco*, has published four novels. [Modifying phrase.]
>
> Alice Adams, *a San Francisco writer*, has published four novels. [Appositive phrase.]

Excessive coordination — stringing main clauses together with coordinating conjunctions for no apparent purpose — can become monotonous for the reader. Excessive coordination also fails to show the proper relation between clauses.

> Alice Adams is a successful writer, and she lives in San Francisco, and she has received grants from the Guggenheim Foundation and the National Endowment for the Arts.

Revise excessive coordination by rewriting the sentence, using dependent clauses, modifying phrases, or appositive phrases.

> Alice Adams, a successful San Francisco writer, has received grants from the Guggenheim Foundation and the National Endowment for the Arts.

Exercise 1

Revise the following sentences to correct faulty or excessive coordination.

1. Eugene O'Neill was an American playwright, and he won a Nobel

   Prize for literature in 1936.

2. O'Neill had an unhappy childhood, and he told the story of his childhood in a play entitled *Long Day's Journey into Night*, and he said it was "written in tears and blood."

3. O'Neill's daughter Oona married Charlie Chaplin, but she married against her father's will.

4. One of O'Neill's plays, *The Iceman Cometh*, is full of symbols and hidden clues about its meaning, and it has probably been written about more than any other American play.

5. Louis Sheaffer wrote a biography of O'Neill, and he spent sixteen years researching and writing it, and his book won a Pulitzer Prize.

16c **Use subordination to distinguish the main clause in a sentence from clauses of lesser importance.**

Indicate the correct relation between main clauses and dependent clauses by the careful selection of subordinators.

COMMON SUBORDINATING CONJUNCTIONS

after	because	provided	until
although	before	since	when
as	how	so that	whenever
as if	if	than	where
as long as	in order that	that	wherever
as much as	inasmuch as	though	whether
as soon as	once	unless	while
as though			

RELATIVE PRONOUNS

that	which	whoever	whose
what	whichever	whom	
whatever	who	whomever	

Be sure to select the appropriate subordinator to show the relation between a dependent clause and a main clause. The choice of which clause to subordinate depends, of course, on your intention, but writers commonly select details of concession, identification, time, cause, condition, and purpose for subordination.

> **CONCESSION** (*as if, though, although*)
> *Although no one was injured,* more than two hundred homes were destroyed.

> **IDENTIFICATION** (*that, when, who*)
> Firefighters, *who came from several neighboring cities,* fought the blaze for two days.

> **TIME** (*before, while, as soon as*)
> Homeowners started sifting through the ashes *as soon as the embers cooled.*

> **CAUSE** (*since, because*)
> *Since you missed the deadline,* you will have to pay extra fees.

> **CONDITION** (*if, unless, provided, since*)
> *If a new storm comes,* the road will be closed.

> **PURPOSE** (*so that, in order that*)
> The promoters installed loud-speakers outside *so that those waiting to get in could hear the music.*

16d Avoid faulty or excessive subordination.

Faulty subordination occurs when the more important clause is placed in a subordinate position in the sentence or when the expected relation between clauses is reversed.

Foreign-made goods are popular with American consumers although their import poses at least a short-term threat to the livelihood of some American workers. [In an article about the problems of the American worker this sentence would take attention away from the worker and incorrectly emphasize *foreign-made goods*.]

Although she easily won the Olympic trial, she had been training for only six months. [This sentence seems to say that she trained in spite of the fact that she easily won the trial.]

Correct faulty subordination by changing the position of the subordinating word or phrase.

Although foreign-made goods are popular with American consumers, their import poses at least a short-term threat to the livelihood of some American workers.

Although she had been training for only six months, she easily won the Olympic trial.

Excessive subordination occurs when a sentence contains a series of clauses, each subordinate to an earlier one.

The lonesome trapper, who was a retired railroad man who lived in a small cabin, enjoyed the rare occasions when a group of hikers wandered by his place, which was inaccessible for most of the year.

This sentence is confusing for a reader. The writer apparently just added information as it came to mind.

To correct excessive subordination, break the sentence into two or more sentences or change some of the dependent clauses to modifying phrases or appositives.

The lonesome trapper, *a retired railroad man*, lived in a small cabin. *Because his place was inaccessible for most of the year*, he enjoyed the rare occasions when a group of hikers wandered by.

One dependent clause, *who was a retired railroad man*, has been changed to an appositive. A second dependent clause, *who lived in a small cabin*, is now the predicate of the first sentence. These changes make the sentence more direct. The subordinator of the third dependent clause has been changed from *which* (identification) to *because* (cause) to show clearly the connection between the inaccessibility of the cabin and the trapper's enjoyment of rare visits.

Exercise 2

Combine each pair of sentences below into one sentence, subordinating one idea to the other.

1. My father took a welding course in night school. He lost his job at the furniture store.

2. I need an English composition course to graduate. I am not planning to take one this year.

3. We dug a drainage ditch from the garage to the street. The rainwater will drain away faster.

4. The home was proposed by a group of bankers from the state capital. The city council rejected the proposal for a high-rise retirement home.

5. Vicki is in Montreal. I want to visit Montreal this summer.

Exercise 3

Revise the faulty or excessive subordination in the following sentences.

1. Daniel J. Boorstin, who has been a teacher at Harvard and the

University of Chicago, is now head of the Library of Congress, which

is located in Washington, DC, and which is the largest library in the

world.

2. Because the Library of Congress is a researcher's dream, it houses

millions of books, films, photographs, and TV tapes.

3. Even though the Library of Congress has copies of every book ever

copyrighted in the United States, many of the books are not important

or even well written.

4. The Library of Congress is open to everyone, which makes it different

from the government libraries of many other countries, which restrict

use of their resources to a select few.

5. Although Boorstin attended Harvard University and won a Rhodes

Scholarship to study at Oxford, he once failed a college entrance

examination in English.

17 Placement of Modifiers *mm/dm*

A writer can confuse a reader by misplacing a modifier in a sentence.
Be sure to place modifiers in your sentences so that a reader will be
certain of the word or words they modify.

17a Place prepositional phrases and dependent clauses as close as possible to the words they modify.

CONFUSING	One of our teachers took belly-dancing lessons to improve her figure at night school.
CLEAR	One of our teachers took belly-dancing lessons *at night school* to improve her figure.
CONFUSING	He sold the article to a magazine publisher that he had worked on for six months.
CLEAR	He sold the article *that he had worked on for six months* to a magazine publisher.

Exercise 4

Revise the following sentences by rearranging the misplaced prepositional phrases and dependent clauses.

1. The woman cashed her check with a French accent.

2. His trial was postponed for three months for tax evasion.

3. The explorer described an earthquake during his lecture.

4. After the party the hostess gave balloons to all the children in the shape of fantastic animals.

5. The senator examined the rocks in his office that the astronauts brought back from the moon.

17b Avoid writing squinting modifiers.

A **squinting modifier** can seem to modify either the word preceding it or following it. The ambiguous result can confuse a reader.

SQUINTING	A person who body surfs occasionally gets injured. [Does *occasionally* refer to *body surfs* or to *gets injured?*]
REVISED	*Occasionally*, a person who body surfs gets injured.
REVISED	A person who *occasionally* body surfs gets injured.

Exercise 5

Revise the following sentences to clarify the confusion created by squinting modifiers.

1. Walking to work occasionally is an interesting experience.

2. News that the water had been shut off completely mystified me.

3. Reading his novel thoroughly delighted me.

4. Taking coffee breaks frequently disrupts production.

5. Young children given an allowance often waste the money.

17c Place limiting modifiers carefully.

Words such as *only, hardly, just, nearly, almost*, and *even* can function in many positions in a sentence. They modify the expression immediately following them. Therefore, as these limiting modifiers change position in a sentence, the meaning of the sentence also changes.

I will go *only* if he asks me. [Otherwise I will stay.]
Only I will go if he asks me. [The others will not go.]
I will go if *only* he asks me. [Please, ask me!]
I will go if he asks *only* me. [If he asks others, I will stay.]

Exercise 6

Write another version of each sentence by moving the italicized modifier to a different position. Briefly describe the difference in meaning in the two sentences.

1. I *just* work here.

2. He is *only* a child.

3. *Even* the boss enjoyed the movie.

4. Her parents wanted her to live *simply*.

5. *Almost* all the passengers on the capsized boat drowned.

17d   Avoid placing a lengthy modifier between the subject and the predicate of a sentence.

> AWKWARD   The cost of attending college, because of inflation and reduced federal support, has risen sharply in recent years.
>
> REVISED   The cost of attending college has risen sharply in recent years because of inflation and reduced federal support.

You may place short modifiers between a subject and a predicate.

> The cost of attending college, *unfortunately*, has risen sharply in recent years.

17e   Avoid placing a lengthy modifier between a verb and its complement.

> AWKWARD   The winning Gran Prix driver seemed, to the surprise of the fans, unhappy.
>
> REVISED   To the surprise of the fans, the winning Gran Prix driver seemed unhappy.

You may place single-word modifiers between a verb and its complement.

The winning Gran Prix driver seemed *terribly* unhappy.

17f Avoid placing a lengthy modifier within a verb phrase.

AWKWARD	He discovered he had been, by all his relatives and friends, deserted.
REVISED	He discovered he had been deserted by all his relatives and friends.

You may use a single-word modifier within a verb phrase.

He discovered he had been *cruelly* deserted.

17g Avoid splitting infinitives.

An infinitive consists of *to* plus the plain form of a verb: *to run, to complain, to contemplate, to speak.*

SPLIT INFINITIVE	When the locusts descended, the prairie residents prepared to *hurriedly* depart.
REVISED	When the locusts descended, the prairie residents *hurriedly* prepared *to depart.*

Occasionally a split infinitive will seem natural and appropriate. In fact, not splitting an infinitive can sometimes create an awkward or misleading sentence.

His inability to clearly explain the issues cost him the election.

In the preceding sentence, the alternatives are more awkward than the split infinitive. *Clearly to explain* and *to explain clearly* sound excessively formal, and *to explain the issues clearly cost him the election* produces a squinting modifier.

Exercise 7

Change the position of the italicized modifier in each sentence to correct the awkward constructions.

1. My horse, *despite a muddy track and a poor start*, won the fourth race.

2. On July 19, 1915, the Washington Senators set a major league record by stealing, *in one inning*, eight bases.

3. In 1982 Jimmy Connors was, *following his win at Forest Hills*, considered the best tennis player in the world.

4. Many of Sally Burton's golf victories result from her ability to, *seemingly without effort*, upset her opponents.

5. I believe that Mike Finnegan will be, *although few fans today have heard of him*, inducted into the Tennis Hall of Fame.

17h Avoid writing dangling modifiers.

A dangling modifier is a phrase or clause that is not clearly attached to any word in the sentence. To correct a dangling modifier, change the subject of the main clause or rewrite the modifier as a complete clause.

DANGLING PARTICIPIAL PHRASE
Walking through the supermarket, the oranges looked tempting.

REVISED
Walking through the supermarket, *I noticed that* the oranges looked tempting. [Introductory participial phrase clearly modifies the new subject, *I*.]

As I was walking through the supermarket, the oranges looked tempting. [Introductory modifier is a complete clause.]

DANGLING INFINITIVE PHRASE

To understand world affairs, a daily newspaper should be read.

REVISED

To understand world affairs, *a person should read* a daily newspaper.

DANGLING PREPOSITIONAL PHRASE

After recovering from the treatments, my doctor told me to be more careful in the future.

REVISED

After I recovered from the treatments, my doctor told me to be more careful in the future.

DANGLING ELLIPTICAL CLAUSE

While a student at Rutgers, Shakespeare was my favorite author.

REVISED

While I was a student at Rutgers, Shakespeare was my favorite author.

Exercise 8

Revise the following sentences to eliminate the dangling modifiers.

1. When only a teen-ager, my grandfather introduced me to trout fishing.

2. Lurching drunkenly down the sidewalk, two police officers came into view.

3. After settling in my seat, the flight attendant served coffee and sandwiches.

4. To remain healthy, a balanced diet is important.

5. Singing in the bathtub, my neighbor rang the doorbell.

18 Pronoun Reference *ref*

Pronoun reference is the relation between a pronoun and its **antecedent.** (See antecedent, p. 3; agreement of pronoun and antecedent, p. 53.) If the pronoun reference is unclear, the sentence will confuse or misinform a reader.

18a Avoid using a pronoun to make a broad reference to an entire sentence or clause.

Sometimes inexperienced writers use *this, that,* or *it* to refer to an entire sentence or clause.

> Mystery is what I felt during my nightly walks through the streets of Paris. That is what I needed. [Does the pronoun *that* refer to *mystery* or *nightly walks?*]

> Good managers know when to delegate responsibility. This allows them to concentrate on the broader aspects of a project. [This what?]

Confusing sentences such as the preceding examples can be made clear by rewriting the sentences or by using a summary noun after *this* or *that.*

> I needed the sense of mystery I felt during my nightly walks through the streets of Paris.

> Good managers know when to delegate responsibility. This knowledge (skill, ability) allows them to concentrate on the broader aspects of a project.

18b　Avoid the indefinite use of *it, they,* and *you.*

In conversation *it* and *they* are often used to make vague reference to people and situations. In writing, more precise identification is usually needed.

VAGUE	In last week's *Time, it* gives an overview of the latest computer technology.
CLEAR	*An article* in last week's *Time* gives an overview of the latest computer technology.
VAGUE	*They* do not allow driving a motorcycle without a helmet.
CLEAR	*Traffic laws* do not allow driving a motorcycle without a helmet.

You is also commonly used in conversation to refer vaguely to people in general. In writing, however, use the more formal *one* or less formal *a person* or *people. You* should be used as a personal pronoun.

VAGUE	In law enforcement *you* must stay alert to the community's changing values.
CLEAR	In law enforcement *a person* must stay alert to the community's changing values.

The use of *you* to refer to "you, the reader" is perfectly appropriate in all but the most formal writing.

> If you plan to spend only two days in Boston, then you must concentrate on visiting the most important historic sites.

18c　Make a pronoun refer clearly to one antecedent.

CONFUSING	After Roth lived with Wiley for a month, *he* discovered that *he* is a creature of habit. [The first *he* seems to refer to Roth, but who is the creature of habit?]

CLEAR	After Roth lived with Wiley for a month, he discovered that Wiley is a creature of habit.
CLEAR	After Roth lived with Wiley for a month, Wiley discovered that Roth is a creature of habit.
CLEAR	After living with Wiley for a month, Roth discovered that he himself is a creature of habit.

18d   Use pronouns ending in *-self* or *-selves* only to refer to another word in the sentence.

Ralph gave me the message *himself*.
They tricked *themselves*.

Avoid using pronouns ending in *-self* or *-selves* in place of other personal pronouns.

INCORRECT	The minister tried to settle the argument between Harold and *myself*.
REVISED	The minister tried to settle the argument between Harold and *me*.

Exercise 9

Correct the faulty pronoun references in the following sentences. You may need to change words or rewrite entire sentences. For example:

Tom showed Ralph the book that he had misplaced weeks before.

Tom found the book that he had misplaced weeks before and showed it to Ralph.

Tom showed Ralph the book Ralph had misplaced weeks before.

1. Mary decided to live with Liz because her roommate had moved out.

2. After months of training, he developed an ability to speak before groups, but this still does not help him practice accounting.

106   *Pronoun Reference*

3. Since my tax return is being audited, they must be out to get me.

4. Among John, you, and myself, the secret will be safe, but if we tell Alice, we will hurt ourselves.

5. Joe Louis and Rocky Marciano were two great heavyweight boxing champions; however, after Marciano beat him in 1950, he never fought as well again.

6. I never buy steaks at butcher shops because they are expensive.

7. As the hand became visible through the window, it opened suddenly.

8. The back house is for ourselves and the front one is for them.

9. Dale survived a six-story fall, which is evidence of his luck.

10. Rick quit his job and then had to move from his apartment. That is a shame.

19 Consistency *shift*

The use of person, number, mood, subject, and voice should remain consistent within sentences. Faulty shifts in any of these elements indicate that the writer's thinking is not clear, and the meaning of the sentences will be obscured. Always review your sentences for consistency.

19a Write sentences consistent in person and number.

Most faulty shifts in person take place between second person and third person.

FAULTY SHIFT	If a *crop duster* is always alert, *you won't* get into trouble.
REVISED	If a crop duster is always alert, *he* won't get into trouble.
FAULTY SHIFT	If *you* do *your* homework thoughtfully, a *student* should be able to pass this class.
REVISED	If you do your homework thoughtfully, *you* should be able to pass this class.
REVISED	If *she* does *her* homework thoughtfully, a student should be able to pass this class.

Number refers to the singular or plural form of nouns and pronouns. Most faulty shifts in number result from the use of a plural pronoun to refer to a singular noun. (See agreement of pronoun and antecedent, p. 53; indefinite pronouns, p. 4.)

FAULTY SHIFT	When a *student* finally graduates, *they* feel proud.
REVISED	When a student finally graduates, *he or she* feels proud. [See sexist language, p. 219.]
REVISED	When *students* finally graduate, *they* feel proud.

19b Write sentences consistent in tense.

Tense refers to the time of an action indicated by the verbs in a sentence. Shifts in verb tense are often required to report time sequences accurately, but faulty shifts can confuse a reader. (See tense, p. 69.)

FAULTY SHIFT	The inventor *experimented* for three years, but he finally *overcomes* the difficulties and *is* ready to market his new camera.
REVISED	The inventor experimented for three years, but he finally *overcame* the difficulties and *was* ready to market his new camera.

FAULTY SHIFT	The escaping driver *speeds* around the corner and *veered* directly into the path of a motorcyclist.
REVISED	The escaping driver *sped* around the corner and veered directly into the path of a motorcyclist.

19c Write sentences consistent in mood.

The mood of a verb can be indicative, imperative, or subjunctive. Statements and questions are in the indicative mood; commands are in the imperative mood; and wishes and statements contrary to fact are in the subjunctive mood. Most faulty shifts in mood occur when a writer fails to follow through with the initial use of the imperative mood. (See mood, p. 76.)

FAULTY SHIFT	Release the clutch slowly, and *you should press* on the accelerator at the same time.
REVISED	Release the clutch slowly, and *press* on the accelerator at the same time.

19d Write sentences consistent in subject and voice.

A shift in subject or from active to passive voice is awkward and possibly confusing.

FAULTY SHIFT	In the game of curling, a *player slides* a heavy stone over the ice toward a target, and the *ice* in front of the stone *is swept* to influence its path.

Because the subject shifts from *player* in the first clause to *ice* in the second clause and the voice shifts from active *(slides)* to passive *(is swept)*, a reader may be confused about who is doing the sweeping.

REVISED	In the game of curling, a player slides a heavy stone over the ice toward a target, and *the player's teammates sweep* the ice in front of the stone to influence its path.

A shift in subject and voice sometimes results in a dangling modifier.

> **FAULTY SHIFT**   *Shaking with fear,* the *sound* of an intruder *could be heard* in the kitchen.

The subject of the main clause is *sound.* The introductory phrase *shaking with fear* is a dangling modifier because it does not sensibly relate to *sound.*

> **REVISED**   Shaking with fear, *we heard* the sound of an intruder in the kitchen.

Now the subject is *we,* which clearly connects to *shaking with fear.*

19e   Avoid unnecessary shifts between direct and indirect discourse.

Direct discourse reports the exact words of a speaker. **Indirect discourse** reports the gist of what a speaker said but not the speaker's exact words.

> **DIRECT DISCOURSE**   Father said, "Be back by 11:30."
>
> **INDIRECT DISCOURSE**   Father said I have to be back by 11:30.
>
> **FAULTY SHIFT**   The manager said to fill out the application form and "Please wait in the anteroom."
>
> **REVISED**   The manager said, "Please fill out the application form and wait in the anteroom."
>
> **RÉVISED**   The manager said to fill out the application form and to wait in the anteroom.

Exercise 10

In these sentences, label each faulty shift in person, number, tense, mood, subject, voice, or discourse and revise each sentence to be consistent. If any sentences are already correct, mark them with a *C.*

1. Until yesterday, Beth Langford had not heard from her brother for months, but last night he telephones her, and then they were talking together in a dingy, underfurnished room on the eleventh floor of the Beckford Hotel.

2. He seemed perfectly calm, and he was obviously enjoying himself.

3. Carefully, he packed the tobacco deeper into the bowl of his pipe and a match was struck.

4. He held the match in his right hand, not bringing it to the bowl, and stares at her.

5. Then he shook the match out and asked her if she was surprised to see him and "Don't you wonder where I've been?"

6. "I can guess where you've been," Beth replied with a laugh, "but I am surprised to see you."

7. "Well, sometimes a man has to come home or you forget where it is," he said, and his lips form a faint smile.

8. She remembered that little smile he had; they always preceded his sharing a special secret.

9. I know why he's home, she thought, but you better not spoil his fun.

10. "Don't tell me now," she said. "Tell me at dinner, and I think you

should call Mom and Dad first."

19f Avoid shifting grammatical plans in a sentence.

> In Faulkner's often anthologized story "Barn Burning" poignantly
> reveals the conflicting loyalties in a young boy's life.

"Barn Burning" is used in this sentence as the object of the
preposition *in,* but it is also used as the subject of the verb *reveals.* A
word or group of words cannot function as both the object of the
preposition and the subject of the main clause.

If the sentence begins with a prepositional phrase, the main clause
has to have a subject of its own.

> In the often anthologized story "Barn Burning," Faulkner poign-
> antly reveals the conflicting loyalties in a young boy's life.

If *"Barn Burning"* is to serve as the subject of *reveals,* the prepositional
phrase must be eliminated.

> Faulkner's often anthologized story "Barn Burning" poignantly
> reveals the conflicting loyalties in a young boy's life.

19g Avoid faulty predication.

Faulty predication occurs when the subject and predicate of a sentence
do not fit together in meaning.

FAULTY PREDICATION	The issue of gun control is an easy solution to a complicated problem. [The issue is not the solution.]
REVISED	The issue of gun control is complicated.
REVISED	Gun control is an easy solution to a complicated problem.

FAULTY PREDICATION	Nepotism is when [or where] officials appoint their relatives to desirable positions. [Nepotism is neither a time nor a place.]
REVISED	Nepotism is the appointing of relatives to desirable positions.
FAULTY PREDICATION	The reason he failed the examination is because he had a toothache.
REVISED	The reason he failed the examination is that he had a toothache.
REVISED	He failed the examination because he had a toothache.

Exercise 11

Revise the following sentences to avoid shifts in grammatical plan and faulty predication.

1. To impersonate is when one person mimics the appearance and behavior of another.

2. The restoration of the old Williams mansion is the chief tourist attraction in town.

3. After filing income tax forms is an occasion to celebrate.

4. The reason I refused the job is because I want to live here in Minnesota.

5. By using reinforced concrete will make the foundation stronger.

20 Sentence Completeness *inc*

The label *incomplete sentence* usually refers to a sentence fragment, but some sentences that are not fragments may still be incomplete because they lack certain words necessary for understanding.

20a Make all comparisons complete, clear, and logical.

INCOMPLETE	I think the Ace Construction Company treats its employees better. [Better than who?]
COMPLETE	I think the Ace Construction Company treats its employees better *than other contracting firms do*.
UNCLEAR	Susan is closer to me than Peggy.
CLEAR	Susan is closer to me than Peggy *is*.
CLEAR	Susan is closer to me than *she is to* Peggy.
ILLOGICAL	To her, the silence of the desert at night was more terrifying than a coyote.
LOGICAL	To her, the silence of the desert at night was more terrifying than *the howl of a coyote*.

20b Do not omit words from the second part of a compound construction unless the omitted words are consistent in grammar or idiom with the earlier parallel words.

In elliptical constructions, writers omit words that are understood.

> There are only two lasting bequests we can give our children: One is roots; the other, wings.

> At eighteen I knew everything; at forty-five, nothing.

In the first example, the verb *is* is omitted before *wings* with no confusion in meaning. In fact, the omission serves to emphasize *wings*. In the second sentence *I knew* is omitted before *nothing*. The comma in each sentence notes the omission of words. (See 23l, p. 143.) Both sentences are strengthened by the omissions. But if omitted words are not consistent in grammar or idiom, a **faulty ellipsis** occurs.

FAULTY	At eighteen I knew everything; now, nothing.
REVISED	At eighteen I knew everything; now *I know* nothing.

FAULTY	Humans have a strong belief and desire for love.
REVISED	Humans have a strong belief *in* and desire *for* love.

Exercise 12

Rewrite the following sentences to make all comparisons complete, clear, and logical and to correct faulty ellipses.

1. My father has confidence and ambition for his children.

2. A Datsun 280Z has more power.

3. The professor is a scholar and his opinions valued by government officials.

4. Irene was surprised and then thankful for the support she received from her former enemies.

5. China has more people than any country on earth.

21   Parallelism   //

Parallelism exists when two or more ideas are given equal weight and are expressed in the same grammatical form in a sentence. Clarity in written English requires that coordinate ideas, compared and contrasted ideas, and correlative constructions be expressed in parallel form — that is, a noun must be matched with a noun, a verb with a verb, a phrase with a phrase, and a clause with a clause. Parallelism can add clarity, interest, and impact to your writing.

21a   Use parallelism for coordinate elements.

To earn a living he worked *as a busboy at the faculty club* and *as a bellhop at the Bayshore Inn*. [Parallel prepositional phrases.]

Clearing tables and *lugging suitcases* often left him *tired*, *disgusted*, and *discouraged* by Sunday night. [Parallel gerund phrases and parallel predicate adjectives.]

If coordinate elements are not expressed in parallel grammatical form, sentences can be awkward and hard to understand.

> **FAULTY**   Her greatest pleasures during the summer were *the dances at Hotspur's* and *sleeping until noon*. [A noun and a gerund phrase as predicate nominatives.]
>
> **REVISED**   Her greatest pleasures during the summer were *dancing at Hotspur's* and *sleeping until noon*. [Parallel gerund phrases.]

Words such as *by*, *in*, *to*, *a*, *the*, and *that* should usually be repeated when they apply to both elements in a parallel construction.

> **FAULTY**   *By not restricting tourism* and *encouraging foreign investments*, the People's Republic of China hopes to make economic progress. [Not clear whether the Chinese government encourages or discourages foreign investments.]
>
> **REVISED**   *By not restricting tourism* and *by encouraging foreign investments*, the People's Republic of China hopes to make economic progress.

Clauses beginning with *and who* or *and which* can be coordinated only with *who* or *which* clauses that precede them.

> **FAULTY**   Our new sales manager is a man *of great ambition* and *who loves his work*.
>
> **REVISED**   Our new sales manager is a man *who has great ambition* and *who loves his work*.

21b Use parallelism for compared and contrasted ideas.

FAULTY   Sandra said she would rather *put up with the hectic pace of life in the big city* than *to waste time in a little backwater town.*

REVISED   Sandra said she would rather *put up* with the hectic pace of life in the big city than *waste* time in a little backwater town.

21c Use parallelism for correlative constructions.

Either . . . or, not only . . . but also, both . . . and, and similar correlative constructions should connect parallel sentence elements.

The same type of construction that follows the first half of the correlative should follow the second half.

FAULTY   The new building code applies not only *to factories, stores, and office buildings* but also *single-family dwellings.*

REVISED   The new building code applies not only *to* factories, stores, and office buildings but also *to* single-family dwellings.

FAULTY   That man across the street is always either *washing his car* or *works in the garden.*

REVISED   That man across the street is always either *washing* his car or *working* in the garden.

Exercise 13

Correct faulty parallelism in the following sentences.

1. The new airline promised not only to schedule more flights but also

   provide better service in flight.

2. Childhood is a time of laughter, tears, hopes, disappointments, and

   growing.

3. The issue is simple: Either we learn to economize or I think trouble lies ahead.

4. I like football, soccer, and basketball, but not to go swimming.

5. Mark Twain was not only a writer but also lectured.

22   Sentence Variety   *var*

A good writer avoids writing monotonous paragraphs and essays by varying the length and structure of sentences. The following paragraph has interesting content but too little variety in sentence length and structure. The monotonous result could put the reader to sleep.

> The first settlers came to Sauk Centre, Minnesota, in 1857. The seven settlers were from New England. They called themselves the Sauk Centre Townsite Company. They built the first residence on a bluff above the reedy swamplands and the sand flats of the river's swell. This first residence was only an excavation lined with poles. They organized the Sauk Valley Claim Association in July of 1857. They built a log house on the river bank and started to build a dam. They didn't complete the dam because winter became too harsh. The partially constructed dam was broken by melting ice in the spring. The residents didn't give up. They established a post office in 1858. They built a frame house in the next year. They finished the dam in 1860. They also built a sawmill and a blacksmith shop in 1860. Joseph Casper, one of the residents, built a general store. Nellie Pendergast was the first white child born there. She was born in 1861. These people built a city where there had been only sand and trails and a few Indians.

Every sentence in the paragraph begins with the subject and follows a similar pattern. Many of the sentences are between five and eight words long, a pattern that gives the paragraph a repetitive dreariness. Most important, each sentence stands as an isolated fact; therefore, the relations between ideas are not made clear.

Now read the way Mark Schorer actually wrote this material:

> Thirty years before, there was nothing here but native earth, rolling prairie, roving Indians, a crossing of stagecoach trails. Then, in 1857, at the point where the Sauk River widens into the nine or ten miles of Big Sauk Lake, the first settlers came — seven New Englanders who called themselves the Sauk Centre Townsite Company. On a bluff rising above the reedy swamplands and the sand flats of the river's swell they established the first residence in this place, an excavation lined with poles. In July of 1857 a first general meeting of settlers organized the Sauk Valley Claim Association, and before the rigor of Minnesota winter locked them in, they had begun the construction of a dam and had built a log house on the river bank. When the ice broke up in the spring of 1858 it swept away the partially constructed dam, but a post office was established in that year, the first frame residence went up in the next, and in 1860 a new dam was finished, a small sawmill was put into operation, and the first blacksmith shop. In 1861 one Joseph Casper built the first general store, and Nellie Pendergast, the first white child, was born.
>
> *—Sinclair Lewis: An American Life*

Of course, the first paragraph was written poorly to illustrate by contrast the value of varying sentence length and word order. Schorer's paragraph differs from the first paragraph in other ways, too, but the point should be clear: Vary the length of your sentences and change the word order as appropriate.

22a Vary sentence beginnings.

Begin with the subject.

> *Travel* presents the opportunity to learn about different customs.

Begin with an adverb.

> *Rapidly*, the secretary shuffled through the stack of papers on his desk.

Begin with a prepositional phrase.

> *On a hill near the Canadian border*, Jake Barnes established his first blacksmith shop.

Begin with a participial phrase.

> *Smacking his lips*, the hungry boy headed for the breakfast table.

Begin with an infinitive phrase.

> *To balance the budget*, the president proposed a reduction in government spending.

Begin with a coordinating conjunction when appropriate.

> They pleaded. They begged. They threatened. *But* Gertrude wouldn't budge.

Begin with a transitional expression when appropriate.

> Some people face adversity with a smile. *However*, some face it with anxiety and gloom.

22b Vary sentence structures.

In a piece of writing you can achieve sentence variety by alternating the structures of sentences. (See sentences, p. 28.)

SIMPLE SENTENCE
I visited the Bower Museum.

COMPOUND SENTENCE
I visited the Bower Museum, but I couldn't find the exhibit of ancient mosaics.

COMPLEX SENTENCE
If I go tomorrow, I will look again.

COMPOUND-COMPLEX SENTENCE
I want to see the mosaic exhibit because my mother saw it in New York City, and she said it was interesting.

22c Vary sentence forms.

A loose sentence (also called a cumulative sentence) has its subject and predicate first, followed by modifiers and other amplification.

> *The family escaped to Illinois*, abandoning the old mansion built by the first Graham in 1763, shortly after he arrived in the New World.

A **periodic sentence** has most of its modification and amplification before the subject and predicate.

> Abandoning the old mansion built by the first Graham in 1763, shortly after he arrived in the New World, *the family escaped to Illinois*.

A **balanced sentence** is a compound or compound-complex sentence in which the clauses are parallel.

> The humid summers drained my strength; the mild winters renewed my energy. [Compound.]

> As the years went by, the mansion faded from their memories, and the new home occupied their efforts. [Compound-complex.]

Exercise 14

For each model sentence, write a sentence that follows the structure, but not the subject matter, of the original.

1. Before we made fire, before we made tools, we made images.

    —Paul Engle

    Sample answer: Because they had strength, because they had purpose, they had victories.

2. When he walked, he clinked, and jangled, and pealed.

    —Richard Rovere

3. When a friend wants to use our place while we are away for a weekend or everyone happens to be out during the day, or a visitor

for whom we do not wish to wait up is spending the night, we tell such a friend that he can pick up the key at the delicatessen across the street.

—Jane Jacobs

4. Paralyzed by the neurotic lassitude engendered by meeting one's past at every turn, around every corner, inside every cupboard, I go aimlessly from room to room.

—Joan Didion

5. The whistle of the locomotive penetrates my woods summer and winter, sounding like the scream of a hawk sailing over some farmer's yard, informing me that many restless city merchants are arriving within the circle of the town, or adventurous country traders from the other side.

—Henry Thoreau

6. And around the sunken sanctuary of the river valley, stretching out in all directions from the benches to become coextensive with the disc of the world, went the uninterrupted prairie.

—Wallace Stegner

7. What Lincoln had just said might make interesting reading in the history books some day; what he would do in the immediate future would determine what sort of history was going to be written.

—Bruce Catton

8. At the door of the emergency room, a policeman stood on one leg, his other foot pressed back against the brick wall, his face devoid of expression.

—Paula Fox

9. To get his description of the landscape correct, he sat all day on a balcony looking through pieces of different-colored glass in order to note the changes in shapes of fields and roads and trees hour by hour.

—Paul Engle

10. The problem of creative writing is essentially one of concentration, and the supposed eccentricities of poets are usually due to mechanical habits or rituals developed in order to concentrate.

—Stephen Spender

Exercise 15

Using the following paragraph as a model, write a paragraph that follows the structure, but not the subject matter, of the original.

> I want a wife who will take care of the details of my social life. When my wife and I are invited out by my friends, I want a wife who will take care of the babysitting arrangements. When I meet people at school that I like and want to entertain, I want a wife who will have the house clean, will prepare a special meal, serve it to me and my friends, and not interrupt when I talk about things that interest me and my friends. I want a wife who will have arranged that the children are fed and ready for bed before my guests arrive so that the children do not bother us. I want a wife who takes care of the needs of my guests so that they feel comfortable, who makes sure that they have an ashtray, that they are passed the hors d'oeuvres, that they are offered a second helping of the food, that their wine glasses are replenished when necessary, that their coffee is served to them as they like it. And I want a wife who knows that sometimes I need a night out by myself.

> *—Judy Syfers*

Exercise 16

Rewrite the following paragraph to make it more interesting. Vary sentence beginnings and combine sentences as necessary.

> A zebra possesses a remarkable form of protective coloration. A zebra is impossible to miss in any light or setting. A zebra's stripes make it stand out against any background. A person on hands and knees can understand how the stripes work to protect a zebra. A lion looking at a zebra sees it from this elevation. The vertical white stripes vanish into the sky from this position. The lion's view of the beast is blurred for a few seconds. The lion cannot clearly see the outline of the zebra. The animal has no distinct shape.

Punctuation

23 The Comma

24 Unnecessary Commas

25 The Semicolon

26 The Colon

27 The Dash

28 Quotation Marks

29 The Ellipsis Mark

30 Parentheses

31 Brackets

32 The Slash

33 End Punctuation

The following section illustrates the correct uses of punctuation. By punctuating your written work correctly, you will be supplying your readers with the cues they need to understand your written thought.

23 The Comma /,

The **comma** serves within sentences mainly to group words that belong together and to separate those that do not. The comma also has several conventional uses, such as in dates and addresses. Since the comma is the most frequently used, and misused, punctuation mark, you will be well on your way to controlling punctuation errors by mastering its use.

23a Use a comma before a coordinating conjunction (*and, but, or, nor, yet, so,* and *for*) linking two main clauses.

> He stormed into the room, but the guests continued to eat.
>
> Professional athletes begin their careers out of love for sports, and a few keep that love.
>
> The road was littered with household goods, for the refugees could not carry the extra weight.

NOTE: Keep in mind that not every coordinating conjunction in a sentence joins main clauses. Often coordinating conjunctions create compound subjects or compound predicates.

> Every Saturday the lawyer walked seven miles to the widow's cabin *and* chopped a week's supply of firewood for her. [The coordinating conjunction *and* joins two verbs, *walked* and *chopped*. It is incorrect to separate two parts of a compound predicate with a comma.]
>
> We enjoy bagels *and* cream cheese for breakfast. [The coordinating conjunction *and* joins two nouns, *bagels* and *cream cheese;* do not use a comma.]

Exercise 1

Insert a comma before each coordinating conjunction linking main clauses. If a sentence is correct, mark it with a *C*.

1. Congress will probably pass the bill early next week but analysts predict a veto.

2. Sunshine penetrated the mist and shone brightly on the leaves and branches of the trees.

3. The stonecutter became increasingly eccentric during his last years and visitors often heard him talk to himself.

4. The students looked worried about missing the lecture for the bus was late that winter morning.

5. Colleges are offering many courses on television yet students and most teachers regard them as watered-down versions of traditional courses.

23b Use a comma to set off introductory phrases and clauses from main clauses.

If the introductory phrase or clause is very short and the sentence cannot be misread, you may omit the comma. (See phrases, p. 19; clauses, p. 25.)

INTRODUCTORY PREPOSITIONAL PHRASE OR PHRASES	*In striking Mexico City,* the earthquake could not have hit a more vulnerable target.
	In spite of the threat of an invasion, Costa Rica has no standing army.
INTRODUCTORY VERBAL PHRASE	*To win the hearts of people,* you must appeal to their emotions.
	Exhausted from hours of negotiations, the diplomats returned to their embassies.
INTRODUCTORY CLAUSE	*If members do not pay their dues,* the club will fold.
	Although many ineffective medical treatments get attention in the news media, the press is usually skeptical about miracle cures.

Be careful to distinguish verbal modifiers from verbals that function as subjects. Verbal modifiers are usually separated from the main clause by a comma; verbals functioning as subjects never take a comma. (See gerunds and gerund phrases, p. 23.)

> *Riding a motorcycle,* John feels a sense of power. [Verbal as modifier.]

> *Riding a motorcycle* gives John a sense of power. [Verbal as subject.]

You may omit a comma after a very short introductory clause or phrase if the omission does not cause a misreading.

CONFUSING	On each weekday morning exercise class begins at six.
CLEAR	On each weekday, morning exercise class begins at six.

Usually no comma is needed to separate adverb clauses placed at the end of a sentence. (See unnecessary commas, p. 144.)

> Presidential news conferences offer more entertainment than information because reporters do not ask pointed questions.

128 *The Comma*

Exercise 2

Insert commas where needed after introductory phrases and clauses in the following sentences. If a sentence is correct, mark it with a *C*.

1. In spite of an apparently inexhaustible supply the numbers of wild creatures are being depleted because of greed.

2. If you are tempted to spend $25,000 for a leopard-skin coat remember that each coat requires the pelts of seven animals.

3. Specializing in killing and stuffing a taxidermist in California illegally offered bighorn sheep to wealthy customers.

4. After exposure he confessed and paid a fine.

5. Handicapped by low budgets authorities seem to be losing the battle against poachers.

23c   Use a comma to set off nonrestrictive elements. Do not use a comma to set off restrictive elements.

A **restrictive element** defines or identifies — that is, it restricts — the meaning of the noun it modifies and is essential to the meaning of the sentence. A **nonrestrictive element** may add important information to a sentence but is not essential to the meaning of the sentence.

RESTRICTIVE   The company *that interests me most* is IBM.

In the preceding sentence, the clause beginning with *that* is essential to the meaning of the sentence. Without the clause, the sentence would mean something else: *The company is IBM.*

NONRESTRICTIVE   IBM, *which has been picked as one of America's best-managed companies,* interests me most.

In the preceding sentence, the clause beginning with *which* adds factual information but is not essential. The basic meaning of the sentence is clear without it: *IBM interests me most.*

1. Restrictive clauses and phrases are *not* set off by commas.

> We encourage children *who are creative.* [The *who* clause defines which children are encouraged.]

> A few artisans *working in wrought iron* have created enduring works. [The participial phrase identifies the kind of artisans being discussed.]

NOTE: Clauses beginning with the relative pronoun *that* are almost always restrictive.

> The new district attorney has won every case *that she has brought to trial.*

> The puzzle *that Joe got for Christmas* is too hard for him to solve.

In a restrictive adjective clause the relative pronoun introducing the clause may be dropped when it does not function as the subject of the relative clause.

> A tax increase is the only way [*that*] *our government can continue to function.*

> Ralph could not find a politician [*whom* or *that*] *he respected.*

NOTE: Clauses and phrases modifying indefinite pronouns are almost always restrictive.

> I gave the report to someone *who was sitting at the desk.* [The *who* clause identifies *someone.*]

> Anyone *running through the park* was punished. [The participial phrase identifies *anyone.*]

2. Nonrestrictive clauses and phrases should be set off by commas.

> The village, *which is isolated at the tip of Baja California,* survives by attracting sport fishing enthusiasts from around the world.

[The clause adds important information but does not restrict the meaning of *village*.]

The cactus spines, *like hypodermic needles*, are three inches long and can easily puncture human skin. [The prepositional phrase adds descriptive information but does not restrict *cactus spines*.]

NOTE: Clauses and phrases that modify proper nouns are always nonrestrictive. (See proper nouns, p. 2.)

Samuel Yellin, *who described himself as a blacksmith to immigration officials*, came to the United States in 1905. [*Samuel Yellin* is a proper noun.]

Sometimes a clause or phrase may be either restrictive or nonrestrictive. The writer must indicate how it is to be interpreted by using or omitting commas.

RESTRICTIVE   The witnesses who were experts in treating alcoholism answered the technical questions. [The *who* clause restricts or defines *witnesses*. The sentence means that not all witnesses answered the technical questions; only the expert witnesses did.]

NONRESTRICTIVE   The witnesses, who were experts in treating alcoholism, answered the technical questions. [This sentence means that all the witnesses were experts, and they answered the technical questions. The *who* clause is not essential to the meaning of the sentence.]

3. Nonrestrictive appositives should be set off by commas; restrictive appositives should not.

A restrictive appositive defines the noun it refers to in such a way that its absence from the sentence would leave the meaning unclear.

NONRESTRICTIVE   Ralph Williams, *a frequent personality on late-night television*, made millions selling used cars.

NONRESTRICTIVE   Baby gray whales, *huge creatures at birth*, consume up to fifty gallons of milk daily.

NONRESTRICTIVE	"Mending Wall," *one of Robert Frost's best poems,* deals with two differing world views.
RESTRICTIVE	The actor *Humphrey Bogart* is best known for tough-guy roles.
RESTRICTIVE	The Greek hero *Perseus* slew the dragon and freed Andromeda.
RESTRICTIVE	James Dickey's poem *"Looking for the Buckhead Boys"* portrays a middle-aged man's attempt to reconnect with his youth.

Exercise 3

In the following sentences, insert commas to set off nonrestrictive clauses, phrases, and appositives. If a sentence is correct as written, underline the restrictive or nonrestrictive element and mark the sentence with a *C*. Be prepared to explain your answers.

1. Freshman Harold Schwartz working night and day finished his first novel four hundred incoherent pages.

2. The manager will give the job to anyone who promises to work eight full hours.

3. We advise patients who experience anxiety and depression.

4. Flight attendant for TWA is one job Richard has had.

5. Ernest Hemingway's novel *The Sun Also Rises* embodies his post–World War I experiences in Paris.

6. I have decided that the personal computer I want has not been made.

7. My uncle Hans who came to Milwaukee at age twenty has worked as a brewer for thirty years.

8. Actors James Cagney and George Raft both of whom began their careers as dancers became famous because of movie roles as gangsters in the 1930s.

9. In 1986 thousands of peace advocates who came from every segment of American society marched from Los Angeles to Washington, DC, to promote world disarmament a cause millions of ordinary citizens are working for.

10. Belinda determined to pass the state bar examination studied sixteen hours a day for two months.

Exercise 4

Combine the following sentences according to the directions given in brackets. After you have combined the sentences, be sure to punctuate them correctly. For example:

> Of all the Crusades, the Children's Crusade shocks us the most. It produced nearly fifty thousand casualties. [Use an adjective clause.]
>
> Of all the Crusades, the Children's Crusade, *which produced nearly fifty thousand casualties,* shocks us the most.

1. The crowd gathered at the palace gates. It listened to the voice coming over the loud-speaker. [Use a participial phrase.]

2. The 1986 senior class purchased a new scoreboard for the school. Its members were the rowdiest the faculty had seen. [Use an adjective clause.]

3. The go-away bird gets its nickname from a call that sounds human. This bird is actually a gray loerie. [Use an appositive.]

4. The old man sat in the back row. He collapsed when the race started. [Use a participial phrase.]

5. Holographic images appear to be three-dimensional. They are created by laser beams. [Use an adjective clause.]

6. Western Samoa has 160,000 inhabitants. My mother was born there. [Use an adjective clause.]

7. Roman invasions brought Britain into contact with the Continent. The invading legions struck in the first century B.C. [Use a participial phrase.]

8. Winston Churchill and Franklin Roosevelt agreed to force Adolf Hitler to surrender unconditionally. Their meeting took place in Morocco. [Use a prepositional phrase.]

9. The central character, John Blackthorne, survives a grueling incar-

ceration. He is shipwrecked in feudal Japan. [Use an adverb clause.]

10. Stephen Crane wrote *The Red Badge of Courage*. It is a novel about a

    soldier in the American Civil War. Crane had never been a soldier

    himself. [Use an adjective clause and an appositive.]

23d Use commas to set off parenthetical expressions that function as transitions, express afterthoughts, or offer supplemental information.

Parenthetical expressions interrupt the flow of a sentence. Transitional phrases such as *for example, on the other hand*, and *in fact* are parenthetical and usually are set off by commas.

> Driving on freeways and turnpikes, *for example,* is four times more dangerous than flying.

Commas are usually needed to set off conjunctive adverbs, such as *accordingly, besides, consequently, furthermore, hence, however, indeed, instead, likewise, meanwhile, moreover, nevertheless, otherwise, therefore,* and *thus.* (See semicolon, p. 151.)

> Several bystanders who witnessed the crime identified the thief; *nevertheless,* he was released from custody because of a technicality. [Before a clause.]

> Several bystanders who witnessed the crime identified the thief; he was released from custody, *however,* because of a technicality. [Within a clause.]

Always use commas to set off *however* when it is used as a conjunctive adverb; do not use commas to set off *however* when it is an adverb meaning "no matter how."

Sixteen engineers gave similar testimony; *however,* the Senate committee was swayed by the attorney general's dissenting view. [Conjunctive adverb.]

However reasonable the expert testimony, the committee still votes according to party attitudes. [Adverb.]

Afterthoughts and supplemental information should be set off with commas.

Mystery writers, *some critics maintain,* try to make sense of murder.

23e Use a comma to set off mild interjections, words of direct address, and *yes* and *no*.

Oh, I didn't mean to buy so many groceries!
Stop playing those video games, *Ed.*
No, I cannot be there early.

Exercise 5

Insert commas as necessary to set off parenthetical expressions and words of direct address in the following sentences. If a sentence is correct, mark it with a *C*.

1. However much Americans love their Big Macs and chocolate shakes,

   many are sacrificing their affair with junk food for a new commitment.

2. Bulging biceps, rippled stomachs, and yes even sinewy necks are the

   new shapes people yearn for.

3. Regardless of the pain and endless hours spent pumping iron men

   and women are dedicating themselves to furious body building.

4. Will chiseled muscles lead to healthier lives? No not if weightlifting

   is an escape from time's relentless craftsmanship.

5. Moreover many body builders express their desire to become the

   next Incredible Hulk or a new-age Rambo.

23f Use commas between words, phrases, and clauses in a
series consisting of three or more items of equal importance.

> Deborah spent her vacation visiting relatives in Montana, Wyoming, South Dakota, and Nebraska. [Nouns.]
>
> Elizabeth flew to Rome, rented a car, and drove to Florence. [Predicates.]
>
> Dave spent his vacation reading Hemingway, camping in the woods, and fishing in the secluded streams of the Sierras. [Participial phrases.]
>
> Hal's dog died, his brother wrecked the new Porsche, and his girl friend eloped with a plumber from Alaska. [Clauses.]

Although the final comma in a series is optional, including it can
prevent misreading.

> I took the following courses: digital computers, software manufacturing, word processing, and data retrieval. [The final comma makes it clear that word processing and data retrieval are separate courses.]

NOTE: No comma is necessary between items in a series all joined
by *and*.

> Bill and Marie and Dave all made the team.

23g   Use a comma between coordinate adjectives not joined by and. Do not use a comma between cumulative adjectives.

Coordinate adjectives are two or more adjectives that modify the same noun or pronoun.

> *Informative, imaginative, appealing* advertising should be more common. [*Informative, imaginative,* and *appealing* modify *advertising.*]

> Advertising is often no more than a *deceptive, dull* appeal to one's insecurity. [*Deceptive* and *dull* modify *appeal.*]

NOTE: A comma is never used between the last adjective in a series and the noun it modifies.

Cumulative adjectives modify the adjectives that follow them as well as a noun or pronoun.

> His life was dedicated to achieving a *single personal* goal. [*Single* modifies *personal* and *goal.*]

> The exhibition of *ancient Tunisian* mosaics will close next week. [*Ancient* modifies *Tunisian* and *mosaics.*]

Two simple tests can help you tell the difference between coordinate and cumulative adjectives. If you can change the order of the adjectives or place the word *and* between them, the series is coordinate and requires commas.

> Imaginative, appealing, informative advertising should be more common.

> Appealing *and* informative *and* imaginative advertising should be more common.

The preceding adjective series meets both tests; therefore, it is coordinate.

> His life was dedicated to achieving a *personal single* goal.
> His life was dedicated to achieving a single *and* personal goal.

The adjective series *single personal* does not meet either test; therefore, it is cumulative.

Exercise 6

Insert commas as necessary within series or between coordinate adjectives in the following sentences. Include the last comma in a series. If any sentence is correct, mark it with a *C*.

1. A lucky photographer might have his photos reproduced on posters postcards and calendars.

2. High-Tec-Rec is a new kind of summer camp where children set aside footballs baseball bats and soccer shoes to spend two weeks writing computer programs.

3. The agile playful aggressive mongoose can kill a scorpion before it has time to sting.

4. Bacteria live everywhere: in water in soil in the air in plants and in animals.

5. Armando Ruiz entered the restaurant glanced quickly around the room and selected a table by the fireplace.

6. The houses were made from economical precut forms.

7. Pamela stared into the dark eerie cave.

8. Well-toned slim bodies dominate fashion magazines.

9. Beyond the nightclubs luxury hotels and mammoth shopping centers lies an exotic refuge of beaches green islands and secluded temples.

10. The huge Asian elephant serves as a political symbol as well as a

beast of burden and a participant in religious ceremonies.

23h Use the comma to set off absolute phrases.

An **absolute phrase** modifies an entire sentence rather than a word or a phrase, but it is not grammatically related to the rest of the sentence.

> *The game having already begun,* we took our seats in a hurry.
> Laura, *her work done,* went to bed.
> The man studied the town, *his eyes narrowing in concentration.*

23i Use the comma to set off contrasting expressions and interrogative elements.

> Defense, *not offense,* wins most football games. [Contrasting expression.]
>
> A newspaper has the responsibility to check the facts behind a story, *doesn't it?* [Interrogative element.]

23j Use the comma to set off expressions such as *he said* or *she wrote* from direct quotations.

> The *Tao Te Ching* says, "Not collecting treasures prevents stealing."
>
> "Writing is an art; and artists are human beings," wrote the eccentric American poet E. E. Cummings.
>
> "One writes out of one thing only," says James Baldwin, "one's own experience."

If the expression comes between two or more sentences of quotation, use a period after the expression to indicate the end of the first sentence.

"The apartment house is nearly finished," she said. "I never thought I would see the day."

(See quotation marks, p. 159; colon, p. 155.)

Omit the comma if a quotation ends with an exclamation point or question mark.

"Why all this indecision?" he asked.

NOTE: When a comma follows a quotation, always place it within the quotation marks, not after or under them.

"Of course," she replied.

Exercise 7

Insert commas as necessary to set off absolute phrases, contrasting expressions, interrogative elements, and explanatory words used with direct quotations. If any sentence is correct, mark it with a *C*.

1. Elected officials need to consider everyone's well-being not just their

   own.

2. Their job being difficult city council members tend to focus only on

   the people who make the most noise.

3. One city council member has said "I see two kinds of people at

   meetings: those who want something done and those who want to

   stop something from being done."

4. People are well behaved at public meetings aren't they? Most of us

   would think so a mistake on our part. Another council member

   remembers a fist fight between two land developers. "They were

going at it in the aisle, tooth and nail" he said "just like a couple of
angry kids fighting over marbles wouldn't you say?"

5. A council seat offers some rewards. "Not money, that's for sure" one
council member said. "But when re-election comes around, you get
to meet people who are glad you're the referee" he added.

23k Use a comma according to established conventions in
numbers, addresses, place names, dates, and friendly letters.

Separate long numbers into groups of three beginning from the right.

    17,325   385,667   186,000,000

In four-digit numbers, the comma is optional.

    4,598 or 4598

Separate each item in an address when the address is run together
in a line. Do not use a comma to set off the Zip Code.

    1204 Curtis Avenue, South Milwaukee, Wisconsin 53172
    1204 Curtis Avenue
    South Milwaukee, Wisconsin 53172

Separate each item in a place name.

    We visited Harvard University, Cambridge, Massachusetts, her
    alma mater.

Separate the month and day from the year in a date.

    On October 31, 1985, two children were lost.

If the day precedes the month, no commas are necessary.

    31 October 1985

Set off a salutation and the close of a friendly letter.

>   Dear Aunt Sally,   Sincerely yours,

Exercise 8

Insert commas as necessary in the following letter, including optional commas.

>   March 16 1986

Dear Pat

I want you to know that I am living at 18 San Juan Drive Costa Mesa California 92626 for the next month. I just made the trip from Indiana University Bloomington where nice houses cost about $55000. But here I am living in a dump they tell me is worth $200000! If I were to buy one like it, the monthly payments would be over $1700. Remember when we paid $65 a month for that cabin outside of Portland? How times change.

>   Your buddy

>   Jerry

231 Use a comma to prevent misunderstanding and to show the omission of an understood word.

To prevent a misunderstanding:

>   **CONFUSING**   On Monday morning schedules will be revised.

| CLEAR | On Monday**,** morning schedules will be revised. |
| CLEAR | On Monday morning**,** schedules will be revised. |

To show an omission:

The French drink wine; the Germans**,** beer.

For Dr. Woodson to give one A is rare; for him to give two**,** unprecedented.

24 Unnecessary Commas *no ,*

Excessive use of the comma may confuse a reader by separating sentence elements that belong together. The following rules specify when a comma is not necessary.

24a Do not use a comma between a subject and its verb unless a sentence element that comes between them requires a comma.

INCORRECT	Fully grown killer whales, are as long as thirty feet and as heavy as ten tons.
CORRECT	Fully grown killer whales are as long as thirty feet and as heavy as ten tons.
CORRECT	Fully grown killer whales, who travel in pods of ten to twenty, are as long as thirty feet and as heavy as ten tons.

24b Do not use a comma between a verb and its complement.

| INCORRECT | A killer whale will eat, anything it can catch. |
| CORRECT | A killer whale will eat anything it can catch. |

24c   Do not use a comma between a preposition and its object.

INCORRECT	Killer whales live in, practically all the tropical oceans of the world.
CORRECT	Killer whales live in practically all the tropical oceans of the world.

24d   Do not use a comma between an adverb and the word it modifies or between an adjective and the word it modifies.

INCORRECT	The killer whale has been described as the most socially, intelligent, animal in the world. [*Socially* modifies *intelligent; intelligent* modifies *animal.*]
CORRECT	The killer whale has been described as the most socially intelligent animal in the world.

(See coordinate adjectives and cumulative adjectives, p. 138.)

24e   Do not use a comma between compound words, phrases, or dependent clauses joined by a coordinating conjunction.

INCORRECT	The engine, and the grill are the most famous features of the Rolls-Royce. [Compound subject joined by conjunction *and.*]
CORRECT	The engine and the grill are the most famous features of the Rolls-Royce.
INCORRECT	A Rolls-Royce has eighty thousand parts, and takes three months to build. [Compound predicate joined by conjunction *and.*]
CORRECT	A Rolls-Royce has eighty thousand parts and takes three months to build.
INCORRECT	The Rolls-Royce is proof that fine work is still being done, and that people will pay any price

for quality. [Two dependent clauses beginning with *that* and joined by conjunction *and*.]

CORRECT The Rolls-Royce is proof that fine work is still being done and that people will pay any price for quality.

(See compound subject and compound predicate, p. 15, 16.)

24f Do not use commas to separate restrictive elements from the rest of the sentence.

INCORRECT The first car, created by Henry Royce and Charles Rolls, was built in 1904. [The sentence falsely suggests that Royce and Rolls built the first automobile.]

CORRECT The first car created by Henry Royce and Charles Rolls was built in 1904.

INCORRECT Fritz Wirth's article, "An Empire on Four Wheels," appeared in January. [This sentence would be correctly punctuated only if Wirth wrote one article.]

CORRECT Fritz Wirth's article "An Empire on Four Wheels" appeared in January.

(See restrictive elements, p. 129.)

24g Do not use a comma after *such as* and *like*.

INCORRECT Some sports, such as, mountain climbing, bicycle racing, and board surfing, build the spirit as well as the body.

CORRECT Some sports, such as mountain climbing, bicycle racing, and board surfing, build the spirit as well as the body.

24h Do not use a comma before the first or after the last item in a series unless a rule requires it.

INCORRECT	Ropes, carbiners, runners, and chocks, enable mountain climbers to scale the huge rock formations of Yosemite National Park.
CORRECT	Ropes, carbiners, runners, and chocks enable mountain climbers to scale the huge rock formations of Yosemite National Park.
INCORRECT	The most famous formations in Yosemite are, El Capitan, Royal Arches, Half Dome, and Glacier Point.
CORRECT	The most famous formations in Yosemite are El Capitan, Royal Arches, Half Dome, and Glacier Point.
CORRECT	Some famous formations in Yosemite are, among others, El Capitan, Royal Arches, and Half Dome. [Rule requires setting off parenthetical expression *among others* with commas.]

24i Do not use a comma to introduce indirect discourse.

Indirect discourse reports what a work, writer, or speaker states but not in the exact words used by the original source.

INCORRECT	The Bible says, that we need more than bread to live.
CORRECT	The Bible says that we need more than bread to live.

24j Do not use a comma before *than* in a comparison.

INCORRECT	Living in Washington, DC, is more exciting, than living in any other capital city.
CORRECT	Living in Washington, DC, is more exciting than living in any other capital city.

24k Do not use a comma with a period, a question mark, an exclamation point, or a dash, all of which stand by themselves.

> INCORRECT   "I won't do it!", Jane shouted.
>
> CORRECT   "I won't do it!" Jane shouted.

Exercise 9: Review

Correct the following sentences by inserting commas where they are needed and by deleting them where they are not needed. Include all optional commas. If any sentence is correct, mark it with a *C*.

1. The life of the Chinese heroine Meng Chiang Nu, the Pumpkin Girl, is an example of loyalty dedication and self-sacrifice.

2. The story begins with two families the Meng and the Chiang.

3. During the planting season one year each family planted pumpkins at the foot of a wall that marked the boundary of their properties.

4. Growing rapidly, pumpkin vines soon began to climb the wall and at the top they joined and produced a pumpkin larger than anyone had ever seen before.

5. According to the story the families agreed to divide the pumpkin but when they cut it open they found a tiny baby girl inside.

6. To show she belonged to both the Meng family and the Chiang family they called her Meng Chiang.

7. At about this same time, the Emperior Shih Huang Ti started to build the Great Wall of China.

8. Each time the emperior's men put up a section of the wall however it collapsed before another section could be built.

9. The emperor who felt discouraged sent for the wisest men in the empire to advise him.

10. One wise man told him the only way to stop the collapse, would be to bury a living person in the wall every mile.

11. Since the wall was to extend ten thousand miles the plan would call for the sacrifice of ten thousand people!

12. Another wise man whispered to the emperor "Your Eminence living nearby is a poor man. Since his name Wan means ten thousand bury him in the wall and your great enterprise will be strong along its entire length."

13. Yes, Wan was poor, but he was not stupid.

14. When he heard of the plan he ran, and ran, and ran, until at nightfall he found himself high, in the branches of a tree in a peaceful isolated garden.

15. Beneath him he saw a beautiful girl bathing naked in a pool.

16. Of course it was Meng Chiang grown to womanhood.

17. She sang softly of love, and said aloud "If any man should see me now I would happily be his wife forever."

18. Wan forgot his own safety for a moment and climbed down from the tree and claimed his bride.

19. Unfortunately the emperor's men arrived just after the wedding seized the bridegroom and carried him off to be buried alive in the Great Wall.

20. Having heard of Wan's fate years later Meng Chiang made the hazardous journey to the wall to search for her husband's body.

21. Out of sympathy for her plight, a section of the wall collapsed, and her husband's bones fell out.

22. She was taken to the emperor who was stunned by her great beauty and vowed to marry her.

23. Seeing that the emperor was determined to marry her Meng Chiang asked only that a high altar be built in memory of her husband.

24. On their wedding day Meng Chiang climbed to the top of the altar

   cursed the emperor for his cruelty and threw herself to her death.

25. The emperor commanded his men to cut her body into little pieces

   but each piece of her flesh turned into a beautiful silver fish and her

   soul lives in these fish as a tribute to faithfulness.

25 The Semicolon   ;

A **semicolon** is used, in a limited number of situations, as a substitute for a period to indicate a close relation between main clauses and as a substitute for a comma to improve clarity.

25a Use a semicolon between main clauses that are closely related in meaning and are not joined by a coordinating conjunction.

> In Irish folklore the Sidhe (pronounced "she") spirits sometimes appear as men and women; other times they appear as birds and beasts. The Sidhe travel as clouds of dust; they rest as blades of grass.

There must be some basis for deciding whether to use two main clauses with a semicolon between them, or two sentences with a period. Generally, the division into separate sentences is better. A semicolon should be used only when the ideas in the two main clauses are so closely related that a period would make too strong a break between them. (See coordinating conjunctions, p. 11; comma splices and fused sentences, p. 39.)

Stylistically, the semicolon may be used to create a balance between closely related clauses.

Mystics trust spirits; realists trust only facts.
Mystics trust spirits; realists, only facts.

(See sentence completeness, p. 113.)

25b Use a semicolon to separate main clauses joined by conjunctive adverbs.

In folklore the Sidhe live under Ireland's rocky soil or beneath the mutinous seas; consequently, some Irish claim the Sidhe are never far from them.

(See note, conjunctive adverbs, p. 12.)

NOTE: When a conjunctive adverb immediately follows a semicolon (as in the preceding example), always put a comma after the conjunctive adverb. When a conjunctive adverb does not immediately follow the semicolon, put commas before and after the conjunctive adverb.

The Sidhe live on cold potatoes and milk left on hearths and at thresholds of Irish homes; when feasting, however, they resort to theft and rob Irish cellars of good wines.

25c Use a semicolon to separate main clauses joined by coordinating conjunctions when the main clauses are long and complex or have internal punctuation.

The Sidhe sing in glens, dance on boulders, and play hurling in the fields; but they also curse, bicker, and fight each other.

25d Use semicolons to separate phrases or clauses in a series if they are long or contain commas.

Partial to humans, Sidhe spirits will help them in their work; aid them in the search for hidden money, lost jewels, and buried gold; treat their sick pets, ailing livestock, and ill children.

25e Avoid misusing the semicolon.

Do not use a semicolon to join dependent clauses or phrases and main clauses.

INCORRECT	According to some enthusiasts; only ten thousand Sidhe exist.
CORRECT	According to some enthusiasts, only ten thousand Sidhe exist.
INCORRECT	Some believe the Sidhe are headed toward extinction; because fewer and fewer people believe in them.
CORRECT	Some believe the Sidhe are headed toward extinction because fewer and fewer people believe in them.

Do not use a semicolon to introduce a list.

INCORRECT	Perhaps the Sidhe will join the ranks of other imaginary creatures; such as unicorns, leprechauns, and magical dwarfs.
CORRECT	Perhaps the Sidhe will join the ranks of other imaginary creatures, such as unicorns, leprechauns, and magical dwarfs.
CORRECT	Perhaps the Sidhe will join the ranks of other imaginary creatures: unicorns, leprechauns, and magical dwarfs.

(See colon, p. 155; dash, p. 158.)

Exercise 10

Delete the unnecessary or incorrect commas and semicolons and insert the correct punctuation in the following sentences. If any sentence is correct, mark it with a *C*.

1. Whereas imaginary creatures may fall from memory; the real mysteries of the world will always arouse our curiosity.

2. One mystery involves strange carvings, many the size of three-story buildings, found on Easter Island, another involves cave drawings at Lascaux, France, painted fifteen to twenty thousand years ago.

3. Easter Island is tiny, volcanic, barren, and isolated; nevertheless, plenty of insects and hordes of rats live there.

4. Mysterious statues dominate the island; their threatening expressions presiding over the landscape.

5. Their faces all share similar features; such as long ears, large eyes, and jutting chins.

6. Some of the statues are toppled over, most, however, still stand, all still have topknots made from red stone.

7. The paintings in the Lascaux caves, are equally mysterious, however the mystery surrounds their purpose, not their origin.

8. Some students claim the paintings represent hunting magic, others see in them a great symbolic idea that is beyond our understanding, still others view them as simply the result of creative impulses.

9. Whatever their motivations; the Lascaux cave painters created groups of pictures in sixty-six caves. This achievement required many skills; including the ability to extract minerals from the ground, pound them to powder, and mix them with grease.

10. As children we huddle together in the darkness and scare each other with tales of mysterious monsters, as adults we curl up under a reading lamp with a good book and wonder about the mysterious creations of people.

26 The Colon :

A **colon** formally introduces sentence elements that explain, illustrate, or amplify earlier portions of the sentence. A colon is also used to introduce formal quotations and to separate subtitles and titles, subdivisions of time, parts of biblical citations, and city and publisher in bibliographic entries.

26a Use a colon to introduce a series following a complete sentence.

The admissions office listed three options: social psychology, linguistics, and computer science.

Three dates stand out in the development of the English language: 450, when the Germanic tribes occupied Britain; 1066, when the Norman French invaded England; and 1607, when English speakers settled in Jamestown.

26b   Use a colon after *the following* or *as follows* to introduce a statement or series.

Agreeing with Orwell, many linguists see the relation between language and thought as follows: Thought depends on language, and language depends on thought.

26c   Use a colon to announce a second main clause that explains the first.

His intention is clear: He is determined to become president no matter how often he must distort the truth.

NOTE: Capitalizing the first word in a sentence following a colon is optional. (See capitals, p. 176.)

26d   Use a colon to introduce a final appositive.

Phrase-makers think they have found a name for the new missile that sounds proud and dependable but has the light touch so necessary for doomsday weaponry: the Hallmark, from those who care enough to send the very best.

26e   Use a colon to introduce a long or formal quotation.

In 1962 Rachel Carson's *Silent Spring* sounded the warning:

The most alarming of all man's assaults upon the environment is the contamination of air, earth, rivers, and sea with dangerous and even lethal materials. This pollution is for the most part irrecoverable; the chain of evil it initiates not only in the world that must support life but in living tissues is for the most part irreversible. In this now universal contamination of the environment, chemicals are the sinister and little-recognized partners of radiation in changing the very nature of the world— the very nature of life itself.

26f Use a colon to separate subtitles and titles, subdivisions of time, parts of biblical citations, and city and publisher in bibliographic entries.

> *Literature*: *An Introduction to Fiction, Poetry, and Drama*
> 12:21 A.M.   1:53 P.M.   Matthew 4:6
> Boston: Little, 1984

(See note, capital after colon in titles, p. 177.)

26g Use a colon at the end of a formal salutation.

> Dear Dr. Agran: To Whom It May Concern:

26h Do not misuse the colon by placing it after a linking verb or a preposition or by placing it in a sentence that lacks a formal introduction for what follows.

INCORRECT	The books you'll need are: *The Bell Jar* and *The Trojans*.
CORRECT	The books you'll need are *The Bell Jar* and *The Trojans*.
INCORRECT	Morgan, a bright young man, is a student of: drama, cinema, and fiction.
CORRECT	Morgan, a bright young man, is a student of drama, cinema, and fiction.
INCORRECT	In the art world, Dada is noted for the irrational and whimsical works it created, such as: the reproduction of the *Mona Lisa* with a mustache.
CORRECT	In the art world, Dada is noted for the irrational and whimsical works it created, such as the reproduction of the *Mona Lisa* with a mustache.

27 The Dash —

The most common uses of the **dash** are to emphasize a sentence element and to indicate a break in tone or thought. Do not use a dash habitually in place of a comma, semicolon, or period. Reserve dashes for situations calling for special emphasis or for the infrequent situations when only a dash will make your meaning clear.

In a typed paper make a dash by joining two hyphens (--) without spaces before or after them.

27a Use dashes to emphasize appositives and parenthetical expressions.

> Judge Sarah Riley sentenced O'Neil — the treasurer of Local 1026 and once the friend of local politicians — to five years. [Appositive.]
>
> The craft of surgery — though some would call it an art — demands the steady hand of a miniaturist to work the scalpel through a web of arteries and veins. [Parenthetical expression.]

27b Use a dash to separate a series that comes at the beginning of a sentence.

> Aching feet and ankles, throbbing shins, clicking knees, and crumbling hip joints — these physical ailments result from running on asphalt or cement.

27c Use a dash for special emphasis or clarity.

> The status game became absurd as soon as pinstripe-suited executives began turning up in denim and sneakers — with no loss of prestige. [Emphasis.]
>
> The police picked up two robbers — an ex-convict and a teenager. [A dash must be used rather than a comma to make it clear that the police picked up two people, not four.]

27d Use dashes to show a break in tone or thought.

"What do you — that is — okay, I'll donate twenty dollars."
"You don't like the necklace?"
"It's too — "
"Too gaudy, maybe?"
"Too — well, too expensive!"

27e Use a dash to precede an author's name after a formal quotation that stands separately from the text, such as an epigraph.

If I had the use of my body, I would throw it out the window.
— *Samuel Beckett*

28 Quotation marks " "

The main use of **quotation marks** is to assist a reader by indicating the beginning and the end of a direct quotation from speech or writing.

28a Use double quotation marks (" ") to enclose direct quotations from speakers or writers.

In a recent lecture on contemporary art, Professor Dunlap said, "Until the general acceptance of Georgia O'Keeffe's work, artists were divided into two groups — artists and female painters. Now we have just one group — artists."

Art historian Sam Hunter sees Georgia O'Keeffe's work as emerging from and going beyond biomorphic abstraction: "O'Keeffe seemed able to invest abstract painting with fresh content and significant new forms."

When quoting a passage that takes up more than four lines in a typewritten paper, do not use quotation marks (unless they appear in the original); instead, set off the quotation from the rest of the paper by putting it in block form. That is, indent the entire passage ten spaces and double-space between the lines. The first line of the passage should be indented an additional three spaces if it marks the beginning of a paragraph.

> While art historians discuss O'Keeffe's work in terms of abstract and biomorphic forms, O'Keeffe, still working in her nineties, talks about art as learning a new language:
>
> > A young potter came to the Ranch and as I watched him work with the clay I saw that he could make it speak. The pots that he made were beautiful shapes—very smooth—near to sculpture. I hadn't thought much about pottery but now I thought that maybe I could make a pot, too—maybe a beautiful pot—it could become still another language for me.

When directly quoting poetry, you should work a quotation of one line into the text and enclose it within quotation marks.

> Gerard Manley Hopkins presents his view of life best in a single line: "The world is charged with the grandeur of God."

A quotation of two or three lines of poetry may be worked into the text or set off. To work the lines into the text, separate them with a slash (with space before and after the slash) and enclose the entire quotation in quotation marks.

Blake ends "The Tyger" with a question: "What immortal hand
or eye / Could frame thy fearful symmetry?"

To set poetry off from the text, begin each line on a new line, indent
it ten spaces unless the poet used varying indentation, and double-
space between lines.

```
Blake ends "The Tyger" with a question:

    What immortal hand or eye

    Could frame thy fearful symmetry?
```

A poetry quotation of more than three lines should be set off from
the text in block form and presented just as it is printed in the
original. Do not use quotation marks and slashes.

When quoting conversation or writing fictional dialogue, put
quotation marks around the exact words spoken. Do not enclose
descriptive phrases or attributions in quotation marks. Begin a new
paragraph for each speaker.

"This work cost an arm and a leg," Max said, leaning against the
railing and staring at a mass of squiggles dripped over a canvas
that hung on the far wall. "But having it makes the pain of getting
it worthwhile."

"Knowing how you operate, I bet it cost the insurance company
an arm and a leg," Grant said. "I see you still have all four of
your limbs."

If one speaker is quoted without interruption for more than a
paragraph, put quotation marks at the beginning of each paragraph
but at the end of only the last paragraph.

NOTE: Do not use quotation marks to enclose indirect quotations
— written or spoken information that you have rewritten or summarized in your own words.

A spokesman for the European Space Agency said that an earth-
quake-predicting satellite will be launched by 1990.

28b Use quotation marks to enclose the titles of articles, short stories, short poems, songs, chapter titles and other subdivisions of books or periodicals, and episodes of radio and television programs.

(See italics, p. 190.)

> Shirley Jackson's "The Lottery" exposes a small community's blind obedience to tradition. [Short story.]
>
> "The Microbe Hunters" is this week's episode of *Nova*. [Television episode.]
>
> Chapter 2, "Entering the Aerobics Program," tells how to take the first step toward improving the cardiovascular system. [Chapter title.]

NOTE: Do not use quotation marks to enclose the titles or section titles of your own papers.

28c Occasionally quotation marks serve to enclose a word used in a special sense.

> I can reduce quantum mechanics to one question: What is the "matter"?

NOTE: Do not use quotation marks in an attempt to create an ironic tone, change the meaning of a word, or justify the use of nonstandard English.

> INAPPROPRIATE His personality is "too totally bizarre" for me.
>
> APPROPRIATE His personality is too bizarre for me.

28d Follow standard practice when using other marks of punctuation with quotation marks.

1. Always place commas and periods that follow a quotation inside quotation marks.

Although Tom Bender said, "Writers who endure will always write about what they know," he spent years describing the journeys of characters who become lost in exotic lands he never visited.

Scanning the crowd for her son, she said, "It's like looking for a needle in a haystack."

2. Always place colons and semicolons outside quotation marks.

Some of Aunt Maude's favorite expressions are "He runs around like a chicken with its head cut off"; "Where there's smoke there's fire"; "Don't count your chickens until they've hatched": expressions from the common pot of American clichés.

3. Enclose dashes, question marks, and exclamation points in quotation marks only if they belong to the quotation.

"What? And miss the chance —" Tom paused, overcome with anger.

After reading "The Love Song of J. Alfred Prufrock" and finding herself confused, Patricia Shaw wrote on the quiz, "Should I ask what is it, or should I return for another visit?"

The protesters shouted, "No more nukes! No more nukes!"

When a dash, question mark, or exclamation point is not part of a direct quotation, do not enclose it within quotation marks.

"The Dancing Bride" — a mystical poem that deals with the marriage between primitive spirit and technological intellect — went unpublished for six years after it was written.

Did the protesters shout, "No more nukes"?

Stop demanding, "Hold still"!

28e Use single quotation marks (' ') to enclose a direct quotation within a quotation.

The senator said, "My approach is like the message I found in a fortune cookie, 'Seek help from those who have the answers.'"

Exercise 11

Supply quotation marks where they are needed and place punctuation marks correctly in the following sentences. If a quotation should be set off in block form, place a *B* to indicate at which point the block would begin and an *E* to indicate where it would end. Make any other changes that would be necessary to handle a block quotation correctly. If no quotation marks are needed in a sentence, mark it with a *C*.

1. Of all Flannery O'Connor's short stories, A Good Man Is Hard to Find best embodies the full range of her style.

2. O'Connor, Michael Finnegan wrote, mastered the use of caricature in character development.

3. The dictionary defines *caricature* as follows: The exaggeration of certain human characteristics in order to create a satiric effect.

4. The portrait of Mrs. Freeman in the short story Good Country People is an example of caricature: Besides the neutral expression that she wore when she was alone, Mrs. Freeman had two others, forward and reverse, that she used in all her human dealings. Her forward expression was steady and driving like the advance of a heavy truck. She seldom used the other expression because it was not often necessary for her to retract a statement. O'Connor even uses the

name *Freeman* ironically because Mrs. Freeman is no more free than the speeding truck she is compared to.

5. To reveal the limited natures of her characters, O'Connor often fills their speech with stock phrases, such as Nothing is perfect; That is life; and You're the wheel behind the wheel.

6. Sometimes her characters seem too strange to be real, but, like all writers who will endure, she draws her material from life, thus following Alexander Pope's dictate: Know then thyself, presume not God to scan; / The proper study of Mankind is Man.

7. She studied people, and the absurdity of much of the world delighted her. Sally Fitzgerald writes about O'Connor's letters, She regaled us with Hadacol advertisements; birth announcements of infants with names that had to be read to be believed; such news items as the attendance of Roy Rogers' horse at a church service in California.

8. Could her intense interest in the absurd behavior of people continue one critic asked and still remain fresh?

9. I've reached the point where I can't do again what I can do well she

wrote in a letter and the larger things I need to do now, I doubt my capacity for doing.

10. Many prefer distant landscapes such as the magical kingdom in Coleridge's short poem Kubla Khan, which begins In Xanadu did Kubla Khan / A stately pleasure-dome decree: / Where Alph, the sacred river, ran / Through caverns measureless to man / Down to a sunless sea.

29 The Ellipsis Mark . . .

An **ellipsis mark (. . .)** indicates that one or more words within a quotation have been intentionally omitted, either to avoid including unnecessary or irrelevant portions of a quoted passage or to mark an unfinished statement in dialogue.

29a Use an ellipsis mark to indicate an omission in a quotation that you have edited to fit the purposes of a paper.

Original passage:

> The last century, we all realize, has witnessed a radical transformation in the entire human environment, largely as a result of the impact of the mathematical and physical sciences upon technology. This shift from empirical, tradition-bound technics to an experimental mode has opened up such new realms as those of

nuclear energy, supersonic transportation, cybernetic intelligence and instantaneous distant communication. Never since the Pyramid Age have such vast physical changes been consummated in so short a time.

—Lewis Mumford

Edited within a paper:

"The last century **. . .** has witnessed a radical transformation in the entire human environment," Lewis Mumford writes, "largely as a result of the impact of the mathematical and physical sciences upon technology**. . . .** Never since the Pyramid Age have such vast physical changes been consummated in so short a time."

Note that when the omission would have completed the sentence or when a complete sentence comes before an omission, as in the sentence above that ends with *technology,* you should place a period at the end of the sentence before the ellipsis mark. Also note that although the quotation is part of a larger work, an ellipsis mark is not used at the end of the quotation.

Keep in mind that you should only use an ellipsis mark to shorten a quotation, never to change the fundamental meaning or shift the emphasis of a quotation.

Type an ellipsis mark by spacing after the period or last word of the quotation and spacing between dots.

29b Use a row of evenly spaced periods to indicate that one or more paragraphs of prose or one or more lines of poetry have been omitted from a quotation.

Earth has not anything to show more fair:
Dull would he be of soul who could pass by
A sight so touching in its majesty:
. . . .
Ne'er saw I, never felt, a calm so deep!

—William Wordsworth

29c   Use an ellipsis mark to indicate an unfinished statement in speech or dialogue.

> The senator sat on the edge of the desk and stared at the smog-shrouded city. "I'm just . . ." His thoughts were wandering; he was unable to concentrate on the danger. "If we had a week, even a day, twelve hours . . . well . . . what can I do?"

30 Parentheses ( )

Parentheses separate incidental information from the rest of a sentence. They serve approximately the same function as commas and dashes in some situations, though each mark gives a different emphasis to the inserted information.

> Mr. Thomas**,** the chairman of the English department**,** led the discussion. [Commas imply that the inserted information is equal in importance to *Mr. Thomas*.]
>
> Mr. Thomas — the chairman of the English department — led the discussion. [Dashes give inserted information more emphasis.]
>
> Mr. Thomas **(**the chairman of the English department**)** led the discussion. [Parentheses imply inserted information is incidental.]

All three of the preceding sentences are correct. Usually, however, commas, dashes, and parentheses are not used interchangeably but are used with different kinds of inserted information. (See comma, p. 126; dash, p. 158.)

> Mr. Thomas**,** the only moderator I have ever respected**,** led the discussion. [Commas used for inserted information that departs from the thought of the rest of the sentence.]
>
> Mr. Thomas — the only moderator I have ever respected — led the discussion. [Dashes used for a strong break in sentence continuity.]
>
> Mr. Thomas **(**Jean's father**)** led the discussion. [Parentheses used for inserted information of only incidental interest.]

30a Use parentheses to enclose parenthetical descriptions or explanations.

Fort Chickery (with a main street no longer than the distance a strong quarterback can toss the pigskin) has six restaurants that serve the best pecan pie in the South. [Description.]

A barber (if he had a steady enough hand to hold the blade at the correct angle) could give a fine shave with Billy John's hunting knife. [Explanation.]

If a parenthetical sentence comes between two sentences, it should begin with a capital letter and end with a period, question mark, or exclamation point.

The largest garbage dump in the world is Fresh Kills on Staten Island, New York. (Can you imagine the smell!) In four months of operation, seven hundred barges dumped 500,000 tons of refuse there.

NOTE: Nonessential elements take no special punctuation other than the parentheses. At times punctuation marks may follow the parentheses if those marks are part of the main sentence.

When I feel my stomach churning from fear (usually on the morning of a midterm or final), I do deep-breathing exercises.

30b Use parentheses to enclose letters or figures that label items in a series.

To begin playing tennis well, you must remember these three fundamental points: (1) tennis is a sideways game, (2) the back-handed stroke makes a loop, and (3) the follow-through should end high.

NOTE: When lists are set off from the text, the letters and figures labeling them are usually not enclosed in parentheses.

31 Brackets [ ]

Always use **brackets** to enclose your own comments that explain, clarify, or correct the words of a writer you quote.

> One red-faced mill worker, who had quit the factory two years earlier and now lives on a subsistence farm, said, "I [used to] work twelve hours [a day] in smoke. Then [I'd] come home and cough till midnight."

> "I used to dream of flying airplanes [he grew up two miles from Edwards Air Force Base] when I was just a kid," Martin said. "Now I only sell them in several-million-dollar orders."

The word *sic*, a Latin term meaning "thus it is," placed in brackets indicates an error that you have let stand in a quotation and that you did not make when you copied the quotation.

> Roberts set the scene: "And then nite [*sic*] seemed to crush the castle under a heavy blanket of gloom."

Use *sic* only for errors, not for disagreements you may have with a writer you are quoting.

32 The Slash /

The **slash** separates lines of poetry worked into the text of a paper. It also indicates two options.

> The off rhyme, or slant rhyme as it is sometimes called, serves especially well to suggest disappointed letdowns or negations, as Blake's couplet illustrates: "He who the ox to wrath has moved **/** Shall never be by woman loved."

> Whether she decides to take the course for credit **/** no credit is a matter of personal choice.

(See direct quotations, p. 159.)

33 End Punctuation

The Period .

33a Use a period to end sentences that are statements, mild commands, or indirect questions.

On his second voyage to the Western Hemisphere, Columbus landed on the island of Dominica. [Statement.]

Put the heavier cartons in front of the truck. [Mild command.]

My father asked why I wanted to fly to New York. [Indirect question.]

33b Use periods with most abbreviations.

Mrs.	Dr.	Ave.	i.e.
Mr.	Ph.D.	Blvd.	e.g.
A.M. (a.m.)	P.M. (p.m.)	B.C.	A.D.

No periods are needed in certain common abbreviations or in abbreviations of the names of well-known companies, agencies, or organizations.

NBA	SEC	CBS	IBM
TV	USA (or U.S.A.)	USSR (or U.S.S.R.)	VW

NOTE: Although the title *Ms.*, used before a name in place of *Miss* or *Mrs.*, is not an abbreviation, it is still followed by a period: *Ms. Hansen.*

Do not use periods after U.S. Postal Service (Zip Code) abbreviations for states.

CA   MA   VT   WY   NY

Do not use two periods at the end of a sentence.

Kathy received her R.N.

The Question Mark ?

33c Use a question mark after a direct question.

What changes led to this increase in production?

33d Use a question mark within parentheses to indicate doubt about the accuracy of a date or number.

Geoffrey Chaucer, born in 1340 (?), is the author of *The Canterbury Tales.*

Do not use a question mark within parentheses in an attempt to indicate sarcasm.

Our chairman, in his wisdom (?), canceled the meeting.

Instead, shape your words to convey your intention.

In his strange administrative wisdom, our chairman canceled the meeting.

The Exclamation Point !

33e Use an exclamation point after interjections, strong commands, and emphatic statements.

Wow! I knew I could do it. [Interjection.]
"Do it!" I told myself. "Do it! Do it!" [Strong command.]
I am not a crook! [Emphatic statement.]

Do not use an exclamation point within parentheses to indicate sarcasm or amazement.

> The necklace was made of genuine (!) pearls.

Instead, shape your words to convey your meaning.

> I was amazed to discover that the necklace was made of genuine pearls.

NOTE: Ordinarily, only one mark of end punctuation is used. Do not combine marks of end punctuation.

INCORRECT	How can you do this to me?!
CORRECT	How can you do this to me?

NOTE: A period is not used as end punctuation for the title of a work. A question mark or an exclamation point is used when appropriate.

> *A Farewell to Arms*
> *Will Samson Win?*
> *Do It Now!*

Mechanics

34 Capitals

35 The Apostrophe

36 Abbreviations

37 Italics

38 The Hyphen

39 Numbers

40 Spelling

Handing in a paper with errors in mechanics is much like giving an after-dinner speech without knowing you have lettuce in your teeth. No matter how brilliant your phrasing, no matter how appropriate your gestures or witty your anecdotes, the audience will be distracted by the green bits between your incisors. You already know the importance of avoiding spelling errors — no other errors are so quickly noticed and condemned — but you should also know the importance of avoiding errors in capitalization, in the uses of apostrophes, abbreviations, italics, hyphens, and numbers. This section covers the conventions of mechanics. By following these conventions, you will avoid distracting a reader's attention from the ideas in your paper.

34 Capitals *caps/lc*

34a Capitalize the first word of every sentence.

> The photographer's black and white images of Hiroshima are haunting.
>
> Whose raincoat was left in the closet?
>
> Please get me more coffee.

NOTE: Capitalizing the first word of question fragments in a series is optional. Both of the following examples are correct:

> How does a writer prove this point? by statistics? by testimony? at the point of a gun?
>
> How does a writer prove this point? By statistics? By testimony? At the point of a gun?

Capitalizing the first word in a sentence following a colon is also optional. (See colon, p. 155.)

34b Always capitalize the interjection *O* and the personal pronoun *I* as well as contractions made with *I*, such as *I've* and *I'm*.

Help them, O God, to see the truth.

When I prepare a stew, I first lay the ingredients on the chopping block.

Although I've been playing soccer for three years, I'm not good enough to make the team.

34c Capitalize the first and last words and every important word in the titles of your papers and of books, plays, short stories, poems, essays, songs, films, and works of art. Do not capitalize coordinating conjunctions, articles, and prepositions of fewer than five letters unless they begin or end a title.

Guinness Book of World Records [Book.]
Raiders of the Lost Ark [Movie.]
"Traveling Through the Dark" [Poem.]

NOTE 1: Capitalize the word immediately following a colon in a title.

The Uses of Enchantment: The Meaning and Importance of Fairy Tales

NOTE 2: Capitalize the first word in a hyphenated compound with in a title. Capitalize the other parts of the hyphenated compound if they are nouns or adjectives or are as important as the first word.

"A Clean, Well-Lighted Place"
"Mysteries of Hide-and-Seek"
The Do-It-Yourself Environmental Handbook

34d Capitalize the first word in directly quoted sentences or dialogue.

> In *Love and Will*, psychologist Rollo May writes, "The striking thing about love and will in our day is that, whereas in the past they were always held up to us as the *answer* to life's predicaments, they have now become the *problem.*"

> "This is illegal," the detective whispered, taking the crisp twenties. "We're in it together, I guess."

NOTE: Do not capitalize the first word after an interruption between parts of a quoted sentence.

> "Medical students must not be squeamish," the editor writes, "for if they are, they will hesitate to put their scalpels to a patient's flesh."

34e Capitalize the first word in every line of poetry.

> To see a world in a grain of sand
> And a heaven in a wild flower,
> Hold infinity in the palm of your hand
> And eternity in an hour.
> — *William Blake, "Auguries of Innocence"*

If the poet does not follow this convention, use the poet's style.

> anyone lived in a pretty how town
> (with up so floating many bells down)
> spring summer autumn winter
> he sang his didn't he danced his did.
> — *E. E. Cummings, "anyone lived in a pretty how town"*

34f Capitalize proper nouns, proper adjectives, and words used to form essential parts of proper names.

PROPER NOUNS	PROPER ADJECTIVES	COMMON NOUNS
Freud	Freudian	psychoanalyst
Texas	Texan	state
France	French	country

The following is a representative list of words that typically are capitalized. Do not capitalize an article that precedes a proper noun unless it is part of the noun.

SPECIFIC PERSONS, PLACES, THINGS

Pat Kubis	the Tower of London
the Atlantic Ocean	Utah
the Washington Monument	the Grand Canyon
Europe	the *New York Times*

HISTORIC EVENTS, PERIODS, MOVEMENTS, DOCUMENTS

the Civil War	the Enlightenment
the Whiskey Rebellion	the Roaring Twenties
the Middle Ages	the Bill of Rights

NOTE: Do not capitalize centuries, as in eighteenth century, nineteenth century, and so on.

DAYS OF THE WEEK, MONTHS, HOLIDAYS

Friday	September	Fourth of July

ASSOCIATIONS, ORGANIZATIONS, GOVERNMENT DEPARTMENTS, POLITICAL PARTIES

American Bar Association	Postal Service
League of Women Voters	House of Representatives
Boston Symphony Orchestra	Republican Party
Metropolitan Museum of Art	Democrats

NAMES OF EDUCATIONAL INSTITUTIONS, DEPARTMENTS, COURSES, DEGREES

Chapman College   History 150
Department of English   Bachelor of Arts

RELIGIONS, RELIGIOUS FOLLOWERS, RELIGIOUS TERMS

Christianity, Christians   Judgment Day
Judaism, Jews   Allah
Buddhism, Buddhists   Holy Ghost
Hinduism, Hindus   the Virgin
God

NOTE: Capitalizing pronouns referring to God is optional in general writing but required in most religious writing. Do not capitalize *who*, *whom*, or *whose* when referring to God.

RACES, TRIBES, NATIONALITIES, AND THEIR LANGUAGES

Native American   European
Iroquois   Gaelic
Afro-American   Asian
Irish   Yugoslav
Chicano

NOTE: Capitalizing *black* and *white* when referring to people is optional. Both of the following examples are correct.

In American cities, Blacks and Whites are struggling to revitalize neglected neighborhoods.

In American cities, blacks and whites are struggling to revitalize neglected neighborhoods.

NAMES OF CELESTIAL BODIES

Mars   the North Star   the Big Dipper   the Milky Way

TRADE NAMES

Atari   Ford   Frisbee   Rolaids   Xerox

34g Capitalize titles when they come before proper names and capitalize abbreviations for academic degrees when they come after proper names.

> Professor Eric Watkins   Eric Watkins, Ph.D.
> President Susan McMahan   Susan McMahan, J.D.

NOTE: Generally, do not capitalize titles that follow a name.

> Teresa Landis, professor of English
> Albert Brooks, president of Ansen and Company

34h Capitalize abbreviations that indicate time, divisions of government, national and international organizations, businesses, and call letters of radio and television stations.

> A.D.   P.M. (or p.m.)   NATO
> B.C.   YMCA   IBM
> A.M. (or a.m.)   FHA   WQXR

34i Avoid common mistakes in capitalization.

Do not capitalize common nouns used in place of proper nouns.

> **INCORRECT**   After I graduated from High School, I traveled around the Country during the Summer.
>
> **CORRECT**   After I graduated from high school, I traveled around the country during the summer.
>
> **CORRECT**   After I graduated from Belmont High School, I traveled around the United States during June, July, and August.

Do not capitalize the seasons or academic years or terms.

> fall   freshman year
> autumn   summer quarter
> spring   winter semester

Do not capitalize words denoting family relations unless they form part of or substitute for proper names.

INCORRECT	I remember my Mother spent a year studying for the bar examination.
CORRECT	I remember my mother spent a year studying for the bar examination.
CORRECT	I remember Mother spent a year studying for the bar examination.

Do not capitalize general directions unless they refer to specific geographical areas.

east	the East
south	the South
southern	Southern California

Exercise 1

Correct all capitalization errors in the following sentences, consulting a dictionary if necessary. If any sentence is already correct, mark it with a C.

1. Last Spring i read *celebration: a journey through human understanding.*

2. The train moves East, up the rocky mountains toward lake horizon and deadwood canyon, before turning North.

3. The Writer Lytton Strachey paraphrased Shakespeare when he wrote, "the time was out of joint, and he was only too delighted to have been born to set it right."

4. Some consider the practice of zen buddhism to be more an attitude than a serious Religious view, such as that held by christians, hindus, and muslims.

5. The book *Patterns Of Culture: a Study of Human Systems* is the best work I've read since majoring in Anthropology.

6. A company called compu-serve, inc., of columbus, offers electronic copies of ten major national newspapers, including the *los angeles times*, on the same day the papers hit the stands.

7. "There is no hope," someone once said, "when good people fail to condemn political evil."

8. Last Summer in washington, d.c., the temperature reached 102 degrees, but tourists continued to visit congress and the lincoln memorial.

9. The Houston oilers are favored over the Dallas cowboys to win the super bowl.

10. Gossip seems to have filled a need from the days when greeks spread rumors about the goings-on of zeus and hera of olympus until today when american columnists chatter about hollywood superstars.

35 The Apostrophe ✔

The **apostrophe** indicates possession, the omission of letters in words or digits in numbers, and the plurals of letters, numbers, and words used as words.

35a Use an apostrophe to form the possessive case for nouns and indefinite pronouns.

To form the possessive of singular nouns, plural nouns not ending in -*s*, and indefinite pronouns (such as *no one*, *someone*, and *everybody*), add -'*s*. (See indefinite pronouns, p. 4.)

> John's novel is about an ex-governor's climb to the presidency.
>
> History exists because of humankind's outstanding achievement: the creation of written language.
>
> If only he could be someone's friend, anyone's — but he felt doomed to be everyone's curse.

To form the possessive of singular nouns ending in -*s*, add -'*s* if it does not make pronunciation difficult. Add only an apostrophe if the additional -*s* makes pronunciation difficult.

> He rushed into the boss's office.
>
> Little is known about Cheryl Moses' life in Paris during the Depression.
>
> James's reptile collection gives me an eerie feeling.

In the following example, only the apostrophe is added because adding -'*s* would make pronunciation difficult.

> James' snake collection gives me an eerie feeling.

To form the possessive of plural words ending in -*s*, add only an apostrophe.

> The writers' convention will be held in Dallas.

To form the possessive of compound words, add -'s or an apostrophe (following the rules for forming possessives) to the last word only.

> My mother-in-law's experience at the board meeting was fruitful.

When two or more nouns show joint possession, add -'s to the last noun in the group.

> Jane, Tom, and Sonya's apartment overlooks the sea. [The three share the apartment.]

When two or more nouns show individual possession, add -'s to each one in the group.

> Jane's, Tom's, and Sonya's apartments overlook the sea. [They each have an apartment.]

Exercise 2

Correct the use of apostrophes in the following sentences.

1. *The Mens Club* did not make Leonard Michaels a household name, but it did establish him as an authors author.

2. A kangaroos hop can span forty-two yards.

3. Joan and Charles's cars each received parking tickets.

4. My brother-in-laws house in Hong Kong is more lavish than Bates' central office.

5. No matter how hard she bites her lip and frowns, Robertas attempts to win at Dungeons and Dragons end up like her children's attempts to find buried treasure in the back yard.

35b   Do not use an apostrophe with possessive pronouns, such as *his, hers, its, ours, yours, theirs,* and *whose.*

> The books are no longer *ours;* they are *theirs.*
> *Yours* is the best answer I've heard.

(See possessive pronouns, p. 3.)

NOTE: Be careful not to confuse the possessive pronouns *its, whose, your,* and *their* with the contractions *it's* (it is), *who's* (who is), *you're* (you are), and *they're* (they are).

35c   Use the apostrophe to mark omissions in contractions.

> it's (it is)
> you're (you are)
> don't (do not)
> o'clock (of the clock)
> class of '57 (class of 1957)

35d   Use *-'s* to form the plurals of letters, numbers, and words used as words.

> Your speech is riddled with *well*'s, *you know*'s, and *uh*'s.
> *R*'s are difficult for young children to pronounce.
> Count off by *3*'s.

NOTE: Letters, numbers, and words used as words are italicized but the *'s* is not italicized as part of the word. (See italics, p. 190.) There is an exception to this convention: When referring to a decade, do not italicize the figures. You may also leave out the apostrophe: the 1920s or the 1920's.

Exercise 3

Correct the use of apostrophes in the following sentences. If any sentence is already correct, mark it with a *C*.

1. Its the door to the right, not her's but his.

2. When the hurricane of 62 hit, wed been living in Florida for six years.

3. These *and*s and *but*s must be deleted.

4. Who's box of plates, their's or our's?

5. We can't hold them responsible for not learning their 6's and 7's

   because their school doesn't require its students to master multipli-

   cation tables until the fourth grade.

36   Abbreviations   *ab*

In most writing, avoid using abbreviations unless they are commonly accepted.

36a   Abbreviate titles before a proper name.

Mr. David Fear	Ms. June Hartman
Mrs. Doreen Dunlap	Dr. James J. Braddle
Prof. Patricia Kline	Rev. Marjorie Reinhart
Gen. Frank C. Rio	Msgr. James Kelly

NOTE: Do not abbreviate a title if it is not used with a proper name.

INCORRECT	There are four guidelines parents should follow when selecting a Dr. for their children.

CORRECT   There are four guidelines parents should follow
                 when selecting a doctor for their children.

36b Abbreviate titles immediately following proper names.

Wesley Root, M.D.   Harold Stacy, Ph.D.
Sarah Walden, LL.D.   Maude Cook, Ed.D.
Marion Feldman, Jr.   Marion Feldman, Sr.

NOTE: You may use abbreviations for academic degrees without
proper names.

After ten years of law school, Brookings finally received his J.D.
with honors.

36c Use familiar abbreviations for names of corporations, organizations, and countries.

NBC   FBI
IBM   USA (or U.S.A.)
AFL-CIO   USSR (or U.S.S.R.)

NOTE: If a name that you plan to use repeatedly is not well known
and can be abbreviated, you may write the full name followed by
the abbreviation in parentheses the first time you use it. You may
then use the abbreviation throughout the paper.

A group of social scientists banded together in Houston as the
American Value System Study Group (AVSSG). Through frequent
surveys that measure material gains and the quality of life, the
AVSSG intends to develop a national self-appraisal.

36d   Use the commonly accepted abbreviations *A.M., P.M., B.C., A.D., no.*, and the symbol *$* with specific dates and numbers only.

12:01 A.M. (or a.m.)	1:00 P.M. (or p.m.)
21 B.C.	A.D. 1061
no. 12 (or No. 12)	$5,501

B.C. always follows a date; *A.D.* always precedes a date.

36e   Use common English and Latin abbreviations in footnotes, bibliographies, and comments placed inside parentheses.

Blair, Walter, et al. *The Literature of the United States.* 63rd ed. 3 vols. Glenview: Scott, 1969.

The ruling committee (i.e., Harper, Laing, and Stokes) voted to table the motion.

36f   In most writing, do not abbreviate personal names, calendar terms, courses of study, divisions of written works, units of measurement, and geographical names.

PERSONAL NAMES

Robert [not Robt.] Brooks studied economics in London.

NAMES OF DAYS, MONTHS, AND HOLIDAYS

Christmas [not Xmas] comes on Friday [not Fri.] this year.

Each December [not Dec.], March [not Mar.], and October [not Oct.] we celebrate family birthdays.

EDUCATIONAL COURSES

For those who wish to see into the mind, we recommend a major in psychology [not psych.] and a minor in literature [not lit.].

DIVISIONS OF WRITTEN WORKS

Read section [not sec.] 2, chapter [not ch.] 4.

UNITS OF MEASUREMENT

He pulled the trigger at a distance of eight feet [not ft.]. The bullet pierced one inch [not in.] of cast iron.

NOTE: Long, familiar phrases such as *miles per hour* are usually abbreviated. The abbreviations may or may not have periods [*m.p.h.* or *mph*].

The Porsche nosed into the turn at 120 mph, fishtailed, and then screeched down the highway.

GEOGRAPHICAL NAMES

The outstanding characteristic of Los Angeles [not L.A.], California [not Calif.], is that it seems to be able to stretch itself from the Mexican [not Mex.] border to San Francisco.

He grew up in Huntington Park [not Pk.] on Randolph Street [not St.] near Miles Avenue [not Ave.].

NOTE: Certain familiar abbreviations for countries are acceptable: USA (or U.S.A.), USSR (or U.S.S.R.)

37 Italics *ital*

Use underlining to represent italic type (a print that *slants to the right*) when distinguishing certain titles, words, and phrases in typed and handwritten papers.

37a Underline the titles of books, periodicals, newspapers, pamphlets, plays and films, long poems and long musical compositions, television and radio shows, and works of visual art.

(See quotation marks, p. 159.)

When underlining a title, be precise. Do not underline an initial article (a, an, the) unless it is part of the title.

BOOKS

The Color Purple
Adventures of Huckleberry Finn

PERIODICALS

the Reader's Digest
Smithsonian

NEWSPAPERS

the Los Angeles Times
The New York Times

PAMPHLETS

Your Assertive Self
How to Say No

PLAYS AND FILMS

The Elephant Man
Star Wars

LONG POEMS AND MUSICAL COMPOSITIONS

Beowulf
Milton's Paradise Lost
The Nutcracker Suite

TELEVISION AND RADIO SHOWS

Dallas
General Hospital
Captain Midnight
I Love an Adventure

WORKS OF VISUAL ART

da Vinci's Mona Lisa
Warhol's One Hundred Campbell's Soup Cans
Segal's The Movie Poster

NOTE: Names of legal documents, the Bible, and parts of the Bible are not underlined.

INCORRECT	The Bill of Rights contains the first ten amendments to the Constitution.
CORRECT	The Bill of Rights contains the first ten amendments to the Constitution.
INCORRECT	The Bible is composed of the Old Testament and the New Testament.
CORRECT	The Bible is composed of the Old Testament and the New Testament.

37b Underline the names of spacecraft, aircraft, ships, and trains.

Challenger   the Titanic
The Spirit of St. Louis   the Orient Express

37c Underline non-English words and phrases that have not become common expressions.

Harrods, Europe's largest department store, tries to live up to its motto — Omnia, omnibus, ubique, everyone, everything, everywhere.

Foreign words that have been absorbed into English do not need to be underlined. For example, the words *cliché* and *genre*, both French, are commonly used in English and, therefore, are not underlined. When in doubt, consult a dictionary to see if a foreign word or phrase should be underlined. (See appropriate language, p. 212.)

NOTE: Although some foreign abbreviations, such as ibid, op. cit., and sic, are sometimes underlined, many common abbreviations never are — R.S.V.P. (r.s.v.p.), i.e., and etc., for example.

37d Underline words, letters, numbers, phrases, and symbols when they are referred to as such.

> When writing a paper, you should not use & for and.
>
> Margaret always printed her A's larger than her M's.
>
> Educational psychologist Harold Swartz claims third graders have more trouble with their 7's than with any other multiplication table.
>
> "Mind your p's and q's" was my grandmother's favorite expression.

NOTE: You can use quotation marks instead of underlining to set off a word you are defining. Both of the following sentences are correct.

> The word "lasso" is purely American and refers to a long rope with a sliding noose at one end.
>
> The word lasso is purely American and refers to a long rope with a sliding noose at one end.

37e Underlining may be used to show emphasis.

> I wrote that I wanted the entire amount.

Excessive underlining, however, will only distract the reader.

> I wrote that I wanted the entire amount.

37f Do not underline the titles of your own papers.

> My Summer Vacation: The Woes of Life on the Road

Underline the title of another work included in your title, however.

> Morality in Nathaniel Hawthorne's The Scarlet Letter

38 The Hyphen *hyph*

Use the **hyphen** to divide words, form compounds, and add some
prefixes, suffixes, and letters to words.

38a Use a hyphen to indicate a word broken at the end of a typed or handwritten line.

> In primitive cultures the old people commu-
> nicate a family's history by telling stories.

NOTE: Be sure to divide words between syllables. Whenever you
are unsure of the syllabication of a word, check a dictionary. The
syllable breaks are usually marked by dots: com•mu•ni•cate. Do not
break a one-syllable word.

38b Use a hyphen to form certain compound words.

cross-reference	clear-cut
mother-in-law	half-moon
deep-fry	bull's-eye
jack-o'-lantern	great-grandfather

NOTE: Since most compound words are not hyphenated, check a
dictionary whenever you are uncertain about whether to hyphenate
a compound word.

38c Use a hyphen to join two or more words that serve as a single descriptive word before a noun.

> The one-eyed, one-armed cowboy could hold his own in any two-
> bit joint he stumbled into.
>
> In Pentagon jargon, two-syllable names indicate jets, and one-
> syllable names indicate piston-driven aircraft.

Since taking a course in crafts, Beth has produced some well-designed furniture.

The twenty-year-old adventurer will lecture tomorrow.

NOTE: When the descriptive phrase comes after the noun, the words usually are not hyphenated.

Beth's furniture is well designed.
The adventurer, who is twenty years old, will lecture tomorrow.

But when such a phrase is used as a noun, it is hyphenated.

The adventurer, a daring twenty-year-old, will lecture tomorrow.

38d Use a hyphen to spell out the compound numbers twenty-one to ninety-nine and fractions.

seventy-five	ninety-nine
one-half	three-fourths

38e Use a hyphen to join certain prefixes, suffixes, and letters to words.

Use a hyphen to join a prefix to a word beginning with a capital letter.

McCarthy labeled his critics un-American.

In American politics the pre-Civil War years seem like an innocent dream.

Use a hyphen between words and the prefixes *self-*, *all-*, and *ex-* (meaning formerly) as well as the suffix *-elect*.

self-control	all-encompassing
ex-student	president-elect

Use a hyphen to join single letters to words.

z-transfer	U-turn
T-shirt	F-sharp

38f **Use suspended hyphens for hyphenated words in a series.**

My mother-, father-, and brother-in-law graduated from Lochlin High School.

38g **Use a hyphen to avoid confusion.**

In creating compound words, use a hyphen rather than doubling vowels and tripling consonants.

The current college administration has an anti-intellectual [not *antiintellectual*] attitude.

When the wind blows, the chimes make bell-like [not *belllike*] music.

The concept of a college without walls is like a wall-less [not *wallless*] room — full of wind.

Use a hyphen to avoid ambiguity.

re-creation (something created anew)
recreation (a diverting activity)

re-sign (to sign again)
resign (to give up a position)

39 Numbers *num*

Follow established conventions when using numbers in written work.

39a **Spell out any number consisting of one or two words.**

Of the *twenty-five* townspeople who volunteered to donate blood, only *sixteen* actually submitted their arms to the needle.

Thomas Camacho, a cool-headed blackjack player, began in Las

Vegas with less than *one thousand* dollars but over *five* years parlayed it into more than *three million*.

(See hyphen, p. 194.)

39b Use figures for any number that requires more than two words to spell out.

The police captain finally admitted that the thief held 102 citizens at bay with a 345-shot squirt gun.

39c Use a combination of figures and words for numbers when such a combination will keep your writing clear.

The Milltown Historical Society celebrated the birthdays of six 90-year-olds who were born in the city.

39d Use figures for dates; time; addresses; scores and other numerical results; percentages, decimals, and fractions; pages and divisions of written works; and exact amounts of money.

DAYS AND YEARS

December 7, 1941   12 B.C.   A.D. 1066

NOTE: The forms *1st, 2nd,* and so on, as well as *fourth, fifth,* and so on, are sometimes used in dates but only when the year is omitted: *June 6th, June sixth.*

TIME OF DAY

8:00 P.M.   1400 hours   12:45

NOTE: If you are not using A.M. or P.M., write the time in words.

seven o'clock   half-past ten   ten in the morning

ADDRESSES

22 Meadow Sweet Way   1236 Grand Boulevard

SCORES, STATISTICS, RESULTS OF SURVEYS

The Rams beat the Cowboys 10 to 3.

The average class score was 83.

The survey showed that of the group of 40, 36 supported the tax cut, 2 had no opinion, and 2 had never heard of the proposal.

PERCENTAGES, DECIMALS, FRACTIONS

52 percent (or 52%)   96.6   16½

PAGES AND DIVISIONS OF WRITTEN WORKS

page 31	chapter 3	volume 11
act 2	scene 3	lines 10th–18

EXACT AMOUNTS OF MONEY

$12.91 $3,421.02 $132 million

39e Spell out any number that begins a sentence.

Sometimes revising the sentence is easier than spelling out the number.

INCORRECT	101 trumpeters blared the message — We won!
CORRECT	One hundred and one trumpeters blared the message — We won!
CORRECT	The message — We won! — was blared by 101 trumpeters.

Exercise 4

Correct the faulty use of numbers in the following sentences. If any sentence is correct, mark it with a *C*.

1. Mayflies, so named because they swarm in May, live only 6 hours but lay eggs that take 3 years to hatch.

2. 29 million people live in Zaire, which has a growth rate of two-point-nine percent.

3. To stay in shape, Fremont used to swim twenty minutes and jog a mile a day besides shooting two weekly rounds of golf in the low 80's.

4. Seven eleven-year-olds are finalists in the spelling bee, which will start at six o'clock on May fifth.

5. On October 18th, 1864, 15 Confederate raiders robbed 3 banks in St. Albans, Vermont, and buried $114,522 in gold and currency, 82½ percent of the town's total capital.

40 Spelling *sp*

Difficulty with spelling is a highly individual problem. Most of us have compiled a personal list of spelling demons, words such as *occasion, separate, rhythm, negotiator,* and *strategy*. When we use a word from our demon list, we remind ourselves to double-check its spelling. We double-check because we know readers consider misspellings among the most serious errors a writer can commit.

Nobody improves poor spelling without working at it. To get started, use a good dictionary to check the spelling of words about which you are uncertain. Keep a list of the words you look up and practice spelling them by using one or more of the following techniques. (See appropriate language, p. 212.)

40a   Visualize the correct spelling of a troublesome word.

Write the troublesome word correctly and concentrate on how it
looks on the page. Then look away and visualize the word. Do this
over and over until you can actually imagine how the word, with the
troublesome letters emphasized, appears on the page.

Some people help themselves visualize a word by capitalizing the
part of the word that is the most difficult to spell.

exisTENTialist	accoMModate
kinDERgarTEN	govERNment

40b   Practice writing a troublesome word several times.

Repeatedly writing a troublesome word will help you break an old
habit and replace it with a new one. Write the word slowly at first
and then rapidly until the correct spelling comes naturally.

40c   Pronounce the syllables of a troublesome word carefully
and accurately.

Mispronunciation often leads to misspelling. If you repeatedly pro-
nounce a troublesome word as it appears in a dictionary, you can
begin correcting some of your misspellings.

ac ci den tal ly	ath lete
(not accident*ly*)	(not ath*e*lete)
light ning	nu cle ar
(not light*en*ing)	(not nuc*ular*)

40d   Proofread your written work for misspellings.

After you've proofread a paper for errors in grammar, punctuation,
and mechanics, proofread it one more time for spelling errors. The

best way to proofread is to read the paper backward — that is, read the last word first, then read the word just before that, and so on, until you reach the first word. This procedure will help you examine the words themselves without being distracted by the ideas in the paper.

40e   Distinguish between *ie* and *ei*.

The vowel combinations in the second syllables of *relief* and *perceive* sound alike, but the syllables are spelled differently. Confused? Apply the familiar jingle to help clear up the confusion: Place an *i* before *e* except after *c* or when pronounced like *a* as in *neighbor* and *weigh*.

> *i* before *e*: chief, grief, belief
> *e* before *i* following *c*: ceiling, conceit
> *e* before *i* when the sound is *a*: eight, sleigh

Exceptions include *either*, *neither*, *foreign*, *forfeit*, *height*, *leisure*, *weird*, *seize*, *sheik*.

Exercise 5

Complete the following words, filling in the blanks with *ie* or *ei*, whichever is appropriate.

1. shr__ __k   6. hyg__ __ne

2. fr__ __nd   7. y__ __ld

3. th__ __r   8. w__ __ght

4. rec__ __pt   9. n__ __ghbor

5. v__ __n   10. f__ __ry

40f   Usually drop a silent final *-e* before a suffix that begins with a vowel.

come + ing = coming   fame + ous = famous
force + ible = forcible   love + able = lovable

EXCEPTIONS: (1) Keep a final *e* to prevent confusion with other words: *dyeing* to distinguish it from *dying; singeing* to distinguish it from *singing*. (2) Keep a final *e* to prevent mispronunciation: *mileage* not *milage*. (3) Keep a final *e* after *c* or *g* to preserve the soft sound of the consonant: *notice + able = noticeable; courage + ous = courageous*.

40g   Usually keep a silent final *-e* before a suffix beginning with a consonant.

arrange + ment = arrangement   care + ful = careful

Exceptions include *awful, ninth*. The final *-e* is sometimes dropped before a suffix beginning with a consonant when *-e* is preceded by a vowel.

true + ly = truly   argue + ment = argument

40h   When a final *-y* is preceded by a consonant, change the *y* to *i* before a suffix except when the suffix begins with *i*.

-y preceded by a consonant:

try + ed = tried
messy + er = messier

-y preceded by a vowel:

obey + ed = obeyed
sway + s = sways

Suffix beginning with *i*:

> apply + ing = applying
> try + ing = trying

40i   Double the final consonant before a suffix beginning with a vowel if (1) the word has only one syllable or is stressed on the last syllable and (2) the word ends in a single consonant preceded by a single vowel.

One-syllable word; final consonant preceded by a single vowel:

> drop + ing = dropping
> stop + ing = stopping

Stress on the last syllable; final consonant preceded by a single vowel:

> forget + ing = forgetting
> submit + ed = submitted

Last syllable unstressed:

> benefit + ed = benefited
> prefer + able = preferable

Exercise 6

Add the final suffix to the words below by writing the words in the right-hand column. Be able to explain the rule that applies to each word. Check doubtful spellings in a dictionary.

1. unwrap + ed   _____

2. stubborn + ness   _____

3. plant + ing   _____

4. ski + ing   _____

5. commit + ed   _____

6. casual + ly   _____

7. move + ing   _____

8. merry + ly   _____

9. argue + ment   _____

10. write + ing   _____

40j   **Observe the conventions for forming plurals of nouns.**

Most nouns form the plural by adding -*s*.

> book, books; chair, chairs; pen, pens

Nouns ending in -*s*, -*sh*, -*ch*, or -*x* form the plural by adding -*es*.

> dress, dresses; bush, bushes; church, churches; fox, foxes

The plural of nouns ending in *y* preceded by a consonant is formed by changing the *y* to *i* and adding -*es*

> enemy, enemies: fly, flies; sky, skies

EXCEPTION: Family names ending in *y* as *McCherry, McCherrys; Haessly, Haesslys.*

The plural of most nouns ending in -*f* or -*fe* is formed by adding -*s*. The plural of some nouns ending in -*f* of -*fe* is formed by changing the *f* to *v* and adding -*s* or -*es*.
Add -*s*:

> chief, chiefs; dwarf, dwarfs; roof, roofs

Change *f* to *v* and add *-s* or *-es*:

> calf, calves; knife, knives; hoof, hooves; leaf, leaves

The plural of nouns ending in *o* preceded by a vowel is formed by adding *-s*. The plural of nouns ending in *-o* preceded by a consonant is formed by adding either *-s* or *-es*.
-o preceded by a vowel:

> radio, radios; studio, studios

-o preceded by a consonant:

> mosquito, mosquitoes; potato, potatoes

EXCEPTION: Musical terms ending in *o* form the plural by adding *-s*.

> piano, pianos; solo, solos

The plural of a few nouns is formed by irregular methods.

> child, children; goose, geese; mouse, mice; ox, oxen; tooth, teeth; woman, women

Some nouns borrowed from French, Greek, and Latin retain the plural form of the original language.

> alumnus, alumni; analysis, analyses; basis, bases; datum, data; medium, media; phenomenon, phenomena

Some nouns are the same in plural and singular forms.

> deer   Chinese   species   trout

The plural of compound nouns written as one word is formed by adding *-s* or *-es*. The plural of compound nouns consisting of a noun and a modifier is formed by making the noun plural.

> leftover, leftovers; strongbox, strongboxes; mother-in-law, mothers-in-law; passer-by; passers-by

Exercise 7

Write the plural forms of each of the following words. Be able to explain your spelling according to the rules for forming plurals. Refer to a dictionary when in doubt.

1. loss   _____

2. Kelly   _____

3. wife   _____

4. son-in-law   _____

5. box   _____

6. tornado   _____

7. eighty   _____

8. company   _____

9. rodeo   _____

10. approach   _____

40k Learn the meaning and correct spelling of commonly confused words.

accept: to receive
except: to exclude

advice: counsel (noun)
advise: to give advice (verb)

affect: to influence (verb)
effect: a result (noun); to accomplish (verb)

all ready: prepared
already: previously

brake: to stop
break: to smash

buy: to purchase
by: near

capital: accumulated wealth; uppercase letter; city serving as seat
         of government
capitol: building in which legislative body meets

cite: to quote
sight: ability to see
site: a place

complement: something that completes
compliment: flattering remark

conscience: moral sense (noun)
conscious: aware (adj.)

coarse: rough (adj.)
course: path, procedure, process (noun)

decent: moral (adj.)
descent: a way down (noun)
dissent: disagree (verb); difference of opinion (noun)

desert: barren land
desert: to abandon
dessert: last course of a meal

formally: in a formal manner
formerly: previously

forth: forward
fourth: after third

hear: to perceive by ear (verb)
here: in this place (adv.)

heard: past tense of *hear*
herd: group of animals

instance: an example
instants: moments

its: possessive of *it*
it's: contraction of *it is*

lessen: to make less
lesson: something learned

loose: to free from restraint (verb); not fastened (adj.)
lose: to misplace; to be deprived of (verb)

passed: past tense of *pass*
past: no longer current (adj.); an earlier time (noun); beyond
         in time or place (prep.)

peace: absence of strife
piece: a part of something

plain: clear (adj.); level land (noun)
plane: airplane; carpenter's tool

principal: most important (adj.); head of a school (noun)
principle: basic truth or law (noun)

right: correct (adj.)
rite: ceremony (noun)
write: to record (verb)

road: a driving surface
rode: past tense of *ride*

stationary: unmoving
stationery: writing paper

their: possessive of *they*
there: in that place
they're: contraction of *they are*

to: toward
too: also; excess amount
two: the number following one

weak: not strong
week: Sunday through Saturday

weather: condition of climate
whether: if; either

who's: contraction of *who is*
whose: possessive of *who*

your: possessive of *you*
you're: contraction of *you are*

401 **Learn to spell frequently misspelled words.**

The following is a list of one hundred commonly misspelled words.

absence	emphasize	occurrence	safety
academic	existence	optimistic	salary
accidentally	familiar	parallel	satellite
accommodate	fascinate	pastime	secretary
achieve	February	personnel	seize
across	foreign	precede	separate
all right	forty	prejudice	sergeant
already	friend	prevalent	similar
apparent	fulfill	privilege	sincerely
appearance	government	probably	sophomore
athletic	grammar	procedure	specimen
attendance	harass	proceed	strategy
believe	height	quantity	subtly
benefited	independent	quiet	succeed
Britain	intelligence	quite	succession
business	license	quizzes	surprise
calendar	luxury	receive	temperament
candidate	maneuver	reference	tendency
cemetery	marriage	referred	thorough
definite	mathematics	referring	tragedy
desperate	misspelled	reminisce	usually
develop	neither	repetition	vacuum
dilemma	ninth	rhythm	vengeance
dining	occasion	ridiculous	weird
embarrass	occur	sacrifice	writing

Exercise 8

Test yourself on the list of frequently misspelled words by asking someone to read the words aloud so you can spell them.

Diction
and Logic

41 Appropriate Language

42 Exactness

43 Conciseness

44 Logical Fallacies in Writing

Diction refers to the choice and use of words. Dictionaries of English are filled with words and their meanings, but so too is the mind of anyone who speaks the language. You know the meaning of words like *child*, *dance*, *sincere*, *immediately*, *theirs*, *after*, and *yellow*. Your knowledge of these and thousands of others enables you to understand them when they are used in combination with other words. Suppose a government official announced

A spy was stopped before discovering Project X15.

You might not know what "Project X15" is, but if you understand the word *spy*, you know the sentence is about a person who was prevented from finding out about a secret project while employed by another government or agency. This information is part of the definition of *spy*. But there is more: the mind's emotional connection with the word *spy*. Most likely you *feel* that a spy is treacherous and deceptive, someone you could never trust.

Now suppose the spy in the announcement was actually a reporter trying to collect information for a story about a project that a government agency wanted to keep secret. For an official to describe the reporter as a spy would not only be inaccurate, it would also color your view of the experience by tugging at your emotions. Indeed, the use of *spy* would have misled you.

Such is just one example of the power and danger in choosing and using words. As a writer, you should use appropriate language and be as accurate and concise as you can be. You must control your diction and keep your thoughts logically consistent — skills discussed in this section.

41 Appropriate Language *appr*

The appropriateness and accuracy of your words are just as important as grammar, punctuation, and mechanics. To develop skill in diction, sharpen your knowledge of words and, after studying the guidelines in this section, trust in your own judgment. Using appropriate and accurate words often has more to do with your sensitivity to the

English language than with your knowledge of its rules. Finally, when in doubt about a particular usage, consult a dependable dictionary, such as one of these:

> *The American Heritage Dictionary of the English Language.* 2nd coll. ed. Boston: Houghton, 1982.
> *Oxford American Dictionary.* New York: Oxford UP, 1982.
> *Webster's New World Dictionary of the American Language.* 2nd coll. ed. New York: Simon, 1983.

41a Use standard American English.

Standard American English is used in literature and printed documents, is taught in schools, is written by political and business leaders, and is propagated by the mass media — television, radio, newspapers, and magazines. In most writing, standard English is appropriate.

Nonstandard English consists of variations of standard English (especially in certain pronoun cases and verb forms) not found in the speech or writing of those who have been trained in standard American English.

STANDARD	The guest *brought* homemade pie for dessert.
NONSTANDARD	The guest *brung* homemade pie for dessert.
STANDARD	Bess is the woman *who* broke the record.
NONSTANDARD	Bess is the woman *what* broke the record.
STANDARD	He sings to *himself.*
NONSTANDARD	He sings to *hisself.*

Standard American English can be **formal** or **informal.** Informal (sometimes called *colloquial*) writing is characterized by common expressions taken from spoken English.

INFORMAL	If the mayor would *get together with* the city manager, *they'd* solve the problem.
FORMAL	If the mayor would *meet* with the city manager, *they would* solve the problem.

| INFORMAL | I *don't get* why the refund took *all these* weeks *to get here.* |
| FORMAL | I *do not understand* why the refund took *several* weeks *to arrive.* |

Contractions, such as *they'd* and *don't*, are common in informal writing; in formal writing the words are usually written out — *they would*, *do not*.

Informal English is appropriate for casual essays, diaries, personal letters or reflections, and creative works whose authors attempt to capture the sounds and rhythms of everyday speech. But because most of the writing you do in college and in a profession — serious essays, theses, reports, and memorandums — will be formal, you should generally avoid words and expressions labeled "informal" or "colloquial" in a dictionary. Also, be especially careful to avoid mixing informal and formal writing in the same work.

| MIXED | According to Philip Larsen's report, two thousand people willingly shell out twenty dollars a year to belong to the Marilyn Monroe Fan Club. For that amount they're considered dues-paying members and are entitled to receive the latest word on the club's publications, on the going price for Marilyn Monroe playing cards or jigsaw puzzles, and on the annual get-together at her graveside. |
| CONSISTENTLY FORMAL | According to Philip Larsen's report, two thousand members of the Marilyn Monroe Fan Club willingly *pay* twenty dollars a year *to learn* about the club's latest publications, the *cost* for a set of Marilyn Monroe playing cards or for a Marilyn Monroe jigsaw puzzle, and the annual *gathering* at her graveside. |

41b   Avoid using slang.

Slang comes from a specialized, often colorful vocabulary that grows out of the experience of a group of people with common interests,

such as actors, astronauts, athletes, computer scientists, copywriters musicians, street gangs, and truckers. Eventually, some slang passes into standard usage; *jazz* and *A-bomb* are two words that once were slang expressions but are now part of standard English. More often slang makes an appearance, increases in use, and then shifts its meaning or becomes dated. The writer of the following sentence uses slang expressions that were current about fifteen or twenty years ago.

> There's something *fishy* going on at work. The *rotten egg* in purchasing had lunch with the *fruitcake* in accounting — a real *sweety pie*, but *bananas*.

Recent slang might express the same thoughts with the words *weird, loony tune, space cadet, fox,* and *bonkers.*

When you wish to use a slang term to create a dramatic effect, use it: "With so much money in campaign donations, Wiener is a *shoo-in.*" But as a general guideline, avoid using slang in your written work because it is imprecise and may be confusing or misleading to a reader.

IMPRECISE	The journalist was *bummed* after the judge *laid a heavy trip on him* for contempt of court.
PRECISE	The journalist was *stunned* after the judge *sentenced him to thirty days in jail* for contempt of court.

41c   Avoid using regional expressions.

Regional differences exist in the use of some words and phrases. Do you carry water in a *pail* or a *bucket*? Do you *draw water* or *run water* from a *faucet*, a *spigot*, or a *tap*? Do you pull down the *blinds* or *shades*? Words such as these will not confuse your reader, but in writing you should avoid expressions that are not generally used outside a particular region.

REGIONAL	The committee had a *right nice* meeting. We wish *you all* could have attended.

GENERAL   The committee had a *productive* meeting. We wish *all of you* could have attended.

41d Avoid using obsolete or archaic words and neologisms.

In a dictionary, items labeled "obsolete" or "archaic" are words or meanings that have fallen from general use. **Obsolete** indicates that a word or a specific meaning is no longer used at all. *Coy* meaning "to caress" and *cote* meaning "to pass" are labeled "obsolete." **Archaic** indicates that a word or meaning appears only in special contexts. *Anon* meaning "at once" and *methinks* meaning "it seems" are labeled "archaic."

Neologisms are words or terms that have come into use so recently that they may still be unacceptable in general writing. Some former neologisms, such as *astronaut, bookmobile, fallout, supersonic,* and *smog,* have become acceptable. But most neologisms pass quickly from use, and you should avoid using them unless they become widely accepted. Such creations include *front runner-up, palimony,* and *usership.*

41e Use technical terms, or jargon, with care.

When writing for a group of literature specialists, you may use the terms *persona, verisimilitude,* and *motif* with confidence that your readers will understand them. These are technical terms that literature specialists freely use. Most fields and activities have technical vocabularies, and a person who studies a field or pursues an activity soon learns the specialized language that characterizes it. A person who has studied finance will use the terms *put, call,* and *margin* with ease. A skier will feel equally at ease talking about *moguls, whiteouts,* and *schussing.* But without explanation such terms are inappropriate for a general audience. When you are writing for a general audience, therefore, avoid using technical terms. If you must use them, be sure to define them.

Exercise 1

Revise the following paragraphs by changing words or phrases that may
be informal, slang, regional, obsolete, or archaic expressions, neologisms,
or technical terms. Feel free to consult a dependable dictionary that
includes usage labels to determine the appropriateness of expressions
and to find suitable substitutes. (See appropriate language, pp. 212–13.)

In 1945 Vice President Harry S Truman unexpectedly became president
when Franklin Roosevelt died in office. When Truman took the oath of
office, he was so jittery that the words would not come to him and his
voice petered out, so he took out a slip of paper with the oath written on
it and held it on top of the Bible. Then his voice began to function, and
he read the words in a real nice manner. The next day he laid his feelings
on a group of reporters: "Boys, if you ever pray, pray for me now!" During
his first months in office, Truman could not duck the decision to use the
atomic bomb against Japan, a decision that not only brought World War
II to an end but also demonstrated that human beings had created the
power to waste the entire world.

After the war, Truman lost the heavy-duty political support Roosevelt
had previously gathered; consequently, in the 1946 midterm elections
Republicans gained control of both houses of Congress for the first time
since 1930. Betwixt the attacks of the opposition party and the sniping

of rebellious members of his own party, Truman appeared to be on the

ropes politically, yet he continued his plans to run for re-election in 1948.

41f Avoid pretentious language.

Write in plain English. Beginning writers often make their writing excessively showy, perhaps from a misconceived desire to sound impressive or even poetic. Unfortunately, the result is often pretentious.

> **PRETENTIOUS** At day's end the evening solitude descended on the sea-swept coast.
>
> **REVISED** At sunset the beach grew quiet.
>
> **PRETENTIOUS** This college is predicated on the belief that diligent and sustained effort will be rewarded.
>
> **REVISED** This college rewards hard work.

To write in plain English, always select the common word over the fancy one. If you want to say something like "Drinking will destroy the liver," do not write "Imbibing alcoholic beverages in vast quantities will lead to the degeneration of one of the body's most important organs."

Exercise 2

In the following sentences revise pretentious phrases by using plain English.

1. After years of regarding it as a flavorful nutrient, most Americans

   now regard salt as a detriment to their physical well-being.

2. When the yacht cruises from the harbor, the passengers may turn

their gaze westward toward the ball of flame sliding into the Pacific seas.

3. No matter how influential the law school they attended, young attorneys who choose private practice will face a difficult period trying to establish themselves in a community.

4. The film's images are infused with the rhythms of the seasons as the charming boy and girl dance through the myriad landscapes.

5. We must face the dangers of an inexorable rise in population today or find an agreed-upon solution for thousands of starving infants and children in the near future.

41g Avoid sexist language.

Changes are taking place in American English usage that reflect a growing awareness of sexism in American society. These changes affect what some social critics describe as a masculine bias embedded in our language. One striking illustration of this bias appears in the use of masculine and feminine pronouns.

You can avoid using singular, masculine pronouns (*he, him, his*) to refer to men and women when the gender of the antecedent is unknown or is composed of both males and females. (See agreement of pronoun and antecedent, p. 53.)

> Each manager must post *his* schedule.
> Each manager must post *his or her* schedule.
> *Managers* must post *their schedules.*

You can also avoid the generic use of *man* to refer to both men and women by substituting *human* or *human beings,* terms that are generally considered less offensive.

> Man dominates the natural world.
> *Humans dominate* the natural world.

Using recent coinages can also help you avoid sounding biased. For instance, you can replace *chairman,* which in the recent past was used to refer to both men and women, with *chairwoman* when a woman holds the position and *chairperson* when the person's gender is unknown.

42 Exactness   *exact*

To be exact in writing, you must find the words that best fit the meaning you wish to convey. Exactness requires not only that you concentrate on the meanings of words you use but that you develop keen sensitivity to the differences in tone of some words. If you are inexact, you risk misleading or confusing your reader, a risk you should always avoid.

42a   Distinguish between a word's denotation and connotation.

Denotation refers to a word's concrete meaning as found in the dictionary. **Connotation** refers to what a word implies or suggests. According to one dictionary, the word *snake* denotes "any of a wide variety of limbless reptiles with an elongated, scaly body, lidless eyes, and a tapering tail." For some people the word *snake* may connote treachery or evil, and for others, wisdom or healing. You must pay close attention to both the denotation and the connotation of the words you use. Otherwise your words might clash, as the words do in the following sentence.

> The speaker manipulated the members of the audience by presenting the evidence to refute their arguments.

Manipulate denotes deviousness on the part of the speaker, but *refute* has the connotation of reasonably proving something false. The two words do not fit well together. To correct the clash of meanings, the writer should use words with more compatible denotations and connotations.

> The speaker convinced the members of the audience by presenting the evidence to refute their arguments.

> The speaker manipulated the members of the audience by presenting only the evidence that would disprove their arguments.

You must also take special care when selecting a word from among **synonyms,** words that have nearly the same meaning. *Depart, retreat,* and *flee; emulate, copy,* and *mimic* are two groups of synonyms. Although synonyms are close in denotation, they usually differ in connotation. It is much different to write "Harold's speech was funny" than to write "Harold's speech was laughable."

When the connotations of words arouse exceptionally strong feelings, we consider the words loaded. **Loaded words** appeal to emotion rather than to reason. A copywriter using loaded language might describe a company as carrying on the tradition of *free enterprise* while claiming that a competitor is *price gouging.* A politician might call himself or herself a *progressive* while calling an opponent a *do-gooder.* Loaded words are the tools of advertisers and other propagandists. If you inadvertently use loaded words, your writing will seem not only inexact but also biased.

Exercise 3

Replace each italicized word with a word that has a similar denotation but a connotation better fitted to the sentence.

1. To be a successful high-fashion model, a woman or man must be

   emaciated and graceful.

2. Success also depends on an ability to improve from hearing a

Denotation and Connotation **221**

photographer's constant *ridicule* and to survive arduous hours in a studio.

3. Unlike actors, models are not hired because of their *quirky profiles*.

4. Instead, their facial features must be *bland*, and their bodies must seem to come from the same mold.

5. Successful high-fashion modeling has its *payoffs* but also its drawbacks — constant routine and *relentless* dieting.

Exercise 4

In the following paragraph replace the loaded words with words that are not as emotionally charged.

In front of the financial aid office, Philip Beach delivered a tirade to a gang of students whose benefits are threatened. He blasted the federal government's prudent cutbacks in financial handouts to education. Judging from the applause, the liberal activist managed to brainwash at least half of his listeners. What will be the result? Probably no more than twenty hate letters designed to influence government policy.

42b Do not rely exclusively on abstract and general words. Be as concrete and specific as you can.

Abstract words refer to qualities, ideas, and actions that we cannot experience through our senses: *culture, friendship, loyalty, democracy.*

Concrete words refer to things we can experience through our senses: *orange, blood, scream, laugh, hug, tick, swamp.*

General words refer to large groups of people or things. The word *athlete* includes everyone who seriously pursues a sport. **Specific words** refer to one particular part of a general group. *Professional athlete* limits the group of athletes to those who are paid for their athletic performances. Other specific words for *athlete* include *professional tennis player, professional female tennis player, top ten female tennis players,* and *Martina Navratilova, one of the top ten female tennis players.* Notice that *general* and *specific* are relative terms and that language becomes more specific as it moves from the general group to a unique example of the group — from *athlete* to *Martina Navratilova* in this case.

Experienced writers know the value of concrete and specific words. Inexperienced writers tend to overuse abstract and general words, and consequently their work is often inexact and lifeless.

GENERAL	In English 101 we studied some of the world's greatest authors.
SPECIFIC	In English 101 we studied *the works of Sophocles, Shakespeare, Dickens, Joyce, and Faulkner* — some of the world's greatest authors.
GENERAL	After major trials, jurors are often interviewed for their opinions.
SPECIFIC	After major trials, jurors are often interviewed *by newspaper and television reporters* who seek to find out *the jurors' versions of the deliberations.*
GENERAL	The amount set by the government as the poverty level for a family of four is not much to live on.
SPECIFIC	The $9,287 set by the government as the poverty level for a family of four *will not buy many $2.50 hamburgers, $3.00 six-packs, $50.00 tickets for Bruce Springsteen concerts, and $12.00 T-shirts, let alone bread, milk, vegetables, and meat for four hungry mouths.*

Exercise 5

Make these sentences more precise by replacing the italicized general words and phrases with concrete and specific language.

1. The *book* was *terrific*.

2. My room is *very small*.

3. *Men* cannot solve her *problem*.

4. The semester was *not the best I have had*.

5. The *administration* disregarded our *suggestions*.

42c   Use idioms correctly.

An idiom is a fixed phrase with a single meaning that cannot be determined from the definitions of the individual words in the phrase. If a person said, "The waiter *flew into a rage*," most native speakers of English would know that the waiter became angry. If, however, a nonnative speaker were to translate the phrase *flew into a rage* word by word, the meaning would seem absurd. People learn the idiomatic expressions of their language naturally and have little difficulty understanding and using most of them. Occasionally, however, even experienced writers make errors in using an idiom that combines an adjective or verb and a preposition. "Independent *of* outside influence" is a meaningful idiom, whereas "independent *from* outside influence" is not a meaningful phrase. Whenever you are in doubt about which preposition to use with a word, look up the word in a dictionary. Here are common idioms and examples of their use.

abide *by*	We must abide by the rules.
according *to*	According to the evidence, he must be innocent.
agree *with* (a person)	I agree with John.

agree *to* (a proposal)	I cannot, however, agree to his proposal.
agree *on* (a course of action)	Moreover, we cannot agree on any plan.
angry *with*	The children are angry with the baby sitter.
charge *for* (a purchase)	The charge for cocoa butter is excessive.
charge *with* (a crime)	The manager has been charged with fraud.
comply *with*	Everyone must comply with the regulations.
compare *to* (something in a different class)	Do not compare psychiatry to witch-craft.
compare *with* (something in the same class)	You can compare a Freudian with a Jungian.
concur *with* (a person)	Jones concurs with Fussel.
concur *in* (an opinion)	I concur in your wish to transfer.
confide *in* or *to*	Philip had no time to confide his secret to me.
	She confides in her roommate.
die *of* or *from*	He may die from grief.
differ *with* (disagree)	Ruth differs with Trent over the presidential candidate.
differ *from* (be unlike)	Gibson's style differs from Redford's.
differ *about* or *over* (a question)	We differ about how food should be cooked.
different *from*	Living in a dormitory is different from living in an apartment.
identical *to* or *with*	One cannot be identical to the other.
ignorant *of*	Sally is ignorant of basic table etiquette.
inferior *to*	Is a life of toil inferior to a life of ease?
occupied *by* (a person)	We found our cabin occupied by two vagrants.
occupied *in* (thought)	He was occupied in thought when the pain struck.
occupied *with* (a thing)	She has been occupied with the book for a year.

| prior *to* | Prior to appearing in court, he wrote the accused a letter. |
| superior *to* | Rhonda often feels superior to Linda. |

42d Use figurative language carefully.

Writers use figurative language to draw a comparison between two things that are essentially different but alike in some underlying and surprising way. By making comparisons writers not only help their readers understand what is being said, but they also add vigor to their prose. The two commonest figures of speech are simile and metaphor.

In a **simile** a writer expresses a comparison directly by using *like* or *as*.

> Her forward expression was steady and driving like the advance of a heavy truck.
>
> *—Flannery O'Connor*

> The bowie knife is as American as the half-ton pickup truck.
>
> *—Geoffrey Norman*

Through **metaphor** a writer expresses a comparison indirectly, without using *like* or *as*.

> A sleeping child gives me the impression of a traveler in a very far country.
>
> *—Ralph Waldo Emerson*

> I refuse to accept the notion that nation after nation must spiral down a militaristic stairway into the hell of nuclear war.
>
> *—Martin Luther King, Jr.*

Personification and hyperbole are less common figures of speech. Writers use **personification** to give ideas, animals, and objects human qualities.

> When the wind swept through the forest, the trees moaned and among their branches birds complained.

Through **hyperbole** a writer creates an exaggeration.

> Mike Finnegan's tennis game has hit bottom, unless he returns to the court another time.

To be exact, a figure of speech must always clarify a writer's thought by making it understandable in other terms. Sometimes, however, a figure of speech will miss the mark or fall flat because it is trite or overblown.

> Her smile is as warm as a crackling fire on a snowy evening. [Trite simile.]

Another figure of speech gone wrong is the *mixed metaphor*, which combines two or more incompatible comparisons.

MIXED META-PHOR	Ideas that *blaze* in his mind often *crash* in his writing.
REVISED	Ideas that *blaze* in his mind often only *smolder* in his writing.
REVISED	Ideas that *race* in his mind often *crash* in his writing.

Exercise 6

Revise the following mixed metaphors to make the comparisons consistent.

1. The scalpel cuts through the flesh, leaving a road of blood.

2. The gorilla paused before the wall of jungle and then stepped into its shadows.

3. She stirs figurative language into her writing the way a cook adds vegetables to a stew — a dash of simile, a pinch of metaphor.

4. His arms flapping, the student aide flew to the lectern and barked for silence.

5. Reformers once imagined that prisons could be lapidary shops where the soul could be polished after the flaws had been surgically cut away.

42e Avoid trite expressions.

A **trite expression,** sometimes called a *cliché* or *stock phrase,* is an expression that was fresh and striking at one time but through overuse has become stale. Trite phrases include exhausted figures of speech *(hit the nail on the head),* wedded adjectives and nouns *(a well-rounded personality),* and overused phrases *(the finer things in life).* Trite phrases may come easily to mind when you feel rushed in your writing. But when you revise your work and come across one, strike it out and reword your thought in a fresh way. These are some common trite phrases to avoid:

a must	in the final analysis
a thinking person	in the world of today
all in all	last but not least
all walks of life	method in his madness
aroused our curiosity	never a dull moment
as a matter of fact	none the worse for wear
at this point in time	pure as newly fallen snow
cold as ice	quick as a flash
depths of despair	sadder but wiser
face the music	silent as the grave
flat as a pancake	smart as a whip
in a very real sense	strong as an ox

Exercise 7

Revise the following sentences, substituting fresh thoughts for trite expressions.

1. It is safe to say that Tod Roberts looks like a timid tax attorney who would feel butterflies in his stomach if he ever heard a raised voice.

2. But looks are deceptive; Roberts is a fierce negotiator who takes the bull by the horns and never gives an inch in collective bargaining sessions.

3. His endurance is such that he can go nose to nose with an opponent for twelve hours straight and leave the table none the worse for wear.

4. Although some see collective bargaining as child's play, Roberts realizes that the incomes of two thousand union members hang in the balance.

5. He takes seriously his responsibility to get the best deal he can and never drops the ball — or a dime.

43 Conciseness *con*

Make your writing concise by cutting words and phrases that add nothing to your meaning. Scrutinize your sentences for empty phrases, needless repetition, jargon, and euphemism. When you find such oversights, cross them out and search your vocabulary for more direct and forceful ways to state your thoughts. Being concise does not necessarily mean your writing will be skimpy; it means your writing will be free of useless words.

43a Avoid empty phrases.

Empty phrases do little more than add useless words to your writing. Whenever they appear in your work, cut them out or revise them.

> **WORDY** In the world of today, eighteen-year-olds find little joy in draft registration. [*In the world of today* is an empty phrase.]
>
> **REVISED** *Today*, eighteen-year-olds find little joy in draft registration.

Many empty phrases develop from such all-purpose words as *angle, area, aspect, case, character, fact, factor, field, kind, nature, process, situation,* and *type.* Watch for them and cut wherever you can.

Often one word will do the work of an entire empty phrase; substitute the single word for the phrase.

FOR	SUBSTITUTE
at all times	always
at this point in time	now
at that point in time	then
at any point in time	whenever
by means of	by
come into conflict	conflict (verb)
due to the fact that	because
for the purpose of	for
for the reason that	because
give consideration to	consider
give encouragement to	encourage
in order to	to
in the event that	if
in the final analysis	finally

FOR	SUBSTITUTE
make contact with	call
of the opinion that	think
regardless of the fact that	although
the fact that	that
until such time as	until

Exercise 8

Revise the following sentences by deleting empty words or phrases or by substituting single words for empty phrases.

1. At the present time sales indicate that biographies of film stars are the type of book more readers want.

2. It is usually the case that these tales give encouragement to the public's fantasies.

3. The 1966 story of Hedy Lamarr's life was so steamy that in order to keep an aspect of her public dignity, she claimed that the book revealed too much and denounced it as obscene.

4. But at this point in time stars seem pleased to reveal shocking details of their lives due to the fact that confession sells books.

5. With big money at stake you can easily come to the realization why Henry Fonda gleefully announced on the cover of a 1980 as-told-to publication, "Here I am, warts and all."

43b Avoid needless repetition.

At times you will repeat words for parallel structure or for emphasis. But careless repetition leads to awkward, wordy sentences.

REPETITIOUS	The grizzly bear is probably the world's most ferocious bear.
REVISED	The grizzly is probably the world's most ferocious bear.
REPETITIOUS	Economists say that the recession will continue, and I continue to believe them.
REVISED	Economists say that the recession will continue, and I *still* believe them.

43c Avoid redundant phrases.

A **redundant phrase** says the same thing twice: *visible to the eye, large in size.*

REDUNDANT	The central character in this novel is a mysterious figure beyond understanding.
REVISED	The central character in this novel is a mysterious figure.

The following list includes some common redundancies. Be aware of them and watch for them and others that appear in your own writing. Whenever you find a redundancy, strike it.

advance *forward*	continue *to go on*
autobiography *of her life*	disappear *from view*
basic fundamentals	*factual* truth
circle *around*	*important* essential
close proximity	refer or revert *back*
combine *together*	repeat *again*
consensus *of opinion*	round *in shape*

Exercise 9

Improve these sentences by revising them for ineffective repetition and redundancy.

1. As far as I'm concerned I believe the value that comes from computer study is worth the time it takes to study BASIC, a language used in computer programming.

2. Nearly square in shape and reddish-brown with yellow stripes in color, the puffer fish is covered with spines that make it look more like a spiny medieval weapon than a fish.

3. Sociologists arrived at a consensus of opinion regarding the attitudes of college freshmen in schools across the country toward careers and marriage.

4. The problem of crime is a major problem for Americans who live in cities, but if police, citizens, and judges cooperate together to stop crime, then crime will stop.

5. Our future expectations are optimistically hopeful

43d Avoid excessive use of euphemism.

A **euphemism** is a word or phrase substituted for other words that are considered harsh or blunt. The funeral industry, for instance, substitutes *loved one* for *corpse, vault* for *coffin,* and *final resting place* for *grave.*

Common euphemisms generally refer to experiences in our daily lives — birth, bodily functions, sex, aging, death — and they are often necessary for tactfulness. No doubt most of us prefer to ask a waiter for directions to the restroom rather than to the toilet.

Indeed, common euphemisms such as *restroom* are harmless, but other euphemisms, especially those created by private and public institutions, often are designed to distract us from the realities of poverty, unemployment, and war. We've become accustomed to the euphemisms of *low-income, inner-city,* and *correctional facility* as substitutes for *poor, slum,* and *prison.* Plumbers may be referred to as *sanitation engineers,* teachers as *learning directors,* and salespeople as *account executives,* yet they still fix pipes, correct papers, and sell products. In war the act of burning villages and herding people into detention camps has been called *pacification,* and the lies of public officials have been euphemistically named *inoperative statements.*

Because euphemism is pervasive in our society, you must guard against its slipping into your finished work. If you identify euphemisms when rereading a passage you have written, rephrase the euphemisms in more accurate, concrete language.

EUPHEMISTIC	The whole area was underdeveloped and crowded with the disadvantaged, who seemed to be living on a marginal diet. Several families often lived together in a small dwelling, sometimes with no more than a single water source to serve them and several other homes together.
REVISED	The whole area was a slum crowded with starving people who seemed to have no more to eat than rice and water. Sometimes several families crammed themselves into two-room hovels made of cardboard and sticks. The only water they had came from a single tap shared by fifteen or twenty such dwellings.

Remember to feel free to use euphemism when tact calls for you to do so, but avoid using it when your work requires a direct rendering of the material. Do not use it to deceive.

Exercise 10

Make these sentences concise by eliminating jargon and euphemism and recasting the sentences in plain, straightforward English.

1. The chairman and the director must resolve the intense feelings that arose during their recent negative encounter.

2. When I was a young girl living in a deteriorating residential section of town, I vowed to develop the capital necessary to buy a penthouse.

3. Beware — pre-owned car dealers embellish information regarding the quality of their products to enhance their monthly revenue.

4. Based on information from visual surveillance, the air force chief of staff ordered the squadron to carry out a surgical bombing action over the enemy's capital.

5. My uncle Ramsey passed away while staying overnight in a nearby motor lodge in the company of a female companion the family had never met.

6. Last summer we chartered a motor coach for our company excursion to the seaside.

44 Logical Fallacies in Writing *log*

Writing that is otherwise excellent — unified, coherent, well organized, adequately developed, consistent in tone, and free of grammatical and mechanical errors — may still be ineffective if it contains
faulty reasoning.

A mistake in reasoning is called a **logical fallacy.** *Fallacy* originally
meant "deception," and although the word now simply means "a
fault in reasoning," fallacies still deceive because they distort the
truth and make it more difficult for the writer to reach sound, logical
conclusions.

The propagandist, the overzealous ad writer, and the misguided
politician seek to influence our decisions through inaccurate conclusions and emotional appeals rather than reasonable arguments. (See
loaded words, p. 221.) The fallacies such writers frequently use are
perhaps intentional, perhaps unintentional, but they are always
damaging to clear thought.

Most fallacies are spoken rather than written. People often say in
haste such things as "You just can't trust repair people" or "Criminals
have all the rights but victims have none." When calm returns, clear
thinking does too, and then the speaker is likely to agree that he or
she overstated things a bit. But in writing, such statements cannot
be so easily dismissed. In writing, to use fallacies consciously is
dishonest; to use them inadvertently is a sign of muddled thinking.
A conscientious writer, therefore, makes every effort to avoid falla-
cious reasoning.

44a Avoid overgeneralizations.

Overgeneralization involves drawing a conclusion from insufficient
or unrepresentative evidence.

> Three regional airlines have just gone bankrupt, and many of the
> larger lines have discontinued flights on certain routes. The
> American commercial transportation system is in ruins.

A few bankruptcies and discontinuations of routes do not justify the conclusion. More evidence is needed, and it should include information about rail and bus transportation.

> In recent years, almost every major college athletic program has been investigated by the NCAA for recruitment violations. Every year, at least one team is placed on probation as a result of these investigations. Why is it that those in charge of college athletics are so immoral?

Are violations of complex regulations always a matter of immorality? Perhaps some of the violations are inadvertent or technical. As for the investigations and penalties, they could be an indication of rigorous enforcement of the rules rather than widespread immorality.

44b Avoid oversimplification.

An oversimplified conclusion ignores essential details of the information from which the conclusion is drawn.

> Getting a good grade in a composition class may involve a lot of your time, but there is nothing difficult about it. All you have to do is meet the required word length and avoid errors in grammar and punctuation.

As you doubtless know by now, a good grade in a composition class also requires clear thinking, organizational skills, and a good deal of effort and practice.

> A survey several years ago showed that students who owned cars had lower grade-point averages than those who did not own cars. I am glad I never bought a car while I was in school.

The writer assumes that car ownership is the only factor contributing to low grades.

44c Avoid faulty *either/or* arguments.

The *either/or* **fallacy** is a type of oversimplification in which a writer assumes only two alternatives when in fact there are many.

> America, love it or leave it!

The preceding statement implies that love of country must be unqualified. The statement is dangerous because the writer attempts to exclude constructive criticism.

> My fellow Americans, we stand at the moment of truth. The issues before us are so monumental that no one can afford to be neutral. Are you going to do nothing? Are you going to stand by idly while this community is brought to its knees by the forces of corruption, or are you going to join me in this righteous crusade?

There are, of course, other things to do. The choice is not between doing nothing or joining one particular crusade.

44d Avoid the *post hoc* argument.

The *post hoc* **argument** assumes that one event causes a second event simply because the second follows the first in time. The complete Latin phrase is *post hoc, ergo propter hoc,* which means "after this, therefore because of this."

> Some people think that microwave ovens are a threat to health, but I know the opposite is true. Our family purchased one three years ago, and none of us have had to see a doctor since.

As stated, the only relation between the purchase of a microwave oven and the good health of this family is that one followed the other in time. Time sequence alone cannot prove the existence of a cause-and-effect relation.

> Church attendance in our city has been on a steady decline ever since we elected our first Democratic mayor in 1964.

Countless other things have happened since 1964, and they cannot all be attributed to one cause. The writer would have to offer other evidence, if it exists, to connect the Democratic mayor to declining church attendance.

44e Avoid *non sequiturs.*

A *non sequitur* is a conclusion that does not follow from the premise. In Latin, *non sequitur* means "it does not follow."

> I am in favor of a large standing army because my sister learned to repair computers while she was in the army, and we need trained technicians.

Having a large standing army is not the only way to train technicians. It may not even be the most efficient way, because an army has other functions to perform.

44f Avoid creating a false analogy.

In a **false analogy** we presume that if two things are alike in one or more respects, they are necessarily alike in other ways.

> Some people cannot be educated. You can't make a silk purse out of a sow's ear.

Applying the apparent wisdom of folk sayings to real-life situations usually results in a false analogy. Education does not change valueless things to valuable things, as the folk saying suggests. It develops already existing intelligence further.

> We should not forget the lessons of World War II, when our leaders assumed that they could negotiate to avoid a war. The best solution to the present state of affairs is to attack our enemies before they attack us.

Conditions today are not the same as before World War II. The atomic bomb is just one factor that has changed world politics. Even if conditions were identical, would such an attack be justified?

44g Avoid the *ad hominem* argument.

Ad hominem means "to the man," and an ***ad hominem*** **argument** is an attack on a person who is connected with an issue rather than an argument focused on the issue.

> The senator has made an interesting case for eliminating the inheritance tax. No wonder! When her father dies, she'll inherit millions!

In this statement the writer ignores the senator's arguments for abolishing the inheritance tax and focuses on the woman's personal situation.

> Don't believe the drama critics. They're all frustrated actors or directors who could not succeed in their own careers.

The writer of this statement attacks the drama critics rather than discussing inaccuracies or bias in their reviews.

44h Avoid the association fallacy.

The **association fallacy** implies that an act or belief is worthy or unworthy simply because of the people associated with it.

> Your Mariner's Club card will prove to everyone that you belong in the company of eminent and distinguished persons because senators, millionaires, and business executives also belong.

But what direct benefits will the card give?

> Eddie Staffer, the famous rock star, uses No Ping in his car. Since he can afford the best, I use No Ping too.

Any product should be selected for its effectiveness, not simply because a celebrity or a person with a lot of money uses it.

Exercise 11

Identify the logical fallacies in these sentences. Be prepared to discuss your choices.

1. I think Mr. Sawyer is the best history teacher at our school. He is so handsome!
2. We must reject gun-control laws or sacrifice a sacred right granted to us by the Constitution.
3. Glenview College always has a winning football team because its coach believes in team spirit.
4. The least promising students achieve the greatest success as adults. Winston Churchill's teachers predicted he would be a failure, and William Faulkner, who won the Nobel Prize for literature, never even earned a college degree.
5. Primitive religious leaders were responsible for the sun's rising because they went to high ground every morning and prayed for the sun god to return.
6. Jim is intelligent and hard-working. There is no doubt he will rise to the top of his field.
7. A brain absorbs information just as a sponge absorbs water. But eventually a sponge becomes saturated; it cannot hold any more water. Students, too, reach a saturation point, and then it is foolish to expect them to soak up more information.
8. If I had not gone out of my way to pick up Margaret this morning, the car would not have broken down.
9. I do not see how young people can enjoy his music; he has been arrested several times, and his wife had to leave him because he was so cruel.
10. Lola Allure, the star of stage, screen, and television, starts every day with Skinny Wafers. Don't you think you should too?

Paragraphs, Essays, and Research Papers

45 Writing Paragraphs

46 Writing the Essay

47 Writing an Analytical Essay About Literature

48 Writing a Research Paper

Each piece of writing has its own audience, its own purpose, and its own content. Moreover, no two writers hold exactly the same views or express themselves in exactly the same ways. Yet despite the unique characteristics of written works and writers, beneath all clear, effective writing is some underlying design that directs the reader's attention from point to point. When reading, you are probably unaware of a design because you seek information to fill the gaps in your knowledge. But when writing, you must create an underlying structure for your work and use it to arrange your ideas as carefully as a mapmaker charts a wilderness for an uninitiated traveler. Paragraphs, essays, research papers — the subjects of this section — all have underlying designs that you can master with practice. But remember: If your written work lacks a clear design, your reader may stumble into a verbal thicket and stray from the main path of your thought.

45   Writing Paragraphs   *par,* ¶

A paragraph consists of several related sentences that develop one unit of content. A paragraph may stand alone as a brief work, but usually it functions as part of a longer piece of writing. The division of prose into paragraphs guides a reader through a paper by presenting content in individually organized, easily digested portions of thought.

A well constructed paragraph is unified (all of its sentences are focused on the same idea), coherent (the thought proceeds logically from sentence to sentence), and fully developed (it contains enough information to convey the idea in a reasonably thorough manner). The end of a paragraph signals completion of the unit of thought and prepares the reader to shift attention, at least slightly, to the beginning of the next paragraph.

In a sense, an essay is created by bringing together a series of related paragraphs, each one a brief composition itself. As you read the selections used as examples throughout this section, be aware that they are one-paragraph excerpts taken from longer essays. As you complete the paragraph length exercises at the end of this section, you will be writing the kind of building blocks you will use for longer papers.

How long should a paragraph be? It's hard to say. Paragraph length depends on many things: the complexity of the idea, the method of development, the length of adjacent paragraphs, and the age, knowledge, interest, and educational background of the intended audience.

The best approach, really, is not to worry much about paragraph length. Instead, concentrate on paragraph unity to avoid long paragraphs that contain several unrelated ideas; also concentrate on including specific supporting information to avoid skimpy, immature paragraphs.

The following is an example of a skimpy paragraph that does not fully develop the idea expressed in the topic sentence.

> Many Americans mindlessly oppose hunting, even in cases where animal populations are dangerously high. In some areas of Alaska, the wolves are so prolific they endanger other animals. In California, deer and sea otters face starvation because of a limited food supply.

The following paragraph fully develops the idea expressed in the topic sentence.

TOPIC SENTENCE	Many Americans mindlessly oppose hunting, even in cases where animal populations are dangerously high. In some areas of Alaska, wolves
EXAMPLE	have become so prolific they are running out of hunting ground and prey heavily on moose, deer, and occasionally dogs. In the past, game managers curbed wolf populations by trapping and aerial hunting without wiping out the species.
EXAMPLE	Still, whenever they propose to do this nowadays, they receive tens of thousands of letters of protest. Growing deer populations in parts of
EXAMPLE	California threaten to starve themselves out. Sea-otter colonies, burgeoning along the Pacific

EXAMPLE   coast, are fast running out of fodder, too, as well
as putting commercial fishermen out of business.

—Lael Morgan, "Let the Eskimos Hunt"

45a State the single idea of a paragraph in a topic sentence.

Frequently a writer uses a topic sentence to announce the content of
a paragraph to the reader. Some paragraphs do not have a topic
sentence, of course, but you should be aware of its value to both the
reader and the writer. For the reader, a topic sentence gives the idea
of the paragraph in a convenient capsule form so he or she knows
what the more specific sentences of the paragraph add up to. For the
writer, a good topic sentence serves as a guide, reminding the writer
of the paragraph's boundaries and therefore helping to assure a well-
unified paragraph. In the following paragraph, the topic sentence —
"What money he could lay his hands on he spent like an Indian
rajah" — is brief and to the point; it announces to the reader that
the rest of the paragraph will consist of information showing that
Richard Wagner, the German composer, spent money lavishly.

TOPIC SENTENCE   *What money he could lay his hands on he
spent like an Indian rajah.* The mere prospect of
a performance of one of his operas was enough

EXAMPLES   to set him running up bills amounting to ten
times the amount of his prospective royalties.
On an income that would reduce a more scru-
pulous man to doing his own laundry, he would
keep two servants. Without enough money in
his pocket to pay his rent, he would have the
walls and ceilings of his study lined with pink
silk. No one will ever know — certainly he never
knew — how much money he owed. We do know

CLOSE   that his greatest benefactor gave him $6,000 to
pay the most pressing of his debts in one city,
and a year later gave him $16,000 to enable him
to live in another city without being thrown
into jail for debt.

—Deems Taylor, Of Men and Music

An effective topic sentence has three characteristics: it includes a subject and a controlling idea; it is limited; and it lends itself to development.

The subject identifies the topic of the paragraph, and the controlling idea identifies what aspects of the topic will be discussed.

> Hong Kong has a fascinating mixture of European and Asiatic traditions.

This sentence placed at the beginning of a paragraph would tell a reader that Hong Kong is the topic and that the writer plans to discuss the European and Asiatic traditions of the city, not its economy, population, or style of government.

The subject and controlling idea of a topic sentence must be limited enough to be discussed fully within a single paragraph.

GENERAL   The works of James Agee often include information from several academic disciplines.

LIMITED   James Agee's *Let Us Now Praise Famous Men* includes content drawn from history, sociology, and philosophy.

GENERAL   Sometimes concerts can be dangerous.

LIMITED   Concert promoters could reduce the number and severity of spectator injuries by following a few simple rules of crowd control.

GENERAL   Bolivia is an interesting country.

LIMITED   Bolivia has some spectacular mountains.

Sometimes the controlling idea of a topic sentence is limited by one or two sentences that follow it, as the next example illustrates.

TOPIC SENTENCE
LIMITATION OF
TOPIC SENTENCE   *My father is the saint of the family.* [He believes] you work at something until you exhaust yourself, so that you can be good at it, and with it you try to improve the lot of the sad ones, the hungry ones, the sick ones. You raise your children trying to teach them decency and

EXAMPLE

respect for human life. Once when I was about thirteen he asked me if I would accept a large sum of money for the death of a man who was going to die anyway. I didn't quite understand. If I was off the hook, and just standing by, and then the man was killed by someone else, why

CLOSE

shouldn't I take a couple of million? I told him sure, I'd take the money, and he laughed his head off. "That's immoral," he said. I didn't know what immoral meant, but I knew something was definitely wrong [with] taking money for a man's life.

—*Joan Baez, "My Father"*

A topic sentence must lend itself to development. The controlling idea has to be one that can be amplified or illustrated. If the controlling idea is strictly factual, it allows no development.

FACTUAL   Northwestern is a university in Illinois.

REVISED   Northwestern, a university in Illinois, is noted for its outstanding drama faculty.

Although placing a topic sentence at the beginning of a paragraph is sound practice, writers sometimes place it in another part of the paragraph or, if the controlling idea can be clearly understood from the discussion within the paragraph, leave it out entirely.

When a writer places a topic sentence at the end of a paragraph, it often serves as a climax to the details that come before it.

DESCRIPTIVE
DETAILS

It was Murdstone who was arrived, and a gloomy-looking lady she was; dark, like her brother, whom she greatly resembled in face and voice; and with very heavy eyebrows, nearly meeting over her large nose, as if, being disabled by the wrongs of her sex from wearing whiskers, she had carried them to that account. She brought with her two uncompromising hard black boxes, with her initials on the lids in hard brass nails. When she paid the coachman she took her money out of a hard steel purse, and she kept the purse in a very jail of a bag which hung upon her arm by a heavy chain, and shut up like a bite. *I had never, at that time, seen such a metallic lady altogether as Miss Murdstone was.*

TOPIC SENTENCE

—*Charles Dickens, David Copperfield*

When a writer leaves out a topic sentence, the discussion must be so clear that the controlling idea of the paragraph is strongly implied. In the following paragraph the implied topic sentence might be stated as "An independent trucker has a difficult time making a living."

An independent trucker working full time can earn close to $20,000 gross compared with the $30,000 or more that a union trucker makes. A union trucker works a 10-hour shift and that's it, whereas the independent trucker is always pushing himself. And even though there are strict laws prohibiting a trucker from driving more than 10 hours a day, with four hours on and four hours off, no independent trucker adheres to that — because if he did, he'd never get the load delivered on time. With the economy as shaky as it is, the competition for loads is fierce and, at times, vicious. There are only so many loads, and truckers will bid on them, the lowest bid getting the load.

—*Roberta Ostroff, "Big Red and Sweet Drifter"*

Often when a writer begins with a topic sentence, he or she will close with a *clincher*, a sentence that restates the controlling idea in different words, summarizes the discussion, or gives the writer's response to the material, which may be ironic or humorous.

TOPIC SENTENCE

REASONS

As sources of ideas, professors simply cannot compete with books. Books can be found to fit almost every need, temper, or interest. Books can be read when you are in the mood; they do not have to be taken in periodic doses. Books are both more personal and more impersonal than professors. Books have an inner confidence which individuals seldom show; they rarely have to be on the defensive. Books can afford to be bold and courageous and exploratory; they do not have to be so careful of boards of trustees, colleagues, and community opinion. Books are infinitely diverse; they run the gamut of human activity. Books can be found to express every point of view; if you want a different point of view, you can read a different book. (Incidentally, this is the closest approximation to objectivity you are likely ever to get in humanistic and social studies.) *Even your professor is at his best when he writes books and articles; the teaching performance rarely equals the written effort.*

CLINCHER

–William G. Carleton,
"Take Your College in Stride"

Exercise 1

These topic sentences are either too general or too factual. Revise each to make it an effective topic sentence.

1. Some states require motorists to wear seat belts.
2. Vandalism is a problem in urban areas.
3. Many Americans try different diets from time to time.
4. Going to college is expensive.
5. Grading policies are different for different classes.
6. Everyone believes that travel is educational.
7. Large stores usually have consumer complaint departments.
8. In spite of all the evidence, my sister believes that spinach alone will give a person tremendous strength.
9. I like people who assume responsibility for their actions.
10. Hollywood films have both good and bad features.

Exercise 2

Using one of the topic sentences you wrote in Exercise 1, develop a complete paragraph.

45b Maintain unity throughout a paragraph.

To achieve **unity** in a paragraph, you not only must have a clear controlling idea but must also stick to that idea. The writer of the following paragraph digresses from the controlling idea stated in the first sentence.

TOPIC SENTENCE   Attending this college can be unexpectedly dangerous. Last week in the parking lot my friend Bill accidentally bumped the side of a pickup truck. Just as he was finishing a note to leave on the windshield, the owner came up, scowled at the grapefruit-size dent, and punched Bill in the nose. He then drove off without looking back or taking Bill's name and address. **DIGRESSION** At least Bill didn't have to pay for the damage. Three days ago a bicyclist wearing portable radio earphones plowed into a psychology instructor, and both went sprawling over the walkway. Yesterday in the zoology lab, a four-foot snake slipped from its cage. No one noticed until it struck at one student, sending him and four others into shock. The lab technician came in, snatched up the snake, and stuffed it back into the cage. **DIGRESSION** No one plans to sue the college, but those students have a good case if any of them would press it.

Because of digressions from the controlling idea, the paragraph is flawed. To correct it, the writer had to revise by deleting some of the unnecessary comments and by subordinating others.

DIGRESSION ELIMINATED   Attending this college can be unexpectedly dangerous. Last week in the parking lot my friend Bill accidentally bumped the side of a pickup truck. Just as he was finishing a note to leave on the windshield, the owner came up, scowled at the grapefruit-size dent, and punched Bill in the nose. Three days ago a bicyclist wearing portable radio earphones plowed into a psychology instructor, and both went sprawling over the walkway. Yesterday in the zoology lab, a four-foot snake slipped from its cage. No one noticed until it struck at one student, sending him and four others into shock, before a lab technician came in, snatched up the snake, and stuffed it back into the cage.

**DIGRESSION
ELIMINATED**

Exercise 3

The following sentences are taken from Robert I. Tilling's "A Volcanologist's Perspective." Several sentences are from one paragraph. Others are from different parts of the article. Determine which sentences should be included in a unified paragraph with the following topic sentence.

Volcanic eruptions have had a profound influence on mankind.

1. Civilizations have flourished in regions blessed with fertile soils derived from the breakdown of nutrient-rich volcanic materials.
2. The volcanoes in the Ring of Fire zone are what scientists call composite volcanoes.
3. The violent, destructive unleashings of volcanic fury that accompanied the catastrophic blast of Mount St. Helens have imprinted their marks on mind and landscape.
4. Some of the world's most majestic and inspirational mountain and seashore scenery, including the entire state of Hawaii, has been created by volcanic action and subsequent erosion.
5. Most of the world's approximately 500 active volcanoes are located along or near such boundaries between shifting plates.
6. The Pacific Basin provides excellent examples of these two types of volcanoes.
7. The earth's surface is broken into lithospheric slabs, or plates.
8. As one volcano dies, however, a new volcano begins to form behind it over the hot spot.
9. More fundamentally, life on earth as we know it would not have evolved at all were it not for volcanic exhalations that occurred over hundreds of millions of years and formed the primitive but life-giving atmosphere and oceans.

10. Composite volcanoes predominantly erupt highly viscous (sticky) magma.

45c Achieve coherence by putting details in proper order.

One way to keep a paragraph coherent is to arrange the sentences in some pattern that will generate an orderly, natural flow of the ideas. Five possible methods are illustrated on the next few pages. You will find these methods useful in some situations, but the most suitable arrangement for any particular paper will depend on your particular purpose and content.

Time order. Narrative paragraphs — those which relate a story or series of incidents — usually arrange themselves naturally in the order in which the events occurred. In the following paragraph from *The Story of My Life*, Helen Keller, who was deaf and blind, relates her first experience with names.

EVENT 1	The morning after my teacher came she led me into her room and gave me a doll. The little blind children at the Perkins Institution had sent it and Laura Bridgman had dressed it; but I did not know this until afterward. When I had
EVENT 2	played with it a little while, Miss Sullivan slowly spelled into my hand the word "d-o-l-l." I was at once interested in this finger play and tried to imitate it. When I finally succeeded in making the letters correctly I was flushed with childish pleasure and pride. Running downstairs to my
EVENT 3	mother I held up my hand and made the letters for doll. I did not know that I was spelling a word or even that words existed; I was simply making my fingers go in monkeylike imitation. In the days that followed I learned to spell in
EVENT 4	this uncomprehending way a great many words, among them *pin*, *hat*, *cup* and a few verbs like *sit*, *stand*, and *walk*. But my teacher had been
EVENT 5	with me several weeks before I understood that everything has a name.

Space order. Descriptive paragraphs lend themselves quite easily to a spatial arrangement — from left to right, from right to left, from near to far, from the center outward, and so on. In this paragraph from "A Hanging," George Orwell presents his material by moving from a distant point to a closer one.

DISTANCE

CLOSER

CLOSER

It was in Burma, a sodden morning of the rains. A sickly light, like yellow tinfoil, was slanting over the high walls into the jail yard. We were waiting outside the condemned cells, a row of sheds fronted with double bars, like small animal cages. Each cell measured about ten feet by ten and was quite bare within except for a plank bed and a pot for drinking water. In some of them brown, silent men were squatting at the inner bars, with their blankets draped round them. These were the condemned men, due to be hanged within the next week or two.

Order of climax. Some paragraphs lend themselves to an arrangement of details or examples according to increasing importance. In the following paragraph from "Shame," Dick Gregory stuns the reader by putting the most dramatic details last.

MAIN IDEA
INTRODUCED

INCREASINGLY
DRAMATIC
DETAILS

The teacher thought I was stupid. Couldn't spell, couldn't read, couldn't do arithmetic. Just stupid. Teachers were never interested in finding out that you couldn't concentrate because you were so hungry, because you hadn't had any breakfast. All you could think about was noontime, would it ever come? Maybe you could sneak into the cloakroom and steal a bite of some kid's lunch out of a coat pocket. A bite of something. Paste. You can't really make a meal of paste, or put it on bread for a sandwich, but sometimes I'd scoop a few spoonfuls out of the paste jar in the back of the room. Pregnant people get strange tastes. I was pregnant with poverty. Pregnant with dirt and pregnant with

CLIMAX
> shoes that were never bought for me, pregnant with five other people in my bed and no Daddy in the next room, and pregnant with hunger. Paste doesn't taste too bad when you're hungry.

General-to-specific, specific-to-general order. Most paragraphs begin with a general comment — usually contained in a topic sentence — and follow with specific details, reasons, or examples that support the generalization. Some paragraphs, however, reverse this order by beginning with specific details, reasons, or examples and ending with a general observation that summarizes the paragraph's meaning.

In the following paragraph from "Football Red and Baseball Green," Murray Ross moves from the general to the specific — from the generalization that football is played like a war to a specific comment by Woody Hayes, former Ohio State coach.

GENERALIZATION

EXAMPLES

SPECIFIC
COMMENT

> A further reason for football's intensity, surely, is that the game is played like a war. The idea is to win by going through, around or over the opposing team and the battle lines, quite literally, are drawn on every play. Violence is somewhere at the heart of the game, and the combat quality is reflected in football's army language ("blitz," "trap," "zone," "bomb," "trenches," etc.). Coaches often sound like generals when they discuss their strategy. Woody Hayes of Ohio State, for instance, explains his quarterback option play as if it had been conceived in the Pentagon: "You know," he says, "the most effective kind of warfare is siege. You have to attack on broad fronts. And that's all the option [a football play] is — attacking on a broad front. You know General Sherman ran an option right through the South."

Scott Momaday, in this paragraph from "The Way to Rainy Mountain," moves from the specific to the general — from physical

details of Rainy Mountain and the surrounding plain to the generalization that one can imagine creation having begun in such a spot.

**SPECIFIC
DETAILS**

A single knoll rises out of the plain of Oklahoma, north and west of the Wichita Range. For
my people, the Kiowas, it is an old landmark,
and they gave it the name Rainy Mountain. The
hardest weather in the world is there. Winter
brings blizzards, hot tornadic winds arise in the
spring, and in summer the prairie is an anvil's
edge. The grass turns brittle and brown, and it
cracks beneath your feet. There are green belts
along the rivers and creeks, linear groves of
hickory and pecan, willow and witch hazel. At
a distance in July or August the steaming foliage
seems almost to writhe in fire. Great green and
yellow grasshoppers are everywhere in the tall
grass, popping up like corn to sting the flesh,
and tortoises crawl about on the red earth, going
nowhere in the plenty of time. Loneliness is an
aspect of the land. All things in the plain are
isolate; there is no confusion of objects in the
eye, but *one* hill or *one* tree or *one* man. To look

GENERALIZATION

upon that landscape in the early morning, with
the sun at your back, is to lose the sense of
proportion. Your imagination comes to life, and
this, you think, is where Creation was begun.

Exercise 4

The following paragraphs were coherent as originally written, but now
the sentence order has been changed. By following a specific order (time,
space, climax, generalization), rearrange the sentences so that the paragraphs are coherent once again.

1. (1) Before I started grammar school, I knew all the neighborhood's
marvelous places: the avocado tree where my friends and I used to
climb to an ancient tree house that had been built by children before
us, the park where old-timers would sit on benches and laugh at our
wild games, the abandoned garage where we used to spy at the

neighborhood through knotholes. (2) My earliest memories center on playing in that house: pushing trucks over the hardwood floors, my pajama knees mopping up the morning dust; rummaging through my mother's pan drawers and banging pans on the linoleum; and hiding behind the overstuffed couch whenever I was called for lunch. (3) Driven out by a severe drought, my parents came from the cornfields of Nebraska to the house where they lived for thirty-five years. (4) I was born in the back bedroom because, as my mother said, "There just wasn't enough time to get to a hospital." (5) When I first began to walk, I remember the back yard seemed to stretch the length of a football field and was the place where I would chase my older brother and sisters until I would fall down, breathless and sweating.

2. (1) The other was thin and reminded me of a deer loping through a meadow. (2) Yesterday, I sat alone in the bleachers and watched the day come to a close. (3) The horizon was turning deep orange while the sun sank behind the ridge of a hill. (4) I felt alone and glanced back at the track to see the joggers like two ghosts fade with the light. (5) They circled the track — four, five, six laps. (6) One was heavy and scuffed along like a tired buffalo, his head bobbing from side to side. (7) On the track below the bleachers two men jogged. (8) The horizon turned indigo, and the sky began to fill with stars scattered like chips of glass tossed on a dark highway. (9) Not far in the distance the university was silhouetted against the orange background, a few lights speckling its dark outline. (10) Soon the light was almost gone.

45d Achieve coherence by using transitional words and phrases.

When a paragraph is coherent, the writer's thought flows from the first sentence to the last. One way to maintain coherence is by using words and phrases that indicate the relation of one sentence to the preceding one. The coordinating conjunctions *and, but, for, or, so, nor,* and *yet* serve this purpose, but English provides a variety of other words that function as transitions. Use them to create clarity in your work.

TO SHOW SIMILARITY

likewise, similarly, moreover

TO SHOW DIFFERENCES OR CONTRAST

but, however, still, yet, nevertheless, on the other hand, on the contrary, in contrast

TO SHOW ADDITION

moreover, and, in addition, equally important, next, first, second, third, again, also, too, besides, furthermore

TO SHOW TIME AND PROCESS

soon, in the meantime, afterward, later, meanwhile, while, earlier, finally, simultaneously, next, the next step

TO SHOW DIRECTION

here, there, over there, beyond, nearby, opposite, under, above, to the left, to the right, in the distance

TO ANNOUNCE AN END

in conclusion, to summarize, finally, on the whole

TO ANNOUNCE A RESTATEMENT

in short, in other words, in brief, to put it differently

TO INDICATE A RESULT

therefore, then, as a result, consequently, accordingly, thus, thereupon

Transitional words and phrases indicating time are italicized in this paragraph:

> At first glance Tod seems to be a typical four-year-old: scruffy, sun-bleached hair, a few freckles, worn cords, short-sleeved shirt, and tattered tennis shoes. *But* behind his boyish appearance he seems to be a loner. *During the first class,* he was the only child who did not raise his hand to answer a question or share an experience. He was attentive *at first* but soon lost interest. *Once* he reached out a finger to poke a boy in front of him, and then stopped, perhaps thinking better of it. *Finally,* his thumb went

into his mouth. *As soon as* the class broke up, he headed for the monkey bars, where he climbed to the highest rung and sat, his eyes staring toward a distant hill. No one tried to approach him, *however*. The other children, most of whom chased around the play yard, seemed to respect his wish for privacy. *Later*, when the class regrouped for story time, Tod didn't show as much interest as he had during the sharing session. He seemed more interested in using a fingernail to trace the cracks in the wall than in listening to *Winnie-the-Pooh*.

45e Achieve coherence by repeating key words and phrases.

A writer maintains coherence by repeating key words and phrases, often with some modification, to stress the major points and to smooth the flow of the sentences. Pronouns referring back to clearly established antecedents function in the same way.

In the following paragraph repeated words are in italics.

> Public speaking differs from acting in that the *speaker* rarely, if ever, reveals any character or personality traits other than his own. A central problem of the *actor* is to create a character for his audience. There are other differences. The *public speaker* usually works alone. The *actor*, unless he is performing a monodrama, usually works with a group. A *public speaker* does not ordinarily use scenery, costume, or make-up to help him express and communicate as the *actor* does. He may on some occasions employ special lighting effects and platform decorations to reinforce his message. Further, the *public speaker* deals only with his own composition while the *actor*, like the oral reader, has all the problems of interpreting the words of another. He serves as a sort of middleman for the playwright and reveals the intentions of a director. Thus, the purposes of the *actor* are at once like and unlike those of the *public speaker*. The *actor* may seek to elicit primarily utilitarian responses or to gain aesthetic responses depending upon the nature of the material with which he works.
>
> *—John F. Wilson and Carroll C. Arnold,*
> *Public Speaking as a Liberal Art*

45f   Achieve coherence by using parallel structure.

By repeating a particular structure in successive sentences, a writer can create a parallel form that will guide a reader smoothly from the first sentence to the last. The repeated structure emphasizes the relation of the sentences to the paragraph's controlling idea. Parallel structures are italicized in the following paragraph from Mark Twain's autobiography.

> As I have said, I spent some part of every year at the farm until I was twelve or thirteen years old. The life which I led there with my cousins was full of charm, and so is the memory of it yet. *I can call back* the solemn twilight and mystery of the deep woods, the earthy smells, the faint odors of the wild flowers, the sheen of rain-washed foliage, the rattling clatter of drops when the wind shook the trees, the far-off hammering of woodpeckers and the muffled drumming of wood pheasants in the remoteness of the forest, the snapshot glimpses of disturbed wild creatures scurrying through the grass — *I can call it all back* and make it as real as it ever was, and as blessed. *I can call back* the prairie, and its loneliness and peace, and a vast hawk hanging motionless in the sky, with his wings spread wide and the blue of the vault showing through the fringe of the end feathers. *I can see* the woods in their autumn dress, the oaks purple, the hickories washed with gold, the maples and the sumachs luminous with crimson fires, and *I can hear* the rustle made by the fallen leaves as we plowed through them. *I can see* the blue clusters of wild grapes hanging among the foliage of the saplings, and I remember the taste of them and the smell. *I know* how the wild blackberries looked, and how they tasted, and the same with the pawpaws, the hazelnuts, and the persimmons; and *I can feel* the thumping rain, upon my head, of hickory nuts and walnuts when we were out in the frosty dawn to scramble for them with the pigs, and the gusts of wind loosed them and sent them down.

Exercise 5

Choose a subject and write a paragraph containing parallel structure.

45g Develop the paragraph according to your subject and purpose.

The controlling idea of a paragraph should be adequately supported with convincing, specific material. Some methods of arranging that supporting material are illustrated on the following pages. They are guides only, not rigid requirements to which your paragraphs must conform. The nature of your content, your paper's purpose, and the way a paragraph fits with others in a larger piece of writing will help you determine the most effective way to develop it.

Examples and Details

One of the commonest ways to develop a paragraph is by using examples and details. Examples and details supply relevant information as well as the specifics a reader needs to understand a writer's point. They are so important that many other methods of development depend on them.

The following paragraph illustrates with examples and details the effects of DDT spraying.

> Soon after the spraying had ended there were unmistakable signs that all was not well. Within two days dead and dying fish, including many young salmon, were found along the banks of the stream. Brook trout also appeared among the dead fish, and along the roads and in the woods birds were dying. All the life of the stream was stilled. Before the spraying there had been a rich assortment of the water life that forms the food of salmon and trout   caddis fly larvae, living in loosely fitting protective cases of leaves, stems or gravel cemented together with saliva, stonefly nymphs clinging to rocks in the swirling currents, and the wormlike larvae of blackflies edging the stones under riffles or where the stream spills over steeply slanting rocks. But now the stream insects were dead, killed by the DDT, and there was nothing for a young salmon to eat.
>
> *—Rachel Carson, The Silent Spring*

Comparison and Contrast

A paragraph developed by comparison and contrast discusses the similarities and differences between two subjects. Each may also be used separately. Sometimes the content of such a paragraph is presented in blocks — all the details about one side of the comparison or contrast are presented first, followed by all the details about the other side. In the following example, information about Old English appears first; the rest of the paragraph shows how modern English is different.

> In grammar, Old English was much more highly inflected than Modern English is. That is, there were more case endings for nouns, more person and number endings for verbs, a more complicated pronoun system, various endings for adjectives, and so on. Old English nouns had four cases — nominative, genitive, dative, accusative. Adjectives had five — all these and an instrumental case besides. Present-day English has only two cases — common case and possessive case. Adjectives now have no case system at all. On the other hand, we now have a more rigid word order and more structure words (prepositions, auxiliaries, and the like) to express relationships than Old English did.
>
> —*Paul Roberts, "A Brief History of English"*

Another way to organize a comparison or contrast paper, particularly when you have many points to make about the subjects, is to move back and forth between the subjects point by point. The author of the following paragraph contrasts the two Americas he sees, item by item.

> There are two Americas. One is the America of Lincoln and Adlai Stevenson; the other is the America of Teddy Roosevelt and the modern superpatriots. One is generous and humane, the other narrowly egotistical; one is self-critical, the other self-righteous; one is sensible, the other romantic; one is good humored, the other solemn; one is inquiring, the other pontificating; one is moderate, the other filled with passionate intensity; one is judicious and the other arrogant in the use of great power.
>
> —*J. William Fulbright, "Two Americas"*

Analogy

Analogy is a figurative comparison that helps explain a complicated or abstract idea by comparing it to a simpler idea or more concrete image. In an analogy, the items compared are from different classes. A writer might compare the life of a human being to a river, for example. In most ways the two are not alike, but in suggestive ways they are alike — both flow smoothly at times, turbulently at other times; both change as they follow their paths; both find destinations that change their very nature. Analogies can help you show things to your reader in different ways, but you must take care not to press an analogy too far, or it can become foolish.

In the following paragraph from *The Mysterious Sky*, Lester del Rey compares the earth's atmosphere to a window. He succeeds because he uses our familiarity with windows to enlighten us about the functions of the atmosphere.

> The atmosphere of Earth acts like any window in serving two very important functions. It lets light in and it permits us to look out. It also serves as a shield to keep out dangerous or uncomfortable things. A normal glazed window lets us keep our houses warm by keeping out cold air, and it prevents rain, dirt, and unwelcome insects and animals from coming in. As we have already seen, Earth's atmospheric window also helps to keep our planet at a comfortable temperature by holding back radiated heat and protecting us from dangerous levels of ultraviolet light.

Classification

Classification is a method of organizing information into general categories. The purpose of such grouping is to clarify the nature of each category. In this sense, classification is a kind of indirect or implied comparison or contrast because the qualities that place an item in one class also distinguish it from items belonging to other classes. In the following example, scientific findings are divided into three classes according to the strength of evidence. The author defines each class in turn and then uses the last three sentences to show the relation between the classes.

> Scientific findings when stated in words are usually classified into *laws*, *theories*, and *hypotheses*. If the evidence indicates that the finding is clearly established and can be stated definitely without too many "ifs, ands, and provideds," then it is called a "law." Examples are the "Law of Falling Bodies" [in physics], "Boyle's Law" [in chemistry], the "Law of Diminishing Returns" [in economics]. Discoveries which are probably true, but for which the evidence is not quite so conclusive, are usually called "theories." It is necessary to emphasize, however, that a theory is not a guess, is not "a notion spun out of thin air," but is a truth for which there exists considerable but not final and conclusive evidence. Finally, there are "hypotheses." A hypothesis is an idea about which we are not yet sufficiently certain to permit us to call it a law or a theory, but there is, nevertheless, some evidence to support it. An idea usually does not remain a hypothesis very long. It is usually soon tested and if found true becomes a theory or a law, if found to be false is discarded. This may, of course, take a long time and require much effort.
>
> *–John F. Cuber, Sociology:*
> *A Synopsis of Principles*

Cause and Effect

Cause-and-effect paragraphs are concerned mainly with exploring why something happened or explaining what happened as a result of something else. Sometimes such a paragraph deals only with causes because the effects are already clear. A paragraph might explore the reasons for a movie star's popularity without needing to demonstrate that the person really was a star, for example. Or a cause-and-effect paragraph could concentrate on effects because a given cause clearly exists, and the only question remaining is "What happened as a result?" Such a paragraph might explain the effects of unemployment or of an increase in taxes. Sometimes it is appropriate to discuss both causes and effects in a paragraph.

The following cause-and-effect paragraph is concentrated on the relation between television violence and real-life violence.

	Much of the research that has led to the conclusion that TV and movie violence could cause aggressive behavior in some children has stemmed from the work in the area of imitative learning or modeling which, reduced to its simplest expression, might be termed "monkey see, monkey do." Research by Stanford psychologist
CAUSE	Albert Bandura has shown that even brief exposure to novel aggressive behavior *on a one-*
EFFECT	*time basis* can be repeated in free play by as high as 88 percent of the young children seeing
CAUSE	it on TV. Dr. Bandura also demonstrated that even a single viewing of a novel aggressive act
EFFECT	could be recalled and produced by children six months later, without any intervening exposure. Earlier studies have estimated that the average child between the ages of 5 and 15 will witness,
DETAILS	during this 10-year period, the violent destruc-
RELATED	tion of more than 13,400 fellow humans. This
TO CAUSE	means that through several hours of TV-watching, a child may see more violence than the average adult experiences in a lifetime. Killing is as common as taking a walk, a gun more
OVERALL EFFECT	natural than an umbrella. Children are thus taught to take pride in force and violence and to feel ashamed of ordinary sympathy.

—*Victor B. Cline*, "How TV
Violence Damages Your Children"

Definition

One kind of definition is the dictionary definition, which provides a synonym (*slice* = to cut) or shows how a word fits into a general class (*astronomy* = the science that studies the universe). Using a paragraph to define a term allows for a thorough discussion. Such a paragraph might begin, as does a dictionary definition, by identifying a term as belonging to a general class and differentiating it from other members of the class; it might also include synonyms. Or it might illustrate the term with examples, discuss the word's origins, compare it to similar words, or tell what it is not.

The following paragraphs go beyond a dictionary definition to show the rich background of urban legends.

GENERAL CLASS   Urban legends are realistic stories that are said to have happened recently. Like old legends of lost mines, buried treasure, and ghosts, they DIFFERENTIATION   usually have an ironic or supernatural twist. They belong to a subclass of folk narratives that (unlike fairy tales) . . . are set in the recent past, involving ordinary human beings rather than extraordinary gods and demigods.

DIFFERENTIATION   Unlike rumors, which are generally fragmentary or vague reports, legends have a specific narrative quality and tend to attach themselves to different local settings. Although they may explain or incorporate current rumors, legends tend to have a longer life and wider acceptance; rumors flourish and then die out rather quickly.

CHARACTERISTICS   Urban legends circulate, by word of mouth, among the "folk" of modern society, but the mass media frequently help to disseminate and validate them. While they vary in particular details from one telling to another, they preserve a central core of traditional themes. In some instances these seemingly fresh stories are merely updatings of classic folklore plots, while other urban legends spring directly from recent conditions and then develop their own traditional patterns in repeated retellings. For example, EXAMPLES   "The Vanishing Hitchhiker," which describes the disappearance of a rider picked up on a highway, has evolved from a 19th-century horse-and-buggy legend into modern variants incorporating freeway travel. A story called "Alligators in the Sewers," on the other hand, goes back no further than the 1930s and seems to be a New York City invention. Often, it begins with people who bring pet baby alligators back from Florida and eventually flush them down the drains.

—Jan Harold Brunvand, "Alligators in Sewers and Other Urban Legends"

Process

A process paragraph explains how to do something or how something works. Process paragraphs are usually developed step by step in a chronological or logical sequence.

The following process paragraph explains how stripes are put into striped toothpaste, following a step-by-step chronology — the construction of the tube, the filling of the tube, and the mechanics of use by consumers.

Although it's intriguing to imagine the peppermint stripes neatly wound inside the tube, actually the stripes don't go into the paste until it's on its way out. A small hollow tube, with slots running lengthwise, extends from the neck of the toothpaste tube back into the interior a short distance. When the toothpaste tube is filled, red paste — the striping material — is inserted first, thus filling the conical area around the hollow tube at the front. (It must not, however, reach beyond the point to which the hollow tube extends into the toothpaste tube.) The remainder of the dispenser is filled with the familiar white stuff. When you squeeze the toothpaste tube, pressure is applied to the white paste, which in turn presses on the red paste at the head of the tube. The red then passes through the slots and onto the white, which is moving through the inserted tube — and which emerges with five red stripes.

—Caroline Sutton, How Do They Do That?

Exercise 6

Write one paragraph for each of the following methods of development. Select your own topic or use a topic from the list. Once you have selected a topic, phrase a topic sentence with a clear controlling idea that seems appropriate for the method of development.

1. Examples and details
   body language
   superstitions
   good teaching
   sports rivalries

2. Comparison and contrast
   dress styles
   artists
   religious beliefs
   political beliefs

3. Classification
   college majors
   rock groups
   lifestyles
   comedians

4. Analogy
   Compare something and a musical instrument.
   Compare education and something.
   Compare something and freeway traffic.
   Compare something and a garbage disposal.

5. Cause and effect
   weather and human behavior
   computers and people
   packaging and retail sales
   noise and health

6. Definition
   respectability
   wisdom
   cowardice
   bigotry

7. Process
   training for physical competition
   cooking for one hundred people
   teaching someone to ski
   making an item of jewelry

46 Writing the Essay *dev*

The papers that you write in most college courses are essays—nonfiction compositions in which you analyze or interpret a limited topic. An essay offers the writer's personal view about a topic. Unlike a journalism article, which objectively reports only who, what, when, and where, or a lab report, which precisely details an experiment, an essay shows the writer's personal, or subjective, understanding of a topic—that is, the writer's personal angle.

"Personal" does not mean that an essay is *about* the writer. It could be, but more often it is not. Rather, the personal viewpoint comes from the writer's analysis or interpretation of a topic through thoughts, insights, and values.

A successful essay comes about through a process of several important steps or stages of writing. In this chapter we will set out the stages one by one, in chronological order. In the process of writing, however, you will frequently move back and forth between the steps as you explore the possibilities of your topic, experiment with content and organization, and decide on the final phrasing of sentences and paragraphs.

To use the process to its best advantage, you should allow yourself as much time as possible to write an essay. Play with ideas. Explore the possibilities of your topic. Consider more than one approach to organization. Finally, accept the necessity and value of revision. Do not expect to write a successful essay in one draft or even in one evening. Even the best writers go back to strengthen phrasing, rearrange ideas, add or delete content, and correct mistakes. Revision will improve your final draft and give you the opportunity to learn more about writing itself.

Every essay should have a purpose: to inform, to entertain, or to persuade. Sometimes these purposes overlap: you might inform your readers about local poverty so that you can persuade them to contribute to a worthy charity. You might write an entertaining essay as an effective way of imparting information about the problems immigrants face. In each case, one purpose dominates: to persuade readers to make a contribution in the first example and to inform readers about the problems facing immigrants in the second.

Every essay should be written for a particular audience, the members of which share interests or backgrounds. Although it is true that classroom writing is usually read only by the instructor, plan your essays as though you were writing for some outside audience

— for example, the members of a car club, first-time voters, or a group of tourists.

Depending on your topic, your purpose and your audience, you might write a narrative, descriptive, argumentative, or expository essay.

A **narrative essay** tells a story by relating a sequence of events. An essay on unemployment, written as a narrative, might trace the chronology of a typical day in the life of a person looking for work.

A **descriptive essay** uses details and images to depict a scene, an event, a person, an object, or an atmosphere. You might write a descriptive essay re-creating the scene in an employment office as people wait in line for job interviews.

An **argumentative essay** attempts to persuade a reader to take some action or to convince a reader to accept your position on a debatable issue. You might try to persuade your reader to join a demonstration of unemployed workers or argue against a government jobs program.

An **expository essay** informs, explains, or analyzes. Most college writing assignments call for expository essays. You might explain the causes of unemployment in a particular industry, analyze the several major approaches to lessening the hardships of unemployment, examine unemployment from a historical perspective, or relate the effects of unemployment in your own life.

The boundaries among these four types of essays are not rigid. You might, for example, use a description or a short narrative in an argumentative essay. You might supply interesting and useful information in a narrative. But every essay generally falls into one of the four categories.

The principles of paragraph writing also apply to essay writing. Just as a paragraph has a topic sentence that expresses the main idea, an essay has a **thesis statement** that states and narrows the writer's purpose. An essay, like a paragraph, should be **unified** — every part must be clearly related to the idea expressed in the thesis statement. An essay should also be **coherent** — the thoughts expressed in the sentences must be connected through the same techniques found in paragraphs, such as repetition of key words and phrases, rephrasing of key ideas, and use of transitional words and phrases. Finally, both paragraphs and essays require thorough supporting explanation and detail to fulfill their purpose.

Within an essay you use the same strategies of paragraph development that you use when writing individual paragraphs. You develop paragraphs by examples and details, comparison or contrast, analogy, classification, cause and effect, definition, or process. (See methods of paragraph development, p. 261.) In fact, within a single essay you might use a combination of these patterns because an essay is composed of several paragraphs.

A typical assigned essay is between 500 and 750 words. No matter how long an essay may be, it follows a general pattern composed of an introduction, a discussion, and a conclusion. The **introduction** presents the thesis statement, usually at the end. The purpose of the introduction is to arouse a reader's interest and limit the territory the essay will cover. The **discussion** is made up of several paragraphs, each organized around a topic sentence that relates to the thesis statement. The discussion paragraphs develop the ideas expressed in the thesis statement in a detailed, thorough manner. The **conclusion** offers a restatement of the thesis statement and provides a sense of completion to the essay.

A Student Essay

Before continuing this section, read the 750-word expository essay, which begins on page 273, that was written by Reuben Langford for an audience of fellow students. Also read the accompanying comments, which will help you understand some of the principles of essay writing. In the rest of the chapter we discuss the processes Reuben used to develop his essay. (See pp. 278–79.)

(*Text continues on page 278*)

The title summarizes the content of the essay.

The introductory paragraph presents the general subject, involves the reader, gives any background the reader might need to understand the essay, and states the thesis.

Thesis statement.

First topic sentence. Three brief examples support the topic sentence.

The discussion develops the thesis statement in several paragraphs. Each discussion paragraph is organized around a topic sentence that develops one aspect of the thesis statement. The individual paragraphs reflect standard methods of paragraph development.

Time to Slow Down

When I first returned to the city after ten months in a forestry camp, I was not ready to re-enter the pace of daily life. For a few uncomfortable days, I had the feeling I was living within the frenetic action of an old silent movie. People around me were rushing as though they were all late for an appointment. At first this activity made me nervous. My experience in the forestry camp had given me a more leisurely approach to daily activities. In the months that followed, I began to understand that the speed of daily living, which had upset me when I returned, was only the most obvious part of a deeper attitude. We are so busy rushing from one experience to another, developing new interests and dropping old ones, that we seldom take the time to do anything well. The impatience and restlessness of our approach to life show in our responses to public affairs, in our educational programs, and in our relationships with each other.

Few of us take time to understand public affairs. We get most of our information about local and national issues from television news programs that devote only a few minutes to even the most complicated stories. State and national political campaigns successfully rely on thirty-second commercials devoted to catchy slogans and unsupported assertions. In local elections for city officials, school board members, and judges, incumbents usually win, not necessarily because they deserve to but because the voters know nothing about the other candidates. As citizens

Second topic sentence, developed through cause and effect. The effects are presented in a series of examples.

Concluding sentence acts as a clincher.

Transitional sentence.

Third topic sentence, developed through analogy.

Statistical support.

in a democracy, we should be willing to study the issues and the candidates, but we are too impatient. We say we do not have enough time.

In education, our admiration for learning combines with our impatience to encourage shortcuts of doubtful value. Advertisements tell us that math can be easy and that a foreign language can be learned in just fifteen minutes a day. For another daily fifteen-minute investment, we can increase our vocabularies or study law or the classics. With a low-cost cassette player we can learn while we sleep. We can read condensed books, digest magazines, and study guides. Even colleges and universities are packaging quick courses that take only a weekend or a few weekly sessions. All these rapid-learning methods have some value, but they also reflect our impatience and subtly direct our attention away from the fact that worthwhile learning takes time.

Our impatient approach to education and public affairs is bad enough, but the real cost of our hurry-up attitude is in our social relations. Too many of our relationships are assembly-line friendships. Just as assembly-line workers know only one aspect of the products they work on, we have only superficial acquaintance with our friends and neighbors. The reason for this is restlessness. In any five-year period, half of the people in the United States change their residences. The average American has been working at his or her present job only three and a half years. Changing jobs and homes so frequently, as they restlessly

Fourth topic sentence, developed through comparison and contrast.

The conclusion echoes the discussion of the thesis statement and brings the essay to a close. It ends by inviting readers to take action.

search for better opportunities, Americans sacrifice the deeper satisfactions that come with stability and loyalty.

Families, too, suffer from the desire to have everything and to experience everything right now. The nuclear family that we used to read about in our primers and see in our neighborhoods consisted of a mother, father, and their children, all living in one home, all sharing meals and time together, and all working toward common goals. The contemporary family is a little different. Single-parent families are now common. Even in two-parent families, Mom and Dad may both have careers that take them out of the home so frequently that they have little time for family matters. Even the children are at home less often. They're taking lessons, playing on teams, and attending club meetings. We get so involved in this activity that we fail to see that much of it is not necessary; it's just our restlessness at work again.

I have thought a lot about these things since I have returned from forestry camp. I am not mounting a campaign to turn the clock back, but I am urging that all of us slow the pace a little. We should take time to study public issues and attend a few meetings where local candidates speak. We should reject the illusion of easy learning and should value thoroughness in edu cation. We should spend more time getting to know each other instead of just doing things together. We should search for satisfaction by doing fewer things, but doing them better and more thoroughly.

Planning the Essay

46a   Select a subject.

You will usually be assigned subjects for your essays, but if the choice is left to you, select a subject quickly rather than wait for inspiration. Your best essays will come from subjects you already know something about, so look first at your own interests and experience. Writing about what you know will give your essay a personal angle — that is, an individual approach to the subject (see p. 269).

If a suitable subject does not come to mind immediately, actively pursue one through the following strategies:

1. If you keep a journal, browse through it, searching for an engaging entry. If an entry engages you, it will engage your reader.

2. Recall a recent lecture. Perhaps a professor stimulated your curiosity or reminded you of a strong opinion you hold, either of which might inspire an essay.

3. Skim a news magazine or newspaper until a subject catches your attention. Jot down your thoughts; use them as a starting point.

You do not need to be an expert on the subject you choose, but you should handle the subject thoughtfully. Your own thoughts, insights, and values—your personal angle — integrated with what you have read or studied will help you write a thoughtful essay.

46b   Narrow the subject to a topic that can be covered in a single essay.

Some writers believe that the broader the subject, the more they will find to say about it. But the opposite is true. A writer can find more informative and interesting things to say about a narrow subject than about a broad subject. A narrow subject forces a writer to use specific material, which requires that more detail be developed.

A personal angle will help you narrow a subject. Suppose your subject is world terrorism. World terrorism is an interesting subject, but too broad. You could do little more than summarize news articles on recent terrorist activity, information most readers would have.

But if you create a personal angle by asking yourself how terrorism affects you and people you know, then you can narrow your subject to a manageable size, such as "the psychological effect of world terrorism on my college campus." By pursuing a personal angle you will develop specific supporting material based on your direct and indirect experience.

Rueben Langford, author of "Time to Slow Down" (p. 273), began with the general subject "American lifestyles." Obviously the subject is too broad for a college essay. Rueben narrowed the subject to "the fast pace of American lifestyles." But he found this subject was still too broad. To include everything that the subject suggests, he would have needed to deal with work schedules, after-work activities, instant communications, the automobile's expansion of community boundaries, the fast-food habit, and many more subtopics. He could have only written one or two sentences about each.

Reuben then settled on "the impatience and restlessness in American life," but soon discovered that he needed to narrow the subject even more. He found a personal angle by recalling his recent forestry-camp experience, which led him to limit his subject to impatience and restlessness in three aspects of American life: public affairs, education, and personal relationships. (See preliminary plan, p. 283.)

Writers often change the scope and phrasing of a topic as they move through the planning and the first-draft stages of a paper. Since writing requires trial and revision, do not hesitate to change your subject if it becomes too difficult to manage or if you see new possibilities.

Exercise 7

Narrow each of the following subjects by writing three progressively more limited topics. For example:

> Music
>
> Country and western music
>
> Male and female relations in country and western ballads
>
> Attitudes toward women in current country and western ballads

1. football
2. shopping malls
3. the business world
4. travel

5. college education
6. skiing
7. music
8. courage

9. health
10. inflation

46c   Use prewriting exercises to generate ideas.

Before you begin writing an essay, you need to examine what you know about the subject and explore the possible ways in which the topic can be developed. The prewriting exercises of listing and clustering can help you in this process.

Listing

You can help focus your thinking about a topic by making a list of items related to it. As you develop a list, try to keep a flow of ideas coming. Do not reject any ideas. Write them all down because one idea, even a weak one, may lead to another. Later you can decide which ideas you will expand upon and include in the essay, but if you edit your list too soon, you may inhibit the flow of ideas.

The writer of "Time to Slow Down" developed such a list for the topic "impatience and restlessness in American life."

> fast food
> horn blowing in traffic — no patience
> people don't listen in conversations, check watches
> computers — no time to think
> moving at a slow pace considered a crime
> jet planes
> Romeo and Juliet summary on TV — "Boy meets girl. Boy dies.
>   Girl dies." — culture in a hurry
> condensed books
> relationships made to solve problems, quickly dissolved
> math made easy
> quick divorce — no time for reconciliation
> abbreviations in correspondence and announcements

TV news
35 minutes for lunch
learn while you sleep
leave jobs easily — no ties
digest magazines
conversation — rapid speech — contractions — swallowed syllables
fall in love quickly
violence — quick elimination of problems
don't know candidates
calculators — no time to add

Reuben listed these items as they came to his mind. He included some of them in the final paper; others he rejected. Nevertheless, the listing process gave him a wealth of ideas to draw from as he began to organize and write the final paper.

Clustering

Listing ideas is an effective way to generate material, but many writers prefer clustering because they find it an easier way to see relations between ideas. To develop ideas through clustering, write your topic in the center of a piece of paper; then as you think of ideas connected with the topic, arrange them around the edges of the page, or in clusters of similar items.

Clustering may make it easy for you to group ideas, but try both methods — listing and clustering — to see which works best for you.

Exercise 8

Select two of the following topics and narrow each to a topic suitable for an essay. For one topic prepare a list of fifteen items; for the other topic, create clusters of at least fifteen items, using secondary clusters when appropriate.

auto racing	messages in dreams
gun control	inspired moments
living in the country	making money
living in the city	bringing joy to others
comedy films	being manipulated
suspense films	obtaining knowledge
effective teaching	improving health
ineffective teaching	destroying health
competitive sports	learning to cook
energy sources	truth in advertising
capital punishment	space travel

46d Plan an essay with a particular audience in mind.

Your audience will influence choices you make about content and vocabulary when writing an essay. If you were separately telling police officers, your parents, and friends about the events at a party, you would select different details to emphasize for each audience and use different words to describe the events. In speech you make this adaptation instantly and naturally, but in writing you must make the adaptation consciously. It is essential, therefore, that before you move too far into the planning of an essay, you should determine your audience. The audience might be quite specific — the city council, for example. Or it might be more general — people over age sixty-five. The audience might be composed only of people of German descent or of people who have never been to Hawaii or of people suffering from stage fright. Whoever the audience is, keep it in mind as you plan an essay. Reuben Langford wanted to write for an audience of fellow students because he felt they would share some of his concerns and could profit from thinking about his ideas.

46e Make a preliminary plan for an essay.

After you have done a prewriting exercise (listing or clustering), examine the items carefully. If you have done listing, look for ways to group the items. Then think about possible methods of developing your essay. (See methods of paragraph development, p. 261.)

Reuben could see at once that his items could not be discussed in the order he had listed them. The first item, "fast food," was not directly related to the second or third, "horn blowing in traffic" and "people don't listen in conversations." But he could pair "fast food" with an item farther down the list, "35 minutes for lunch."

He continued to study his list, looking for related items, and organized them into five groups:

```
technology
        calculators — no time to add
        computers — no time to think
        jet planes
eating habits
        fast food
        35 minutes for lunch
personal relationships
        leave jobs easily — no ties
        relationships made to solve problems, quickly dissolved
        fall in love quickly
        quick divorce — no time for reconciliation
        conversation — rapid speech — contraction — swallowed
           syllables
        people don't listen in conversations, check watches
        abbreviations in correspondence and announcements
        horn blowing in traffic — no patience
        moving at a slow pace considered a crime
```

> political
>> TV news
>> don't know candidates
>> violence — quick elimination of problems
>
> educational
>> condensed books
>> digest magazines
>> learn while you sleep
>> math made easy
>> Romeo and Juliet summary on TV — "Boy meets girl. Boy dies. Girl dies." — culture in a hurry

Next Reuben considered possible methods of development for his essay. He ruled out analogy, process, and definition because the items on his list did not seem to be appropriate for those methods. He could see that his items were all examples; he could select a few of the most important ones, flesh them out, and use examples and details as his method of development. He also thought he could write a comparison or contrast paper if he developed a parallel list of items for a different time or place. He considered making such a list for his stay in the forestry camp. Cause and effect also seemed to be workable. Impatience and restlessness cause the behaviors on his list. Although he had arranged his items in five categories, he rejected classification because the categories did not represent different kinds, or classes, of impatience and restlessness; they were simply different activities in which the results of impatience and restlessness could be seen.

After further consideration, Reuben tentatively decided to try cause and effect. That method would allow him to use the examples on his list as examples of effects. It was preferable to comparison or contrast because he wanted to focus the paper on his observations about the typical daily life of people around him, not those of some other place or time. If cause and effect did not work when he reached the formal planning stage, he could go back to examples or comparison or contrast.

After evaluating his five groups, Reuben decided that the most important ones were "political," "educational," and "personal relationships." "Technology" and "eating habits," he decided, were trite and obvious. He decided he might mention them in the introduction but not make them important parts of the essay. The other three groups were matters of concern to him and perhaps to others. He knew he would have to add more items to the political aspect of his essay, and he was not sure that all the items listed under "personal relationships" were equally valid, but he felt confident that he had a reasonable plan for an essay addressed to an audience of fellow students.

So far, Reuben had taken the following steps:

1. He thought about his own experience and chose a subject — "American lifestyles."
2. He narrowed his subject to a topic he believed he could cover in an essay — "impatience and restlessness in American life."
3. He made a prewriting list of items related to his topic.
4. He decided to address his paper to fellow students.
5. He made a preliminary plan for his essay by grouping the items on his prewriting list and by deciding that he would use cause and effect as his method of development.

It is important to remember that Reuben could still change his decisions. A writer should be prepared to modify a plan or shift direction if such changes will produce a more effective essay.

Exercise 9

Examine the results of the prewriting and clustering exercise you completed on page 282. Select either the list or the cluster and develop categories in which to group the items.

46f Write a clear, limited thesis statement.

A thesis statement serves the same purpose in an essay as a topic sentence does for a paragraph: It states and imposes limits on a narrowed topic. The thesis statement usually appears at the end of the introduction to an essay. Sometimes a thesis statement indicates the subtopics of the topic or suggests the method of development.

Reuben's first thesis statement was too vague:

> Americans live impatient and restless lives.

This sentence presents the topic, but it does not fully reflect the thinking Reuben had already done. It ignores his decision to include only the "political," "educational," and "personal relationships" categories from his prewriting list.

His second attempt included a further limitation:

> The impatience and restlessness of Americans show in our political affairs, our educational system, and our personal relationships.

He felt this statement was better. It limited the scope of the essay more clearly, and the words *show in* at least hinted at a cause-and-effect method of development. He decided to use the sentence as his tentative thesis statement.

Later, while writing his introductory paragraph, he came back and changed the wording of his thesis statement to fit the context of the paragraph.

Reuben's final thesis statement was the following:

> The impatience and restlessness of our approach to life show in our responses to public affairs, in our educational programs, and in our relationships with each other.

This sentence states the topic, limits the topic, states the subtopics of the essay, and suggests a cause-and-effect method of development.

To be effective, a thesis statement must be not only limited but also concrete.

VAGUE	Jogging daily is great. [What does *great* mean?]
CONCRETE	Jogging daily improves a person's health, endurance, and self-esteem.

| VAGUE | The California condor is in danger. [What danger?] |
| CONCRETE | The California condor will be extinct in ten years. |

Exercise 10

The following thesis statements are vague. Rewrite them to make them more concrete.

1. If you're planning to go cross-country skiing, you had better be prepared.
2. Studying American literature teaches us many things.
3. I think many seniors are unhappy.
4. People today are exposed to many health hazards.
5. Great music is very important.

Exercise 11

Write thesis statements for the topics you wrote in Exercise 8, page 282.

46g Make a final plan for an essay.

The final plan for an essay should be developed after the tentative phrasing of a thesis statement and before writing the first draft. It usually takes the form of an outline of the ideas and supporting details to be covered in the essay.

An outline can be written in topic or sentence form. The main items are identified by roman numerals, the first sublevel of items by capital letters, the second sublevel by arabic numerals, the third sublevel by lowercase letters, the fourth sublevel by arabic numerals enclosed in parentheses, and the fifth sublevel by lowercase letters enclosed in parentheses. All letters and numbers at the same level are indented to fall directly under one another.

```
I.
  A.
  B.
    1.
    2.
      a.
      b.
        (1)
        (2)
          (a)
          (b)
II.
```

You will rarely need all six levels. Notice that each level is a division of the level above it. Therefore, there must be at least two items at every level because, logically, a topic cannot be divided into one item. Of course, there may be more than two items at any level.

All items at the same level must be expressed in parallel grammatical structure.

INCORRECT	II. Shortcuts in education
	A. Study in fifteen-minute periods
	B. Learning while asleep
	C. Condensed books and digests
CORRECT	II. Shortcuts in education
	A. Studying in fifteen-minute periods
	B. Learning while sleeping
	C. Using condensed books and digests

A, B, and C are now grammatically parallel. In this case each is a participial phrase.

Do not use such terms as *Introduction, Discussion Section,* and *Conclusion* to label portions of the outline because these labels will not appear in the essay.

Begin the first word of each item with a capital letter.

The following example is a topic outline of "Time to Slow Down." Notice that Reuben added some material that was not on his original prewriting list. He also eliminated items from the lengthy "personal relationships" category and divided it into two sublevels. Notice too that the thesis statement is still tentative. This is a topic outline and is not written in complete sentences, and so there is no end punctuation.

> *Thesis statement:* The impatience and restlessness of Americans show in our political affairs, our educational system, and our personal relationships.

  I. Adverse effects of impatience and restlessness
     A. On me
     B. On political affairs, the educational system, and personal relationships
 II. Political affairs
     A. Public issues
     B. State and national campaigns
     C. Local elections
III. Educational system
     A. Advertisements offering effortless learning
     B. Colleges offering quick courses
 IV. Relationships with friends
     A. Frequent moves
     D. Frequent job changes
  V. Relationships in families
     A. Increasing number of one-parent families
     B. Increasing number of outside activities
 VI. Solution
     A. Study public issues
     B. Reject illusion of easy learning
     C. Spend time to know each other
     D. Take time to do fewer things better

Your instructor may ask you to make a sentence outline, particularly if your essay is long or complex. A sentence outline is more thorough than a topic outline and therefore serves as a better guide to writing the first draft. Each item is written as a declarative sentence, but the sentences are not necessarily written as they will appear in the final essay. (For a sample sentence outline, see pp. 353–55.)

Exercise 12

Develop a topic outline or sentence outline for the material you worked with in Exercise 8, page 282.

46h Use a suitable tone.

Before you actually begin writing, decide on an appropriate tone. Tone reveals your attitude toward your readers and your topic, so you must be sensitive to the nuances of your words and sentence structures.

Tone ranges from formal — impersonal and objective — to informal — personal and subjective. For example, the tone of a report written for businessmen might be very formal:

> Five years ago, the government forced cosmetic manufacturers to warn consumers that hair-dyes contain an ingredient that can penetrate skin and has been determined to cause cancer in laboratory animals.

In contrast, the same material written informally for readers who are suspicious of cosmetic manufacturers might be written in the following tone:

> About five years ago, the Food and Drug people were on their toes. They forced hair-dye makers using a chemical called for short 4-MMPD to warn buyers that it might cause cancer. Cancer! The industry went into shock.

If your tone is not right — too flippant, stuffy, bossy, patronizing, or angry — you should modify it.

Rueben Langford chose an informal tone for his essay because his readers were fellow students and he was basing his conclusions on his personal analysis of American behavior. Rueben used one tone consistently. A serious paper may be enlivened with occasional humor, but changes in tone from paragraph to paragraph are irritating and confusing to readers.

Writing a First Draft

Your first draft will grow naturally from the planning stages you have completed. You will not need to stare at a blank piece of paper or gaze off into the distance hoping for inspiration. Instead, remind yourself of your purpose, audience, and tone; review your outline; and begin to write.

Do not worry about making the first draft perfect. As we mentioned before, the stages of the writing process are not distinct. You will find yourself making some minor revisions even as you write your first draft, but your main purpose at this stage is to get a draft completed so that you can revise it later. The excerpt from Reuben Langford's first draft on page 292 illustrates this process.

46i Write an introduction that includes the thesis statement and captures a reader's interest.

An effective introduction presents the thesis clearly, in a way that will draw the reader into the essay. Traditional introductory methods consist of some of these elements:

1. Descriptions of personal experience that allow a reader to identify with the writer
2. Statements of striking facts or statistics that surprise a reader
3. A provocative quotation or interesting question
4. A definition, but not merely taken from a dictionary
5. A glance at an opposing argument or attack on a common opinion
6. An anecdote or narrative closely related to the topic
7. A discussion that leads naturally to the thesis statement

Reuben opens his essay with a discussion that provides some background information a reader might need to understand the situation. He also establishes his personal angle — returning home after ten months at forestry camp. He concludes the introduction with the thesis statement.

46j Develop the thesis statement in the discussion section of the essay.

The discussion section of an essay develops the idea advanced in the thesis statement. If you have written a thorough topic outline or sentence outline, you have done most of the work already. Each of the main points of the outline needs to be turned into a topic sentence of a paragraph. The sublevel items in your outline, rephrased, become the supporting sentences in each paragraph.

Reuben followed his topic outline to write the paragraphs of the discussion section. The section on "political affairs" is shown below in outline form and in draft form. The final draft of the entire essay is on pages 272–77.

> II. Political affairs
>   A. Public issues
>   B. State and national campaigns
>   C. Local elections

Reuben first had to phrase a topic sentence that was about political affairs. Then, he had to develop a paragraph that included all his subtopics.

> Few of us take time to understand public affairs. ~~Our knowl-edge of~~ local and national issues ~~is gained mostly~~ from news pro-grams that devote only a few minutes to even the most complicated storis. ~~Political campaigns at the state and national levels are characterized by a~~ relance on thirty-second ~~spot~~ commercials devoted to catchy slogans and unsupported assertions. Local elections are usually won by incumbents because voters ~~don't~~ know ~~who else to vote for.~~ As citizens in a democracy, we should be willing to study political affairs, but we are impatient.

(handwritten edits: "We get most of" above "Our"; "information about" replacing "knowledge of"; "television" above "from"; "e" above "storis"; "S" capitalizing "state"; "successfully y" with "relance"; "e" in "incumbents"; "nothing" replacing "who else"; "about other candidates" replacing "to vote for"; comma after "democracy")

As you write the discussion section of your essay, use methods of development appropriate for your content and purpose. (See methods of paragraph development, p. 261.)

46k Signal the end of an essay with a short concluding paragraph.

A successful essay concludes; it doesn't just end. Conclusions and introductions are important because they are the first and last contact a writer has with a reader. The introduction arouses a reader's interest and presents the thesis statement, and the conclusion completes the discussion, echoing the thesis and the supporting points. There are several standard ways to conclude a paper. An effective conclusion can consist of any of these techniques:

1. An answer to a question or a solution to a problem raised in the introduction and explored in the discussion; or a statement that no clear answer or solution exists, thus showing the complexity of the issue
2. A quotation, especially one that amplifies the thesis statement or verifies another quotation already presented in the introduction
3. A relevant anecdote which the reader will be likely to remember and which echoes the thesis statement
4. A rephrasing of the thesis statement and supporting points, followed by a sentence or two that turn the reader's thoughts to the implications of the paper

In the conclusion of "Time to Slow Down," Reuben offers a personal solution to the problem he discussed in the essay (see p. 277).

A word of caution: The conclusion must grow from the paper; it should not open a new subject by raising questions unexplored in the discussion.

46l Create a title that briefly indicates the content of an essay.

The best time to compose a title is after you have written your essay because only then will you know the complete contents.

A title should be brief: "Calisthenics for Health," "Helping Children Handle Stress," "Hank Williams: Country Music Giant."

Reuben wanted a title that would suggest his main idea — that we are too impatient and restless. First he chose the title "Impatience and Restlessness," but he soon realized that his essay was really about the effects of impatience and restlessness, not about these qualities themselves. Next he tried "The Effects of Impatience and Restlessness." But his paper certainly didn't deal with *all* the effects of impatience and restlessness, and as he reread his conclusion, he decided he should try to convey the idea that there are things we can do about the situation. Then he tried "Take the Time to Slow Down" and finally shortened it to "Time to Slow Down," which conveyed the same idea in fewer words.

46m Revise the first draft thoroughly.

If you set your essay aside for a few days before you revise it, you will be more objective in your evaluation and better able to see its strengths and weaknesses. But if you cannot delay your revision, you must still try to approach the essay from a reader's point of view. Review the essay slowly, concentrating on its overall clarity. Try doing this review while reading out loud. It will help you find confused or inconsistent areas. For the first reading, ask yourself these questions:

1. Is the thesis statement clear? Does it indicate the scope and direction of the essay?
2. Is the essay unified? Does every sentence and paragraph have a clear relation to the thesis?
3. Is the tone consistent?
4. Is the essay organized logically and effectively?

If you need to make changes, make them and then read the essay again, concentrating on smaller elements of it and using the following questions as a guide.

1. Are the paragraphs developed with sufficient detail and explanation?

2. Does the essay move smoothly from paragraph to paragraph? Is the essay coherent?
3. Is the introduction interesting and to the point? Does it lead naturally to the thesis statement? Does the concluding paragraph bring the essay to a satisfactory close without being unduly repetitious or introducing a new subject?

During a third reading you should concentrate on even smaller elements. One way to do so is to read the essay backward sentence by sentence. By reading each sentence out of context, you may find it easier to answer these questions:

1. Are the sentences clear, grammatical, and free from sentence errors?
2. Is the paper consistent with the conventions of punctuation and mechanics?
3. Do the words convey your intended meaning? Are they spelled correctly?

If all this sounds like a lot of work, it is. But excellence is not born in first drafts. It is achieved through thoughtful and painstaking revision.

Exercise 13

Write an essay according to the guidelines presented in this chapter. If your instructor has not assigned a subject, read the following list for some ideas. Because these subjects are very broad, you will need to narrow the one you select to manageable size.

technology	careers	literature
politics	education	prejudice
television	athletics	medicine
crime	art	competition
government	childhood	music
holidays	conservation	nutrition
fashion	entertainment	law
violence	leisure	censorship

47 Writing an Analytical Essay About Literature *dev*

The process of writing analytical essays about literature involves breaking up a work of fiction, poetry, or drama into its component parts and concentrating on a single element of the work.

47a Select an appropriate subject for analysis.

When selecting a single element as the subject of your analysis, be sure that the element is central to the work's meaning. If the author of a short story made little use of symbols, then you would be mistaken to analyze the use of symbols in that story. If the psychological development of a character, however, were central to the story, then writing a character analysis would be appropriate.

Traditionally, analytical essays have concentrated on several subjects, many of which are discussed in the following paragraphs.

Characterization refers to the way in which an author presents the characters within a work. Two types of characters appear in fiction and drama — flat and round. A *flat character* usually has a single outstanding trait and stays the same throughout a work. A *round character* may have several traits and usually learns from his or her experiences and changes in the course of the work. An analysis of character might begin with the following questions: How is this character developed? What is he or she like? In what ways does he or she learn or change?

Plot usually refers to the meaningful arrangement of events in a narrative. Authors arrange events in patterns and establish causal relations among them. For the most part, plot is generated by conflict. At a simple level, conflict arises when a character wants to achieve something but must overcome barriers to reach his or her goal. Conflict is usually external or internal. *Internal conflict* takes place within the mind of a character, whereas *external conflict* takes place between characters or between a character and the forces of nature. To write about the plot of a narrative work, begin your analysis with these questions: What conflicts does the work embody? How are the conflicts related? Which conflicts are external and which are internal? How does conflict affect the characters?

Point of view refers to the means by which a work is narrated. At the simplest level, a narrative can be told through the first person (a character in the work) or the third person (the author is implied as the narrator). When using first person, an author must sustain the work's psychological reality by using the language and reflecting the attitudes and opinions of the character who is telling the story. Because of its complexity, a first-person narrative is often a better subject for analysis than a third-person narrative. Begin such an analysis by asking: Who is telling the story? How does the narrator reveal his or her personality? Is the narrator trustworthy? What irony develops because of the narrator's limitations?

Setting comprises physical details of the place and time in which a work unfolds and the social environment of the characters. Setting often has little significance in a story, play, or poem, but at other times it is indispensable. To examine setting, begin by asking some of the following questions: Where and when does the action take place? What relation does setting have to the characters? How long does it take for the events to occur? How do the manners or customs of the social environment affect the characters? How does the physical environment affect the characters?

Symbols are actual objects and places infused with emotional significance that goes beyond their concrete qualities. Symbols do not stand for abstractions, such as *love* or *hate;* instead they hint at or suggest a meaning. Not every work embodies symbols, but if symbols are important in a work you are examining, ask yourself: What do the symbols suggest about character? How do they relate to the action? How do they support the theme?

Theme is the central idea that emerges from a work. A successful theme comments on the larger human experience, not just on the experiences of individual characters. Theme, therefore, is the general application of the central idea embodied in a literary work. To deal with the theme of a narrative work, begin by asking: What is the work's subject? What does the author seem to be saying about the subject? In what ways do characters, setting, plot, and symbols contribute to the theme?

Sometimes an analytical essay combines several approaches. One such essay is an **explication,** a line-by-line analysis of a short poem or a passage from a long poem, work of fiction, or play. Explications are thorough, detailed examinations that are often concentrated on such elements as the uses of words, rhythm, rhyme, and images. A **critical review** also combines several approaches. Critical reviews deal with book-length works, such as a collection of poems or short stories or a novel, and evaluate the work's strengths and weaknesses.

47b Review the text for evidence.

Once you have identified a general subject for an essay about literature, review the work to find key passages which relate to the subject and which might serve as evidence in your paper.

Incidents, details of setting, character traits, symbols, paraphrases, and summaries of long passages can all serve as evidence. Of course, the most convincing evidence is a direct quotation and your explanation of its meaning as it relates to your subject.

47c Formulate a thesis statement and develop a plan.

No one can examine every aspect of a literary work in a brief essay; consequently, you must decide on a topic by selecting a single aspect of your subject. Then develop a limited thesis statement that announces the topic and expresses your attitude toward it. (See thesis statement, p. 285.)

> In "The Chrysanthemums," John Steinbeck portrays a character who senses but cannot understand the need to communicate her deepest feelings.

> "Buffalo Bill's defunct" by E. E. Cummings creates an ambiguous image of an American folk hero.

Once you have developed a working thesis statement, you can sift through the evidence you have identified and develop a plan as you would for any essay. (See preliminary plan, p. 283; final plan, p. 287.)

47d Assume that your reader has read the work.

Do not include excessively long quotations or unnecessary summaries merely to familiarize your readers with the work. Instead, assume that they have read the work at least once and that your job is to enrich their experience by pointing out elements and patterns that a closer examination uncovers.

47e Write an introduction that presents the thesis statement and supplies background information.

The introduction should include the name of the author, the title of the work, and a clear thesis statement. It should also have enough background information, which might include a brief quotation, to prepare the reader for what follows. (See introduction, p. 291.) In an introduction to Guy de Maupassant's short story "Moonlight," one student wrote the following:

> Guy de Maupassant's "Moonlight" deals with an awakening. The principal character, Father Marigan, is a self-satisfied woman-hater who believes he understands "God ... His plans, His wishes, His intentions." Marigan's awakening comes when he is seduced by moonlight into realizing, to his dismay, that God's plan includes love between a man and a woman. In this story de Maupassant uses setting to reinforce the characterization of Father Marigan and to convey the idea that love is natural and good.

Thesis Statement Introduction **299**

Clearly, this student's analysis will show how setting supports characterization and reflects the theme of the story. But whether you are writing an analysis of setting, theme, characterization, symbols, plot, or point of view, the introduction should always include the author's name, the title of the work, necessary background information, and the thesis statement.

47f Write a discussion consisting of several paragraphs.

Arrange the discussion according to significant ideas. Do not feel bound by the structure of the story, novel, play, or poem you are examining. Your discussion should consist of several paragraphs, each supporting one aspect of the thesis statement and each unified by a fully developed topic sentence.

One way to develop the topic sentence is by combining your comments with a quotation that supports them, as in the following discussion paragraph from an analysis of Flannery O'Connor's "Revelation." (See direct quotations, pp. 327–30.)

> O'Connor creates a conflicting portrait of Mrs. Tur-
> pin. We see her from the inside and the outside. Through-
> out the story she professes Christian love and charity,
> but in her mind she judges others by superficial stan-
> dards. For example, at night before sleeping she catego-
> rizes and judges people by their economic condition:
>
> > On the bottom of the heap were most colored peo-
> > ple ... next to them—not above, just away from—were
> > the white trash; then above them were the homeowners,
> > and above them the home-and-land owners, to which she
> > and Claud belonged. Above she and Claud were people

with a lot of money and much bigger homes and much
more land.

This judgmental vision of Mrs. Turpin ends in confusion
when rich blacks who own land and "white trash" who've
grown rich don't fit into her scheme, but she solves the
problem by mentally consigning everyone—white, black,
rich, and poor—to boxcars headed for a gas oven, a grim
reference to Nazi Germany and the result of categorical
thinking when carried to its limits.

Other paragraphs in the discussion might be developed by accurately summarizing the content of a work as it relates to your point, as the following discussion paragraph from an analysis of *Oedipus Rex* illustrates:

Sophocles uses the imagery of sight and blindness
ironically throughout the play. It is blind Tiresias, the
prophet of Apollo, who is the god of foresight and in-
sight, who sees more clearly than those who have eyes.
Early in the play, Oedipus promises to bring the dark secret of Laius' death to light for all to see, yet he does
so while still blind to his own moral faults. After blind-
ing himself near the play's end, Oedipus sees who he
really is and what he has done. Ironically, through the
play, Oedipus prides himself on his clear-sightedness, but
by the end he recognizes that this pride has blinded him.

You might also combine very brief quotations from a work and your comments on them, as this discussion paragraph from a critical evaluation of *Serpentine* does:

> A minor flaw in the book comes from Thompson's fla-
> grant use of clichés in place of more thoughtful prose. He
> writes, "It was the dead of winter, 1967, and the prison
> walls were cold as ice." He refers to Sobhraj's courtroom
> chicanery as a "bag of tricks." His girl friend clung to
> him "like moss on an oak." He tries to pass off their taw-
> dry affair as an "epic romance more poignant than Romeo
> and Juliet." Trite expressions such as these mar every
> page and blemish an otherwise powerful work.

47g   Write a conclusion.

The conclusion to your analytical essay should briefly summarize your thesis and the major thoughts in your paper, and it should end with your general view of the work. Here is an effective conclusion from an analysis of Flannery O'Connor's "Revelation":

> Clearly, O'Connor's "Revelation" takes a careful
> reader into the shadowy mind of a bigot who gains aware-
> ness through a personal catastrophe. O'Connor seems to be
> offering a positive message--that is, there is even hope
> that a bigot such as Mrs. Turpin can learn not to judge
> others by the weight of their wallets or the color of
> their skin.

47h   Create a precise title.

The title of your essay should be brief and should express the ideas your essay examines. If the title of the work you analyze is included in your essay title, only it should be italicized or put within quotation marks, as appropriate. (See quotation marks, p. 159; italics, p. 190.)

> E. E. Cummings's "Buffalo Bill's defunct": The Backside of a Folk Hero
>
> Imagery in Oedipus Rex
>
> Mrs. Turpin's Revelation

47i   Identify your quotations and specific references.

In a brief essay about literature, you might be allowed to omit complete citations for primary sources. If so, you should still identify the location of each quotation and specific reference you make. After the quotation or reference, place the page number or numbers from the original work in parentheses and close the sentence with the end punctuation mark after the last parenthesis.

> Hemingway ends the story on an ironic note: "After all, he said to himself, it's probably only insomnia" (p. 72).
>
> Near the end of his life we find that Gimpel has achieved peace. He now understands that soon all illusion will be swept away. He believes he will truly see without the confusion of ridicule and deception. He will see what is real (pp. 85–86).

47j Use the present tense of verbs.

The dominant verb tense in an essay about literature — whether fiction, drama, or poetry — should be the present. (See present tense, p. 69.)

> In The Executioner's Song Mailer re-creates life as
> it is lived in the rural West. He evokes people struggling
> to make a living in gas stations, roadside cafés, movie
> theaters, small factories, country stores, and on farms.
> It is a world filled with pickup trucks, six-packs, coun-
> try music, Monday Night Football, deer hunting, motorcy-
> cles, and honky-tonk violence. The city slicker is sus-
> pect, and the easy buck is hard to find. The four-wheel-
> drive Blazer, not the sleek Mercedes, is the status sym-
> bol.

47k Avoid common mistakes in essay writing.

Do not summarize excessively. Summarize only enough of a work to clarify your thought or a point. Summary should always serve a clear purpose.

Do not refer to authors by their first names or as Dr., Prof., Mr., Mrs., Miss, or Ms. After giving an author's full name in the introduction, refer to him or her by last name throughout the rest of the essay.

Do not miscopy a direct quotation. Always recheck any quotation you use to be sure you've copied it accurately.

Do not set off the title of a work with commas when it follows the word book, poem, or play.

INCORRECT	In his poem, "Traveling Through Dark," William Stafford reflects on humans' relation to nature.
CORRECT	In his poem "Traveling Through Dark," William Stafford reflects on humans' relation to nature.

Exercise 14

Visit your library and select an anthology of literature that includes fiction, poetry, and drama, such as X. J. Kennedy's *Literature* or Sylvan Barnet, Morton Berman, and William Burto's *An Introduction to Literature*. Browse through the books to find a work that interests you. After reading the work several times, begin a five-to-seven paragraph explication of a brief poem or passage, critical evaluation, or analytical examination with character, plot, point of view, setting, symbol, or theme as the subject.

48   Writing a Research Paper

A research paper is a formal composition based on an investigation of other writers' ideas about a topic rather than solely on your own attitudes and experiences. No doubt you have personal opinions about a number of topics, but unless you have taken many courses or read extensively, you probably do not have an *informed* opinion. Writing a research paper offers you the opportunity to develop an informed opinion and to apply your thinking and writing skills to an objective discussion of a topic. Unlike the personal essay, which grows from personal experiences and viewpoints, the research paper grows from an in-depth study and careful examination of the ideas of other writers.

A research paper is more than a summarized version of what others have said or written, however. Ideally, your research paper represents a synthesis of your own perceptions, attitudes, ideas, and experiences supported by information gained from other sources. In most cases, those sources are materials in your own college or community library. You can use these materials to enlarge, to strengthen, to define, or otherwise to complement your own basic views about a subject. No one expects you to solve a major world problem as a result of your research, but if you have done your work seriously and thoroughly, it will result in a broader and more informed view than any one source alone has yet provided.

48a Find and limit a topic suitable for research.

If your instructor has not already given you a specific research assignment, allow yourself time to select an appropriate topic for research. The best way to start your search is by examining your own interests and experiences.

1. Begin with topics that interest you.

Your favorite section of the newspaper, the kinds of books, magazines, or films you enjoy, or a particular textbook chapter that excited your curiosity are all strong clues to your real interests. The best ingredients for a successful paper are your own understanding of and enthusiasm for a subject.

2. A suitable topic allows room for discussion.

To choose an appropriate research topic you also must be aware of what your paper can achieve. Since most research papers attempt to add new dimensions or perspectives to a body of ideas already expressed by others, process or "how-to" papers or those that merely summarize already known information ("the major decisions during John F. Kennedy's presidency") are not good choices. Strictly philosophical subjects or topics based on personal beliefs — "The nature of reality," "Loyalty to one's government comes before loyalty to one's family," "Public nudity should be left to personal choice" — should be avoided because they are based on opinion and often do not require research for objective evidence and do not lend themselves to objective discussion. Look for a topic that allows you to explore areas that still need discussion or review, such as an unsettled and continuing problem or a little-known situation. "Whether the sale of handguns should be controlled in this country," for example, might prove a suitable problem to investigate for a research paper. Or an examination of the social and economic impact of credit cards (as in the sample research paper by Leslie Webster beginning on page 351) could produce an informative, researched discussion.

3. Narrow the topic to manageable size.

The topic for your research paper should allow you to generate enough discussion to fulfill your instructor's requirements about length and about the kinds of sources you should use for your research. A subject that is too narrow, such as "whether the shopping mall provides enough security for Christmas shoppers," or too recent, such as "How video games influence children's patterns of play," will not work because there will not be enough written for you to build on.

Likewise, some topics may be so large or already have so much written about them — "The events leading up to President Nixon's resignation," for example — that you cannot expect to learn enough in a few weeks' time to write about them convincingly. In such instances, you will need to narrow the focus of your paper, just as you did when developing a thesis or writing the personal essay.

Sometimes reviewing the general sources for a broad subject can help you see particular ways to narrow the approach or shift the emphasis of a topic. Often the topic itself becomes more refined only after you have begun researching it; and it may not evolve to its final form until the completion of the paper. For instance, if you were to begin with a broad topic such as "art" or "psychology," you might find yourself moving gradually toward a narrower topic in the manner illustrated on page 308.

Narrowing a topic from general to specific is seldom as smooth or orderly as these illustrations might make the process seem. Usually you will have several false starts, but reading in a general subject area will help you find your way. Business major Leslie Webster, the author of the sample paper, moved quickly from the broad subject of "business" to "merchandising," her college minor. Because she was taking an investment course, she found herself exploring how merchandisers, especially department stores, finance their inventories. Preliminary research yielded very little information on the topic. At first she was blocked, but she kept reading anyway. Soon she realized how much information was available on consumer credit.

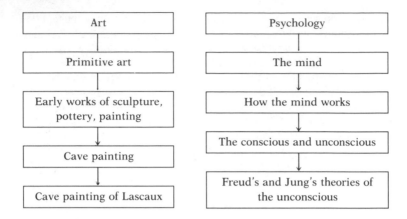

Art	Psychology
Primitive art	The mind
Early works of sculpture, pottery, painting	How the mind works
Cave painting	The conscious and unconscious
Cave painting of Lascaux	Freud's and Jung's theories of the unconscious

She quickly shifted her reading to the subject of "consumer credit" and finally concentrated on credit cards, which became her topic.

Do not rush this essential step of narrowing the topic to something that interests you and that can be easily researched. Careful selection of the right topic can save you much time and work later, and it can provide an early foundation for a successful finished product.

48b Use available library sources.

Use reference books to get an overview of your topic and to evaluate its appropriateness for your assignment. In addition to encyclopedias, dictionaries, almanacs, indexes, guides, atlases, and book reviews, your library's reference section probably contains a large selection of special reference sources, ranging from the *Encyclopedia of Banking and Finance* (1983) to the *Guinness Book of World Records* — both of which were valuable sources for Leslie Webster's paper about credit cards.

A complete listing of the hundreds of reference books would, of course, be impractical here. The following is a sampling of the variety of sources available. But you should survey your own library for the reference books most applicable to your topic, and you can also consult Eugene P. Sheehy's *Guide to Reference Books*, 9th edition, for a comprehensive catalogue of reference books.

GENERAL ENCYCLOPEDIAS

Encyclopedia Americana (1983)
The New Encyclopaedia Britannica (1985)

THE ARTS

Art Books: A Basic Bibliography on the Fine Arts (1968)
Encyclopedia of World Art (1959–83)

BUSINESS AND ECONOMICS

American Business Dictionary (1957)
Encyclopedia of Computers and Data Processing (1978)
The Encyclopedia of Management (1982)
Marketing Terms: Definitions, Explanations and/or Aspects (1973)

HISTORY

Dictionary of American History (1976)
An Encyclopedia of World History (1972)

LITERATURE, THEATER, FILM, AND TELEVISION

Bibliography of American Literature (1955–73)
Contemporary Authors (1962–   )
The International Encyclopedia of the Film (1972)
International Television Almanac (1956–   )
Modern Drama: A Checklist of Critical Literature on Twentieth Century Plays (1967)
Short Story Index (1953–   )

MUSIC

Encyclopedia of Pop, Rock, and Soul (1977)
The New Harvard Dictionary of Music (1986)
The New Grove Dictionary of Music and Musicians (1980)

PHILOSOPHY AND RELIGION

The Encyclopedia of Philosophy (1973)
The Interpreter's Dictionary of the Bible (1976)

SOCIAL SCIENCE

A Dictionary of Psychology and Related Fields (1974)
Foreign Affairs Bibliography (1976)
Handbook of Social Science Research (1979)
The Literature of Political Science (1969)

SCIENCES

Cambridge Encyclopedia of Astronomy (1977)
The Environment Handbook (1978)
The International Dictionary of Physics and Electronics (1961)
The Larousse Encyclopedia of Animal Life (1967)

UNABRIDGED DICTIONARIES

The Oxford English Dictionary (1933–76)
Webster's Third New International Dictionary of the English Language (1966)

SPECIAL DICTIONARIES

Dictionary of Modern English Usage (1965)
Modern American Usage (1966)
The New Roget's Thesaurus of the English Language in Dictionary Form (1978)

BIOGRAPHICAL REFERENCE

Dictionary of American Biography (1928–81)
Who's Who in America (1899–   )

ATLASES AND GAZETTEERS

Columbia Lippincott Gazetteer of the World (1962)
Rand McNally Cosmopolitan World Atlas (1971)

ALMANACS AND YEARBOOKS

Britannica Book of the Year (1938–   )
Facts on File Yearbook (1940–   )
World Almanac and Book of Facts (1868–   )

1. Use the card catalogue to find books on your topic.

The best guide to the books available to you for research is your library's card catalogue. Whether in a book, on a computer printout, or in the traditional card tray, the library's catalogue alphabetically lists and cross-references its holdings by subject, author, and title. Special information given with each entry can supply useful data about a book's publication date, whether it includes illustrations, and its length. You can locate books on your topic by looking under the author, title, or subject heading. There are two widely used classification systems — the Dewey decimal system and the Library of Congress system. The system a library uses has no effect on your library work; it merely determines the call number of any book.

2. Use periodicals for more focused information about your topic.

Periodicals are valuable sources of more specific or current information. Many different indexes catalogue the various kinds of jour-

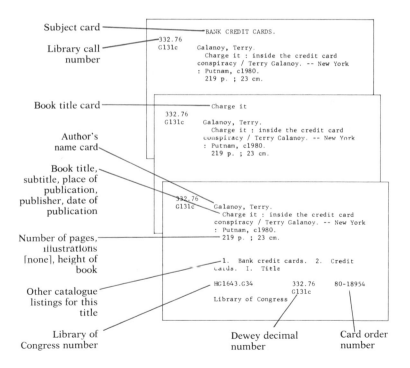

Subject card

Library call number

Book title card

Author's name card

Book title, subtitle, place of publication, publisher, date of publication

Number of pages, illustrations [none], height of book

Other catalogue listings for this title

Library of Congress number

Dewey decimal number

Card order number

BANK CREDIT CARDS.

332.76
G131c   Galanoy, Terry.
            Charge it : inside the credit card
         conspiracy / Terry Galanoy. -- New York
         : Putnam, c1980.
            219 p. ; 23 cm.

Charge it

332.76
G131c   Galanoy, Terry.
            Charge it : inside the credit card
         conspiracy / Terry Galanoy. -- New York
         : Putnam, c1980.
            219 p. ; 23 cm.

332.76
G131c   Galanoy, Terry.
            Charge it : inside the credit card
         conspiracy / Terry Galanoy. -- New York
         : Putnam, c1980.
            219 p. ; 23 cm.

         1. Bank credit cards. 2. Credit
         cards. I. Title

HG1643.G34   332.76   80-18954
                     G131c
Library of Congress

nals, magazines, newspapers, and other periodicals, and certain guides are more useful to the general researcher than others. One such source is the *Readers' Guide to Periodical Literature*, which provides a monthly, quarterly, and annual index to the most widely circulated magazines in the United States.

Articles listed in the *Readers' Guide* are cross-referenced under author, title, and subject. Information about each entry is listed in a condensed form explained in the front of every volume of the *Guide*. Below, for example, are entries on "credit" and "credit cards" that Leslie Webster used for her research paper.

In addition to magazines, newspaper articles are important contemporary sources for research. While most libraries can store no

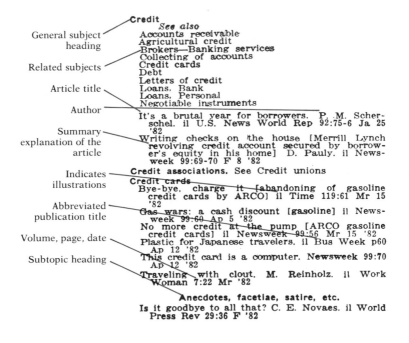

General subject heading

Related subjects

Article title

Author

Summary explanation of the article

Indicates illustrations

Abbreviated publication title

Volume, page, date

Subtopic heading

Credit
See also
Accounts receivable
Agricultural credit
Brokers—Banking services
Collecting of accounts
Credit cards
Debt
Letters of credit
Loans. Bank
Loans, Personal
Negotiable instruments
It's a brutal year for borrowers. P. M. Scherschel. il U.S. News World Rep 92:75-6 Ja 25 '82
Writing checks on the house [Merrill Lynch revolving credit account secured by borrower's equity in his home] D. Pauly. il Newsweek 99:69-70 F 8 '82
Credit associations. See Credit unions
Credit cards
Bye-bye, charge it [abandoning of gasoline credit cards by ARCO] il Time 119:61 Mr 15 '82
Gas wars: a cash discount [gasoline] il Newsweek 99:60 Ap 5 '82
No more credit at the pump [ARCO gasoline credit cards] il Newsweek 99:56 Mr 15 '82
Plastic for Japanese travelers. il Bus Week p60 Ap 12 '82
This credit card is a computer. Newsweek 99:70 Ap 12 '82
Traveling with clout. M. Reinholz. il Work Woman 7:22 Mr '82
Anecdotes, facetiae, satire, etc.
Is it goodbye to all that? C. E. Novaes. il World Press Rev 29:36 F '82

more than a few nationally circulated or local newspapers, most university and college libraries have copies of several major newspapers on microfilm. Articles are usually listed in a separate index, such as *The New York Times Index*, according to subject or author. These listings supply the section, page, and column of the paper in which the article appeared and the date of the newspaper. Leslie Webster used the *Wall Street Journal Index* to find an article about consumer debt that she cited in her research paper. Below you will find a sample subject entry from *The New York Times Index*.

Besides the *Readers' Guide* and newspaper indexes, most libraries contain other indexes to periodical literature on general and specialized subjects. The list on the following page is representative of the most common indexes to periodical literature. You should investigate your own library's holdings and use such sources to compile your bibliography.

Related topic **CREDIT Cards and Accounts. See also** Airports – NYC
headings Met Area, Ja 4. Bankers Trust NY Corp, Ag 20, N 5.
Credit – Puerto Rico, Ap 16. Credit – US, Ap 27, Je 9.
Credit – US – Consumer Credit, Ja 6,22, F 4,6,7,23, F 25,27,
Mr 1,2,8,9,13,17,18,20, Ap 1, My 5,10, Je 11, Je 25 par,
Je 27, Jl 19, Ag 16,19, S 25, O 17, N 17, D 3. Credit – US –
Frauds, Ja 4, F 5, Ag 9,19, O 24. Data Processing, My 7.
Hotels etc – NYS, Ap 14,19. Indiana, S 10. Liquor – US,
My 15. Oil – US, My 9. Prostitution, Ja 15. Roads – NYC –
Parking, Ap 12. Stocks and Bonds – US – Mutual Funds,
My 18,19,27, S 2,22, O 15. Travel, My 10. US – Cong (HR)-
Ethics, N 24. Names of issuers, eg, Amer Express Co,
Diners' Club Inc
Article titles American Express forms joint venture with Banco
Bamerindus and Banco Economico to market American
Express Cruzeiro Card throughout Brazil (S), My 21,IV,4:5
Advice on choosing a credit card; drawing (M), My 30,
30.1
Date, section, Visa International chief executive Dee Ward Hock
page, column discusses worldwide expansion plans, interview;
organizational diagram; portrait (L), Je 7,III,4:3
Correction on May 30 advice article, Je 9,II,1:6
Sydney H Schanberg comment on American Express
criteria for rejecting credit-card applicants as redefining
middle-class (M), Ag 15,23:6

Abstracts of Popular Culture (1976–   )
Alternative Press Index (1969–   )
The American Humanities Index (1975–   )
Applied Science and Technology Index (1958–   )
Bibliography and Index of Geology (1969–   )
Biography Index (1946–   )
Biological Abstracts (1926–   )
Book Review Digest (1905–   )
Book Review Index (1965–   )
Business Periodicals Index (1958–   )
Cumulative Index to Periodical Literature (1959–   )
Economics Abstracts (1969–   )
The Education Index (1929–   )
Humanities Index (1974–   )
Index Medicus (1960–   )
Index to Jewish Periodicals (1963–   )
International Political Science Abstracts (1951–   )
*MLA International Bibliography of Books and Articles on the Modern
    Languages and Literatures* (1921–   )
The Music Index (1949–   )
Poole's Index to Periodical Literature (1802–1906)
Popular Periodical Index (1973–   )
Social Sciences Index (1974–   )
United States Government Publications (1895–   )

3. Use computer data bases to supplement your library's resources.
Perhaps your library subscribes to one or more of the numerous
computer data base services that give users immediate access to a
vast library of information on a multitude of subjects. Using such
data bases, you can peruse a comprehensive bibliography of your
subject, read related encyclopedia articles, and find answers to specific
factual questions. You can also have all the on-screen information
printed so you can keep a copy and use it when you wish. We suggest,
though, that you begin your search for information in your local
library and turn to computer data bases only to fill a gap in the
library's resources. The reasons are simple. Commercial data bases
charge users a fee for every minute on-line, and research can take a
great deal of time. Each data base has its own methods and termi-

nology, and often considerable experience is needed to search efficiently. And once you have a list of sources, you may be unable to locate many of them or you may discover that they are expensive to purchase.

4. Use primary and secondary sources in your research.

Secondary sources are written materials about your topic, including books, magazine and newspaper articles, encyclopedia entries, pamphlets, and other works that examine, analyze, or report facts. Leslie Webster used several books, reference works, and articles as secondary sources of information to complete her paper.

Primary sources are the original materials about which secondary sources are written, including novels, short stories, plays, poems, letters, journals, government documents, surveys, reports of experiments, and interviews. Leslie used a primary source when she viewed and reported on a television commercial in her paper.

Using primary sources puts you in direct contact with the raw material from which your paper will develop. Through this contact your own analysis can become an integral part of your research paper.

48c Gather information and prepare a working bibliography.

When you have decided on a topic, you will be ready to start gathering information about it. Most of your research data will probably come from the reference books, general books, and periodicals available in your college or community library. Systematically investigate each of these three major sources to establish a preliminary bibliography for your paper.

A working bibliography helps you determine whether your chosen topic is researchable in your library. It helps you keep track of the available sources you need to seek out. Finally, the working bibliography provides a handy source of information you will need for evaluating your sources during the writing stage, for citing sources in your text, and for completing your list of works cited.

1. Keep your working bibliography on index cards.

The working bibliography is most conveniently kept on 3-by-5-inch index cards, with a separate card for each source you consult. To find the source easily or for reference if you need the work later, record the library call number in the upper-right-hand corner. List the essential information about the source in standard bibliographic form, as explained in the next section.

2. Follow standard bibliographic form.

Recording your sources in standard bibliographic form will provide a complete and handy guide when you later use them in your text and complete a Works Cited list.

Bibliographic formats vary not only among colleges and universities but also among disciplines. They all, however, have the same intent — to encourage you to include the information a reader needs to check your sources. The following are several standard works that include guidelines about bibliographic form:

> *The Chicago Manual of Style.* 13th ed. Chicago: U of Chicago P, 1982.
>
> Turabian, Kate L. *A Manual for Writers of Term Papers, Theses, and Dissertations.* 4th ed. Chicago: U of Chicago P, 1973.
>
> *CBE Style Manual.* 5th ed. Bethesda: Council of Biology Editors, 1983.
>
> Gibaldi, Joseph, and Walter S. Achtert. *MLA Handbook for Writers of Research Papers.* New York: Modern Language Association, 1984.
>
> *Handbook for Authors.* Washington: American Chemical Society, 1978.
>
> *Publication Manual of the American Psychological Association.* 3rd ed. Washington: APA, 1983.
>
> *Style Manual for Guidance in the Preparation of Papers.* 3rd ed. New York: American Institute of Physics, 1978.

At the top of the facing page is a sample bibliography card for Leslie Webster's paper on credit cards.

The forms presented in this list follow the guidelines of the Modern Language Association and the *MLA Handbook* (1984), which it publishes. But before beginning to record bibliographic information,

```
                        332.76
                        G131c

        Galanoy, Terry. Charge It!
        Inside the Credit Card
        Conspiracy. New York:
        Putnam's, 1980.
```

check with your instructor about the format you should follow for your research paper. American Psychological Association (APA) guidelines are discussed on pages 340–43. Then carefully follow the handbook, taking care during the final typing of your paper to use the spacing and punctuation shown in the illustrations. Also be sure to notice how bibliographic form, the form you will use in your Works Cited list, differs from in-text citation form. (See parenthetical citation, pp. 334–40.)

General Books

BOOK WITH ONE AUTHOR

Galanoy, Terry. *Charge It! Inside the Credit Card Conspiracy*. New York: Putnam's, 1980.

TWO BOOKS WITH THE SAME AUTHOR

Veblen, Thorstein. *The Theory of Business Enterprise*. New York: NAL, 1958.

———. *The Theory of the Leisure Class: An Economic Study of Institutions*. New York: Mod. Lib., 1934.

BOOK WITH MORE THAN ONE AUTHOR

Meyer, Martin J., and Mark Hunter. *How to Turn Plastic into Gold: A Revolutionary New Way to Make Money and Save Money Every Time You Buy Anything — with Credit Cards.* 2nd ed. New York: Farnsworth, 1974.

Goldman, Bruce, Robert Franklin, and Kenneth Pepper. *Your Check Is in the Mail: How to Stay Legally and Profitably in Debt.* New York: Workman, 1974.

[For a book with two or three authors, use either of these forms. For a book with more than three authors, cite the first author's name followed by "et al.," the abbreviation for the Latin *et alii*, "and others," as the following example shows.]

Young, Ralph A., et al. *Personal Finance Companies and Their Credit Practices.* New York: Nat. Bur. of Econ. Res., 1940.

BOOK WITH A CORPORATE AUTHOR

Credit Research Foundation. *Credit Management Handbook.* 2nd ed. Homewood: Irwin, 1965.

BOOK WITH A LATER EDITION

Meyer, Martin J., and Mark Hunter. *How to Turn Plastic into Gold: A Revolutionary New Way to Make Money and Save Money Every Time You Buy Anything — with Credit Cards.* 2nd ed. New York: Farnsworth, 1974.

BOOK IN MORE THAN ONE VOLUME

Kroos, Herman E., ed. *Documentary History of Banking and Currency in the United States.* 4 vols. New York: Chelsea, 1969. [Always include the total number of volumes, placing this information between the title and the publishing information.]

BOOK REPRINTED OR REPUBLISHED BY A DIFFERENT PUBLISHER

Marshall, Alfred. *Money, Credit and Commerce.* 1929. New York: Kelley, 1960.

BOOK IN A SERIES

McCleod, Robert W. *Bank Credit Cards for EFTS: A Cost-Benefit Analysis.* Research for Business Decisions 14. Ann Arbor: UMI, 1979.

BOOK WITH AN EDITOR

Levine, Sumner N., ed. *The 1982 Dow Jones–Irwin Business and Investment Almanac*. Homewood: Dow–Irwin, 1982.

BOOK WITH TWO EDITORS

Colton, Kent W., and Kenneth L. Kraemer, eds. *Computers and Banking: Electronic Funds Transfer and Public Policy*. New York: Plenum, 1980.

BOOK WITH AN AUTHOR AND AN EDITOR

Kohns, Donald P. *Credit and Collections*. Ed. Harland E. Samson. Cincinnati: South-Western, 1980.

BOOK WITH AN INTRODUCTION, FOREWORD, OR AFTERWORD

Bishop, James, and Henry W. Hubbard. *Let the Seller Beware*. Introduction Betty Furness. Washington: National, 1969. [When citing the book's author.]

Furness, Betty. Introd. *Let the Seller Beware*. By James Bishop and Henry W. Hubbard. Washington: National, 1969. v–xi. [When citing the author of the book's introduction, foreword, or afterword. Include page references — in this instance, lowercase roman numerals.]

BOOK THAT HAS BEEN TRANSLATED

Von Mises, Ludwig. *On the Manipulation of Money and Credit*. Trans. Bettina Bien Graves. New York: Free Market, 1978.

BOOK THAT INCLUDES A REFERENCE TO ANOTHER WORK

Manso, Peter. *Mailer: His Life and Times*. New York: Simon, 1985. [See indirect sources, p. 339. The citation identifies McClure as the source of the quotation, but Manso's book, which quoted McClure, is listed in Works Cited.]

SELECTION FROM AN ANTHOLOGY, COLLECTION, OR CRITICAL EDITION

Lawrence, D. H. "The Rocking-Horse Winner." *Literature: An Introduction to Fiction, Poetry, and Drama*. Ed. X. J. Kennedy. 3rd ed. Boston: Little, 1983. 297–307.

Howe, Irving. "Henry James and the Millionaire." *Tomorrow* 9 (1950): 53–55. Rpt. in *The American*. By Henry James. Ed.

James W. Tuttleton. New York: Norton, 1978. 442–45. [If the cited work is a previously published article or essay, also identify the original publication, the publication date, and the inclusive page numbers followed by the publication facts of the book in which it was reprinted, as illustrated in this entry for a Norton Critical Edition.]

AN ANONYMOUS BOOK

The Times Atlas of the World. 7th ed. New York: New York Times, 1985. [If the work cited has no author's name on the title page, begin the entry with the title and alphabetize by the first word other than an indefinite or definite article.]

Periodicals

UNSIGNED ARTICLE IN A MAGAZINE

"Getting Off the Credit Treadmill." *American Educator* May 1981: 21–24.

SIGNED ARTICLE IN A MAGAZINE

Small, Linda Lee. "Credit Cards: What You Should Know Now." *McCall's* Mar. 1981: 76 + . [If a month and day are cited, begin with the day and abbreviate the month except May, June, or July. For example, 25 Mar. 1982. When citing an article not printed on consecutive pages, type only the first page number and a plus sign.]

ARTICLE IN A JOURNAL WITH CONTINUOUS PAGINATION

Kent, Richard J. "Credit Rationing and the Home Mortgage Market." *Journal of Money, Credit and Banking* 12 (1980): 488–501. [*Continuous pagination* means that a publication numbers its pages continuously through an entire volume composed of several issues. For instance, if the first issue in a volume ends on page 85, then the second issue will begin on page 86.]

ARTICLE IN A JOURNAL WITH SEPARATE PAGINATION

Dreyfus, Hubert L. "What Expert Systems Can't Do." *Raritan* 3.4 (1984): 22–36. [*Separate pagination* means that a publication numbers its pages separately for each issue of a volume, always beginning with page 1. Most such publications will have an issue number as well as a volume number. In this example, *3* is the volume number and *4* is the issue number.]

UNSIGNED AND SIGNED NEWSPAPER ARTICLES

"Four Big Banks Post 3rd-Quarter Operating Gains." *Wall Street Journal* 20 Oct. 1982, sec. 1: 5.

Abramson, Rudy. "Economic War Being Won, Reagan Says." *Los Angeles Times*, 26 Sept. 1982, Orange County ed., sec. 1: 5. [If the city of publication is not part of the newspaper's name, include it in brackets after the name: *Daily Pilot* [Costa Mesa, CA]. Newspaper citations sometimes require the inclusion of particular editions — evening, morning, city, election, county.]

LETTER TO THE EDITOR

Gay, Jill. Letter. *Progressive* May 1985: 7.

UNSIGNED AND SIGNED EDITORIALS

"Magic Words for Colleges." Editorial. *Los Angeles Times* 3 May 1985, sec. 2: 6.

Birnbaum, Norman. "The Center Holds." Editorial. *Nation* 1 June 1985: 660–61.

Encyclopedias

UNSIGNED ARTICLE FROM AN ENCYCLOPEDIA

"Credit." *Encyclopaedia Britannica: Micropaedia.* 1982 ed. [Volume and page numbers are not required for an article appearing alphabetically in an encyclopedia.]

SIGNED ARTICLE FROM AN ENCYCLOPEDIA

Baird, Robert N. "Credit Card." *Encyclopedia Americana.* 1981 ed. [Encyclopedia articles are sometimes signed only with the author's initials, which are usually identified in the index or the front of a volume.]

Other Sources

UNSIGNED AND SIGNED PAMPHLETS

Bank Fact Book. Washington: American Bankers Assn., 1978.
Beach, Richard. *Writing about Ourselves and Others*. Urbana:
NCTE, 1977. [Cite a pamphlet as you would a book. In this
example, the publisher, National Council of Teachers of English, appears on the MLA list of acceptable shortened publishers' name, and so the abbreviation NCTE is used. The American Bankers Association in the above example does not appear
on this list.]

GOVERNMENT PUBLICATION

United States. Board of Governors of the Federal Reserve System. *Federal Reserve Bulletin* 9. Washington: GPO, 1982. [Begin
with the name of the government. The abbreviation *GPO* is
used for Government Printing Office, the agency responsible
for printing most U.S. government materials.]

UNPUBLISHED DISSERTATION

Williams, Edward Cameron. "Some Effects of State-Imposed
Consumer Finance Rate Ceilings." Diss. U of North Carolina,
Chapel Hill, 1982.

UNPUBLISHED DISSERTATION LISTED IN *Dissertation Abstracts* OR
Dissertation Abstracts International

Williams, Edward Cameron. "Some Effects of State-Imposed
Consumer Finance Rate Ceilings." *DAI* 42 (1982): 5229A. U of
North Carolina, Chapel Hill.

FILM AND VIDEO TAPE

Roll Over. Dir. Alan J. Pakula. IPC Films, 1981. [Begin with the
film title, followed by the director, distributor, and year of
release.]
Sakharov. Video cassette. Dir. Jack Gold. Prism, 1984. [After the
title, insert the words *video cassette*, followed by the director,
distributor, and year of release.]

TELEVISION OR RADIO PROGRAM

Good Morning America. ABC. KABC, Los Angeles. 4 Oct. 1985.
   [After the title, include the network, local station, city, and the
   date of broadcast.]

PLAY

Hay Fever. By Noel Coward. Dir. Robert Fryer. Ahmanson Theater, Los Angeles. 8 Apr. 1983. [In addition to the basic information, also give the theater, the city, and the date of the
   performance.]

RECORDING

Eliot, T. S. *The Waste Land and Other Poems.* Caedmon, TC 1326,
   1971. [After naming the manufacturer — Caedmon in this
   example — include the catalogue number.

INTERVIEW

Rossiter, John. Personal interview. 12 Dec. 1985.

LECTURE OR ADDRESS

Ruiz, Armando. Lecture. Psychology 100 class meeting. El Cam-
   ino College, Torrance, 2 Oct. 1985.
Kübler-Ross, Elisabeth. "Life, Death, and Transition." Church of
   Religious Science. Huntington Beach, 28 June 1985.
[Include the title of the lecture if you know it; if you do not
know the title, use a descriptive label as the first example illustrates.]

CARTOONS

Arno, Ed. Cartoon. *New Yorker* 24 June 1985: 39.

48d Read for a tentative thesis and working outline.

When you have set up a working bibliography (usually about fifteen
sources for a college paper), you will be ready to examine your
research materials more closely. Your first efforts should be directed
toward preliminary reading and establishing a tentative thesis and
working outline.

Preliminary reading consists of skimming the most promising materials in your bibliography to give yourself an expanded overview of the topic. You should gain a more detailed sense of the scope and complexity of the topic and a familiarity with the kinds of information you will compare and analyze during the research process. Work quickly by using tables of contents and indexes to locate information. At this point, take notes only for general information about the topic. Once you have explored enough material, you will start to form an idea (or sharpen an already existing one) of the central point you want to develop in your paper.

1. Develop a tentative thesis statement.

Begin to develop a tentative thesis statement, no more than one or two sentences, that presents and limits your topic. The tentative thesis may actually change during further research or in the writing stage of the paper, but at this point it will add focus and organization to your research. Leslie Webster's preliminary reading revealed two major ideas about credit cards — that they had advantages and disadvantages in the way they affected society and that their future use is uncertain. She decided to include these ideas in her research paper, so she formulated the following as a *tentative* thesis statement:

> Credit cards seem to have advantages and disadvantages, and their future is doubtful.

2. Develop a working outline.

Your preliminary reading and your tentative thesis statement should aid you in establishing a working outline for the paper. Like everything you have done so far, the working outline need not be in permanent form; it is an early guide, a flexible blueprint to aid you in organizing your research, arranging your ideas logically, and making sure you have not left out any important aspects of your topic. The working outline may simply state the tentative thesis and then list supporting ideas. Leslie's working outline was roughly organized around the divisions of her tentative thesis.

> Credit cards seem to have advantages and disadvantages, and their future is doubtful.

Advantages
— Credit cards are available and widely accepted; that is, well established.
— There is a history of credit card use in American society — people feel comfortable using credit cards.
— Credit cards provide a convenient way to pay for goods and services.
— Some credit cards create a sense of prestige for those who possess them.

Disadvantages
— Wide credit card use generates extra costs for goods and services, especially for those who use cash.
— Hidden costs of credit cards are high.
— Wide use of credit cards may fuel inflation.
— Undisciplined use of credit cards leads some consumers into bankruptcy.
— Credit counseling services are being created to advise people about credit card abuse.
— Credit card users tend to spend more on purchases.

Future of credit cards
— Many predict the wide use of "debit cards," a more sophisticated credit card.
— Debit card use demands advanced technology to develop interlocking credit systems.
— The development of global data banks would threaten individual privacy and could be dangerous in the hands of governments.

Notice that the outline need not be complete at the outset. At this stage, it is useful in roughly charting the direction the paper may finally take and in pointing out the research that still needs to be done.

48e Take detailed notes.

For this step in the research process, you will need to use note cards for recording information and your own observations as you read. The most convenient note cards are 4-by-6-inch index cards, which can be easily distinguished from the smaller 3-by-5-inch bibliography cards you have been keeping. The larger note cards also allow more room for note taking, are more durable than loose slips of paper, and can be more easily organized than notebook entries.

Using your working outline headings as categories, and adding others as needed or as your reading suggests them to you, first skim and then read closely all your sources, taking notes and analyzing information as you proceed. Be sure to include the author and the page number for each item of information you record on a note card (other necessary data are already recorded on your bibliography cards). Use a separate card for each note, even if two notes are in the same category or from the same source. The following sample note card shows how Leslie Webster summarized one of her source's comments.

The preceding note card presents a summary of information from an original source. In summarizing, you condense an original statement to a brief sentence or two phrased in your own words. You leave out less important ideas and include useful ideas, taking care not to distort the essential meaning of the source. The source of Leslie Webster's summary note appears at the top of the next page.

> Credit cards as big business
>
> Galanoy 42
>
> Credit cards accounted for $55 billion of spending in 1979. People spent more because credit cards had given them a potential $260 billion more to spend – on credit purchases.

The bank card helps create inflation in two ways. First, the cards allowed $55 billion to be spent on credit during 1979; $55 billion of money other than cash and checks, which was added to the economy. Two-thirds of that created money was being borrowed and financed and was not offset by immediate cash payment. Second, with over a total of $260 billion available for spending on all cards, everyone could become a big spender. People were no longer limited to what cash they had, what checks they could write.

> *–Terry Galanoy, Charge It! Inside the Credit Card Conspiracy*

In addition to summarizing, note taking generally includes three other methods: paraphrase, direct quotation, and quotation and paraphrase combined. In paraphrase, you adapt the language and ideas of the source to your own style of expression without losing the content and flow of the original. (See acknowledging sources, p. 333.) With direct quotation, you record the exact language and punctuation of the original, condensing or altering them by following the rules for using brackets and ellipses. (See ellipsis mark, p. 166; brackets, p. 170.) To combine quotation and paraphrase, you structure the note's language and content to suit your needs, but you must be scrupulously careful not to distort the meaning of the original.

The sample cards on pages 328 and 329 show the different uses and methods of taking notes. They are based on the same passage, quoted above, that Leslie Webster summarized. Since research material can be used for different purposes in a paper, each card is titled with the purpose it might serve. Of course, Leslie would not have created all these cards for her paper; they are presented here to illustrate different ways of handling research material. Here are some guidelines for the use of quotations and paraphrases.

1. Handle quotations with care.

Any time you quote the exact words of a source, you must place quotation marks around the quotation and cite your source. (See bibliographic form, p. 315; acknowledging sources, p. 333.) Separate, ordinary single words need not be treated as a quotation, but put quotation marks around any unusual single word or any groups of

PARAPHRASE CARD

> Credit cards vs. cash and checks
>
> Galanoy 42
>
> The $55 billion spent with credit cards in 1979 was money circulated in addition to cash and checks, and ⅔ of that amount was being borrowed and financed. Also the $260 billion available credit power allowed people to spend more, regardless of the cash or checks they had to back up their purchases.

QUOTATION CARD

> Credit cards and inflation
>
> Galanoy 42.
>
> "The bank card helps create inflation in two ways. First, the cards allowed $55 billion to be spent on credit during 1979.... Two-thirds of that created money was being borrowed and financed and was not offset by immediate cash payment. Second, with over a total of $260 billion available for spending on all cards ... [consumers] were no longer limited to what cash they had."

Credit cards and debt

Galanoy 42

Two-thirds of the created $55 billion credit dollars spent in 1979 "was being borrowed and financed and was not offset by immediate cash payment." With $260 billion available from credit cards, everyone could become a big spender.

words–phrases, sentences, or short paragraphs. You can integrate the quoted material into your own sentence structure.

> Many parents feel they must "teach, preach, and bribe a morality of money" or watch their children grow confused in today's materialistic world.

You can attribute the quotation to a speaker with a phrase such as *he said, she commented, the president remarked,* or *the report stated.*

> Barbara Long said, "Parents today must teach, preach, and bribe a morality of money into their children."

You can introduce a quotation with a sentence followed by a colon. (See colon, p. 155.)

> No one has a clearer understanding of the role of parent in a material world: "Parents today must teach, preach, and bribe a morality of money into their children."

Quote accurately and sparingly. Give the reader only enough quoted material to convey and support your ideas. Be careful, however, not to distort the original or quote out of context. Use quotation only when the original language is needed for its effectiveness or authority. A paragraph or a whole paper that consists of no more than a series of quotations shows that the writer has not understood the material well enough to synthesize his or her own ideas with those of sources.

2. Paraphrase with effectiveness and fairness.

Paraphrase when you express a source's ideas in your own language. Good paraphrasing is true to the original sense, but it is not simply a translation of the original into different words. Merely altering the original will not result in a fair or effective use of paraphrase. Note the differences in the following examples of poor and good paraphrasing.

ORIGINAL

With their use so widespread, it seems hard to believe that the bank credit cards as we know them today got started barely a decade ago when four California banks jointly issued a single card that became known as "Master Charge." Each bank agreed to honor the sales slips submitted by merchants who had joined any of the bank plans.

– *Glen Walker*, "Credit Where Credit Is Due"

POOR
PARAPHRASE

The use of the bank cards as we know them today is so common that believing they actually began hardly ten years ago — when four banks in California issued the first "Master Charge" card — may be difficult. The banks all agreed to accept sales slips from merchants who subscribed to their card organization.

BETTER
PARAPHRASE

Surprisingly, the common bank card of today began less than a decade ago when four California banks issued the first Master Charge card. They agreed to honor any card receipts from merchants belonging to their new program.

The second example shows that a paraphrase should be more

concise than its source, without distorting ideas. The poor paraphrase does little more than twist the syntax of the original, making the information more difficult to comprehend. Like a quotation, a paraphrase must be followed by adequate citation of its source. (See bibliographic form, p. 315; acknowledging sources, p. 333).

48f   Revise the thesis and outline.

After completing the reading and note taking for your paper, you probably will have changed your conception of the paper's content and organization. At this point you will start to revise your thesis and then your outline. Begin by sorting the note cards by topic and then arrange them in a way that parallels your tentative outline. This process will show whether you have adequate material to support the points in your outline. Once the sorting is completed, evaluate your tentative thesis and working outline with an eye for revision. Then begin to rearrange the note cards and rework the tentative thesis to fit the concept you see emerging from the material you have collected.

After reading and taking notes, Leslie Webster found that in her tentative thesis the terms *advantages* and *disadvantages* seemed too objective for the information she had found. She also decided her assumption that the future use of credit cards is doubtful was completely wrong. In fact, she discovered that credit cards were growing in popularity and that no creditable source expressed a fear for the loss of individual privacy. All this led her to revise her tentative thesis.

TENTATIVE THESIS	Credit cards seem to have advantages and disadvantages, and their future is doubtful.
FINAL THESIS	The availability and convenience of credit cards are both a blessing and a curse, but the cards will continue to grow in popularity.

After sorting the cards and revising her thesis, Leslie also found that her outline needed substantial revision. She decided to begin with a brief history of credit cards because she had a great deal of useful information in that area. Also, a discussion of credit card history was the logical place to begin because she was ending her paper with comments on the future use of credit cards. Consequently, the history of credit cards would be an entire section, whereas in the tentative outline she had listed it under "advantages" to support the conclusion that consumers had become comfortable using credit cards. Following are the first sections of the tentative outline and the revised outline.

TENTATIVE OUTLINE	REVISED OUTLINE
Advantages	*History*
— Credit cards are available and widely accepted; that is, well established.	— Prior to 1950 America had only gasoline credit cards.
— There is a history of credit card use in American society — people feel comfortable using credit cards.	— In the 1950s and 1960s millions of cards were issued.
— Credit cards provide a convenient way to pay for goods and services.	— By the 1980s nearly half of all American families used cards.
— Some credit cards provide a sense of prestige for those who possess them.	— Success of credit cards
	— Credit cards are readily available.
	— Credit cards are a convenient way to buy goods and services.
	— Some credit cards create a sense of prestige for those who possess them.

Once Leslie completed this stage of the revision process and arranged her notes according to the revised organization — that is, according to the headings of the revised outline — she was ready to develop the final outline by following the formal outline form. (See final plan for essay, p. 287.) Leslie's formal sentence outline is on pages 353–55, preceding her research paper. If you compare the formal outline to the tentative and revised outlines, you will see how much more information she included and how she rephrased the sentences for accuracy in the formal outline.

48g Write the first draft.

You can begin writing your paper at any point in the outline, perhaps writing the middle paragraphs before the introductory and concluding paragraphs. Leslie, for instance, began writing her research paper at the point she felt was most interesting — the section dealing with the future of credit cards. She then wrote the section covering the economic disadvantages of credit cards. She postponed the introduction until last because she could not decide how to begin. The appropriate introduction occurred to her while she was watching a television commercial for Arco, a major gasoline company. At that point she had already written two-thirds of her paper, but she was alert, as a good researcher is, to information that might fit into her project.

48h Acknowledge your sources.

Acknowledging sources for your paper lends it authority and credibility as well as providing readers with information to locate your sources for themselves. In addition, the value of your paper's content and your own integrity as a writer depend to a significant extent on how fairly you make use of ideas from other sources. Whenever you are indebted to any source for a quotation, for a summary or paraphrase, or for a particular line of reasoning or explanation, you must acknowledge that indebtedness. Any failure to give credit for words or ideas you have borrowed from others is **plagiarism**. Done consciously or not, plagiarism in any form is the same as stealing, punishable in most colleges by immediate failure or even dismissal from the school. Plagiarism most often results from inattention and a too-casual attitude toward giving credit for what one takes from another. You can avoid this serious breach of ethics by scrupulously rechecking your note cards during and after the writing stage to make sure you have used and acknowledged all your sources accurately.

MLA Documentation Style

Give credit to your sources by acknowledging them in brief parenthetical citations. Traditionally, the Modern Language Association (MLA) recommended that sources be acknowledged in notes identified consecutively by numbers throughout the text and placed either at the bottom of appropriate pages in footnote form or at the end of the paper in endnote form. Now the MLA recommends that sources be acknowledged within parentheses placed directly in the text. In this new system of parenthetical citation, numbered notes, though rarely necessary, serve only to identify supplementary or explanatory comments. (See p. 340.)

Parenthetical Citations: MLA Style

Use parenthetical citations to acknowledge quotations (except for common sayings or well-known quotations), summaries, paraphrases, the opinions of others, lines of thinking you adopt, and statistics. In short, use parenthetical citations whenever you borrow information that is not commonly known or believed, especially by people generally acquainted with your subject. Do not provide parenthetical citations for facts or common knowledge, such as that hydrocyanic acid is a colorless, poisonous liquid or that Abraham Lincoln was the sixteenth president of the United States.

Because a parenthetical citation must always designate a specific entry alphabetically listed in Works Cited, the information in the citation must clearly direct a reader to that entry. Usually, but not always (see examples below), the author's last name and a page reference are enough to identify the source and the specific location from which you have borrowed material.

> First, in 1950, came the Diners Club card, originally honored at only twenty-two restaurants and one hotel in New York City (Galanoy 62).

Page references never include *p.* or *pp.* If you are referring to several consecutive pages, join the page numbers with a hyphen — for example, (Galanoy 123–28). When referring to two or more individual pages in one citation, use commas to separate them — for example, (Galanoy 12, 23, 129).

Keep parenthetical citations as concise as possible so that the interruption in your text is minimal. You are only required to give enough information to guide a reader to the specific source you have fully identified in Works Cited. If you have integrated into your text any information that should be included in the parenthetical citation, such as the author's name, you need not include that in the citation.

> Wilson Bryan Key has taken the mystery from subliminal-advertising discussions. He claims to have found subliminal messages in vodka ads (99).

To keep your paper as readable as possible, insert parenthetical citations before a period or comma as close to the borrowed material as possible and outside quotation marks, if you are directly quoting a source.

> In her 1979 essay collection *The White Album*, Joan Didion sounds confused by random violence and personal terror (15–20), but by 1982 its meaning has become clear to her, "I came to understand, in a way I had not understood before, the exact mechanism of terror" (*Salvador* 21).

If the borrowed material is set off from the text, the parenthetical citation follows the final punctuation. (See quotation marks, p. 159.)

> In contrast to great art works, Oates sees literary criticism as a refined form of communication between writer and reader. She writes,
>
>> If the greatest works of art sometimes strike us as austere and timeless, with their private music, as befits sacred things, criticism is always an entirely human dialogue, a conversation directed toward an audience. (2)

To acquire skill in accurately acknowledging your sources in parenthetical citations, study their use in Leslie Webster's paper (pp. 351–387) and review the following examples, paying close attention to the details of form and punctuation.

ENTIRE WORK

At times you may wish to acknowledge an entire work rather than a specific part of the work. In this case, include the author's name in the text rather than in a parenthetical citation. Since the reference is to a work in general, you are not required to cite a page number.

> Peter Brooks's analysis of plot and plotting is established on basic psychoanalytic principles.

PART OF AN ARTICLE OR OF A SINGLE-VOLUME WORK

When you refer to specific passages or when you quote directly from a work, you must give the relevant page reference in the parenthetical citation.

> Campbell's point is stunningly clear, "Communication is not confined to radios, telephones, and television channels. It occurs in nature, wherever life exists" (67).

> Most people spend more time picking a car than they do a doctor and hospital (Mathisen 63–64), but obviously you can't kick tires in a doctor's office and if you attempted the equivalent in a hospital — laying your foot into a $600,000 CAT scanner — you would get some very nasty looks indeed.

If another author listed in Works Cited has the same last name as the one you are acknowledging, give the first name as well as the last — for example, (Lawrence Sanders 34).

For a work with two or three authors, give all the last names. If, however, there are more than three authors, give one last name followed by *et al.* — for example, (Scholes et al. 28–29).

If you have more than one work by a single author listed in Works Cited, give the title or a shortened version after the author's name — for example, (Barthes, *Images* 12–13).

MULTIVOLUME WORK

In the parenthetical citation for a multivolume work, include the volume number followed by a colon, a space, and then the page reference — for example, (Kroos 1: 210–15). If you refer to an entire volume in general rather than to specific pages, place a comma after the author's name and include *vol.* — for example, (Kroos, vol. 1). If you place the information in your text, write out *volume* and the numeral — for example, "Kroos's volume 1 covers the first . . . ." Use arabic numerals rather than roman numerals to indicate volume numbers.

> "Feeling-toned complexes" were defined by the early psychiatric community as "failures to react" (Jung 8: 93).

> At first the prose is groping, unsure of its footing, but midway through the work sharp portraits of avant-garde artists emerge (Nin, vol. 1).

WORK LISTED BY TITLE

For a work alphabetized by title in your Works Cited, use the title or a shortened version of the title in the parenthetical reference. To make tracing the reference easier for your reader, begin the citation with the word by which the work is alphabetized. If you are acknowledging a one-page article, omit the page reference.

> A debit card, according to MasterCard's president Hogg, "looks like a credit card but works like a check" ("Now It's the No-Credit Card").

> The *Planning Commission Handbook* clearly states that land development is not the landowner's god-given right, but is a privilege granted by a public agency (31–32).

WORK BY A CORPORATE AUTHOR

Because the names of corporate authors are often long, identify them in your text and cite the specific page reference in the parenthetical citation. When necessary, you may offer a shortened version of the name in the parenthetical citation.

> The Commission on Post-Secondary Education in California states that remedial education in the University of California and State University systems has dramatically increased (5–10).

FICTION, POETRY, DRAMA, AND THE BIBLE

When citing the Bible and other literary works available in more than one edition, include the appropriate unit — that is, chapter, book, scene, line. In general, use arabic numerals rather than roman numerals in citing volumes or divisions of a work. Roman numerals may be used in citing acts and scenes of a play.

For a novel, give the page number first, a semicolon and space, and then the divisions, using appropriate abbreviations with periods.

> Politics, the undercurrent of the novel, sweeps Julien from one extreme to another. Nowhere is this more evident than in the description of the king's visit to Verrières (Stendhal 115–26; pt. 1, ch. 18).

For extended works of poetry give the division reference first, followed by the line reference. Use a period with no space to separate the two. Do not give a page reference.

> Antenor described Odysseus's power as a powerful orator: "But when he let the great voice go from his chest, and the words came/ drifting down like the winter snows, then no other mortal/man beside could stand up against Odysseus" (Homer 3.221–23).

If the poem is short or not divided into books or cantos, give only the line reference. When acknowledging only line numbers, use *line* or *lines* in the citation, but after you have established that the numbers designate lines, use only numbers.

> "For the Anniversary of My Death" begins with the suggestion that after death the soul starts a journey through time "Like the beam of a lightless star" (Merwin, line 5). The poem ends with Merwin's affirmation of concrete experience, behind which lies the mystery of existence.
>
> > As today writing after three days of rain
> > Hearing the wren sing and the falling cease
> > And bowing not knowing to what. (11–13)

For a play give the act, scene, and line references, using periods without spaces to separate the divisions. You may use roman numerals in citing acts and scenes.

> The imagery of futile battle is also found in the "To be, or not to be . . ." soliloquy (Shakespeare 3.1.56–89).

For the Bible give the book title, chapter, and verse, using periods to separate the divisions. Within the parenthetical citation (but not in the text itself), you may abbreviate a book title, using a period to end the abbreviation — for example, "Gen." for *Genesis*, "Rev." for *Revelation*.

> In the opening verses of the Book of Job (1.1–5), Job appears to have fulfilled the blessing that God had bestowed on humankind when Adam and Eve were created, "Be fruitful, multiply, fill the earth and conquer it" (Gen. 1.28).

INDIRECT SOURCES

Whenever possible, draw your material from an original source, but at times you will need to rely on an indirect source for information. For instance, you may need to use someone's published account of what another person has said. When you do quote or paraphrase from an indirect source, you must indicate in the parenthetical citation that you have done so by putting *qtd. in* ("quoted in") before the acknowledgment of the source, unless, of course, you have clearly indicated in your text that you are relying on an indirect source.

> Poet Michael McClure claims Mailer had a strong belief that he would only be listened to if he were irreverent. When people asked Mailer to moderate his irreverence, he would say, "Hey, I *feel* irreverence, and there's truth in the irreverence" (qtd. in Manso 281).

TWO OR MORE SOURCES IN A SINGLE PARENTHETICAL CITATION

To acknowledge more than one source in a single citation, cite each work as you normally would but separate the citations with a semicolon and a space.

> Whenever we open another novel, we embark on an adventure in which we have a chance to become a new person in the sense both that we can assume the imaginary role the writer thrusts at us and that we can reformulate ourselves by discovering what had previously seemed to elude our consciousness (Gibson 265; Iser 294).

Acknowledging Sources: MLA Style **339**

When multiple references in a single citation would be too long, acknowledge them in a note instead. (See explanatory notes below.)

Explanatory Notes: MLA Style

Explanatory notes have a limited use in the MLA's system of documentation. Notes are used to offer definitions, provide translations, make comparisons between sources, or generally furnish information not strictly pertinent to the immediate discussion in the text. (See explanatory notes on p. 383.)

Identify notes in your text by numbering them consecutively throughout with raised arabic numerals. The numerals correspond to notes appearing either in footnotes at the bottom of the page or on a page titled "Notes" placed at the end of the paper before Works Cited. (See p. 383.)

TEXT REFERENCE

Complex computers will keep track of everyone's "money," crediting and debiting records as each person earns credit from another's account or spends it from his or her own. [4]

NOTE

[4] For a discussion of the major concerns and implications of debit cards and the "cashless society," see Colton, Kent W., and Kenneth L. Kraemer, eds. *Computers and Banking: Electronic Funds Transfer Systems and Public Policy*. New York: Plenum, 1980.

APA Documentation Style

The American Psychological Association (APA) style of documentation is frequently used in courses in psychology and other social sciences. Although all documentation styles require essentially the same information, each has its own conventions of arrangement, punctuation, and abbreviation.

As you study the following examples of APA in-text parenthetical citations and reference listings, notice carefully the order in which information is given, the use of punctuation and capitalization, and spacing between items.

Only the most frequently encountered situations are illustrated here. For a comprehensive guide, consult the *Publication Manual of the American Psychological Association.* 3rd ed. Washington: APA, 1983.

Parenthetical Citations: APA Style

The APA style begins with the last name of the author and the date of publication. For some citations, these two items of information are the only ones necessary, but page references should be added when you present a direct quotation or refer to specific information rather than general concepts.

AUTHOR AND DATE ONLY

Today, in their wallets and purses, Americans carry millions of plastic credit cards, which they use to buy everything from groceries to blue-chip stocks (Small, 1981). [For general reference only the author's last name and date of publication appear in the citation. Notice that no title is given for any APA in-text citation if the author's name is known. A reader can find the title in References.]

DATE ONLY

Linda Lee Small (1981) estimates that Americans carry over 500 million plastic credit cards, which are used to buy everything from groceries to blue-chip stocks. [When the author's name is given in your text, only the date of publication is given in the citation.]

AUTHOR, DATE, AND PAGE

Although welcomed and used by almost everyone, the credit card is also becoming for many people a symbol of costly affluence, "the agent of debt, of spending addiction, of inflation, of loss of both privacy and freedom" (Galanoy, 1980, p. 35). [For direct quotations, include the page number. Use "p." for *page* and "pp." for *pages*.]

A WORK BY SEVERAL AUTHORS

First citation:

Often credit cards are issued even to applicants without a bank account, good credit history, or regular employment (Goldman,

Franklin, & Pepper, 1974, p. xiii). [Include last names of all authors the first time you cite a work. Use "&" for *and*.]

Second and later citations:

(Goldman et al., 1974, p. 23). [Substitute "et al." for all but first author's name in later citations.]

UNSIGNED ARTICLE

A spokesperson for Arco admitted that the customers who had been "paying cash were, in effect, subsidizing those buying on credit . . ." ("No More," 1982). [Use a shortened version of the title to identify an unsigned source. The full title is given in References.]

References: APA Style

In APA style, the works cited are listed at the end of the paper in a section titled "References." If you are using APA guidelines, notice the conventions of punctuation, capitalization, abbreviation, and the order in which information is presented.

BOOK WITH ONE AUTHOR

Galanoy, T. (1980). *Charge it! inside the credit card conspiracy*. New York: Putnam's. [Use the initial only for the author's first name. Only the first word of the title is capitalized; other words are lowercase unless they are proper nouns.]

BOOK WITH MORE THAN ONE AUTHOR

Meyer, M. J., & Hunter, M. (1974). *How to turn plastic into gold: a revolutionary new way to make money and save money every time you buy anything — with credit cards* (2nd ed.). New York: Farnsworth. [List all authors. Use "&" for *and*.]

BOOK IN MORE THAN ONE VOLUME

Kroos, H. E. (1969). *Documentary history of banking and currency in the United States* (Vol. 4). New York: Chelsea House.

BOOK WITH AN EDITOR

Levine, S. N. (Ed.). (1982). *The 1982 Dow Jones–Irwin business and investment almanac*. Homewood, IL: Dow Jones–Irwin.

SIGNED ARTICLE IN A MAGAZINE

Small, L. L. (1981, March). Credit cards: what you should know now. *McCall's*, p. 76. [Do not use quotation marks or underline to indicate article title. Use "p." for *page* and "pp." for *pages*.]

UNSIGNED ARTICLE IN A MAGAZINE

Credit causes inflation. (1981, May 10). *Forbes*, p. 65.

UNSIGNED ARTICLE FROM AN ENCYCLOPEDIA

Credit. (1982). *Encyclopaedia Britannica: Micropaedia.*

48i   Finish the final draft.

After you have completed the first draft, put your paper aside for a day or two if possible. This will give you a chance to return to it with a fresh approach. Reread the entire draft carefully several times and at least once aloud to listen for missing transitions or awkward constructions. Watch for careless grammar, spelling, or punctuation mistakes. More important, examine the content to see that you have kept to your thesis, provided ample evidence to support the assertions in your topic sentences, and integrated your own views with those of your sources to create a balanced whole. As a last step, check your citations and list of works cited to be sure they are correct in form, content, and punctuation.

Guidelines for Typing the Research Paper

Formats for research papers vary, and you should follow those suggested by your instructor. The following guidelines are the most common practices for typing the title page, outline (if required), quotations, citations, and Works Cited. Unless otherwise noted, all typing should be double-spaced. Additional information is covered in Chapter 49.

Title page. Center the title about a third of the way down the page. Do not underline it or put quotation marks around it unless the words would also be underlined or quoted in the paper's text. Ten lines down from the title, center the word *By*, capitalized, followed by your name, centered, two lines beneath it. Ten lines down from your name, type the course title, the instructor's name, and the date, each on a separate line.

Your instructor may prefer that you follow the 1984 MLA guidelines, which recommend not using a separate title page. If you do, present the identifying information on the first page of the text. Place your name, your instructor's name, the course number and section, and the date on separate double-spaced lines in the upper-left-hand corner of the page, observing the same left-hand margin as the text. Double-space below the date and center your title on the page; then quadruple-space between your title and the first line of the text.

Outline. Begin on a separate page, with the word *Outline* one inch from the top. Two lines below, type the thesis statement, followed by the outline itself. Use standard outline form, with the various topic levels successively indented and numbered with roman or arabic numerals and small or capital letters as required. The outline included in Leslie Webster's research paper begins on page 353.

Quotations. Indent quotations requiring more than four typed lines ten spaces from the left margin, double-spacing throughout. Do not put quotation marks around an indented quotation. When quoting two or more paragraphs, indent the first line of each paragraph three additional spaces. The parenthetical citation appears at the end of the indented quotation, following the period or other end mark. Shorter quotations, not indented, should be enclosed in double quotation marks.

Other punctuation marks. Brackets are made on the typewriter with the slash mark (/) and the underscore (raised for the top of the bracket). You can write brackets in neatly by hand with a pen if you wish. The typed dash is two unspaced hyphens (--) typed without space on either side.

Notes. Starting on a new page, center the word *Notes* one inch from the top, with the first entry two lines below the title. Indent the note number, raised, five spaces from the left margin, leaving one space between the number and the first word of the note. All subsequent lines of the note begin at the left margin. Double-space within each note and between notes.

Works Cited. Type the words *Works Cited* on a new page, one inch from the top. Begin the first alphabetized entry at the left margin two lines below the title. Remember to cite the first author with the last name first; subsequent authors' or editors' names are typed in regular order; subsequent lines of an entry are indented five spaces. When you have more than one work by the same author, the name is not repeated; instead, type three hyphens followed by a period. Double-space throughout.

After you have typed the final version of the paper, carefully read it again for errors in typing. Include, in order, an outline, the text of the paper, the notes, and the list of works cited. Other sections, such as an appendix or glossary, if they are included, precede the notes. When you are satisfied that you have written and typed the paper in a manner that fulfills your own goals and the requirements of your instructor, make a photocopy to keep for yourself and present the original copy to your instructor.

48j Questions and answers from research writers.

Research is a complicated activity that raises innumerable questions. The following are a few of the most common questions asked of instructors, with answers that may help your own research.

1. I want to write a paper arguing against child abuse. I know a lot has been written on the subject. Is that a good choice for a topic?

First, who would argue against you in favor of child abuse? That is, are there two sides to the question? A topic like this might lead you into a discussion of morality, which would be too philosophical for a research paper. You would need to concentrate on arguing a thesis about some unsettled issue or problem related to child abuse, such as prevention, laws, or some aspect that needs further investigation.

2. I have scoured all the reference indexes and the card catalogue, but I have found only three sources on my topic. Where do I go next?

There are other places to look — pamphlets, other libraries, or some community sources of information. At this point, though, you may need to reconsider your topic. It might be too recent an idea, and perhaps not much has been written about it. Or it might be so narrow or so broad that it is not identified in any indexes or catalogues. Try to redefine the topic along the lines of other ideas you have seen in sources, or develop another topic entirely.

3. A book I need for my research is not available in any convenient libraries. Is there any way for me to get the book or find out about it?

Yes. You can ask the school's librarian to get the book on interlibrary loan from another college or university. Or use the *Book Review Digest* or a similar guide to find a comprehensive review of the book. You may find the information you need in the review, which itself will serve as a research source for your paper.

4. For my paper I want to interview a friend who was once arrested for drunk driving. Is that a good primary source?

Use interviews with careful judgment. In most cases the people you choose to interview should be in a position to speak objectively and knowledgeably about the subject. They should also be able to give you insights or information not available in regular, published sources — that is why you have to interview them instead of using the library. If your friend or anyone else fits these broad criteria, use that person as a source to reaffirm or illustrate the information you obtain from more broadly available and recognized authorities.

5. I couldn't find a date of publication, but I found a copyright date. How do I cite that date?

In most cases, the copyright date and date of publication are treated as the same. If both are supplied, give the publication date. If only the copyright date is included, give that date.

6. My book source was published in three different cities. Which do I cite?

Cite the first city or place listed.

7. Can I use a political rally poster I found on my campus bulletin board as a reference source?

Yes. Any item from which you get information is a legitimate source for research.

8. Out of a total of twelve sources so far, six of my preliminary works cited are from one major magazine. Is that all right?

Your list of works cited should be balanced in terms of both the categories of sources you use (books, magazines, and so on) and the specific publications within each category. Any one source or category of source presents a limited point of view. Try to include as many viewpoints as possible, although you do not have to ignore any source.

9. My paper topic has a long and fascinating history. How much of that history should I include?

Include only as much history as is relevant to your thesis or to a current situation. For the most part, keep histories to a minimum, focusing your paper's content on the development and support of your thesis statement.

10. I need to use a number of technical terms in my paper. What is the best way to make sure my reader understands them?

For general college papers, keep technical vocabulary to a minimum. Recast technical terms in familiar wordings whenever possible. Refer, for example, to *microdont creatures* as "small-toothed animals." Or use descriptive phrases to define unfamiliar terms: "Such pinnate, featherlike leaves are common to these plants." Finally, ask yourself if the terms are really necessary for you to convey your point. If not, leave them out.

11. My paper seems like a paragraph-by-paragraph summary of my sources. Where do my own ideas come in the paper, and how do I express them?

Your thesis statement is *your* most important opinion in the paper and should control the organization and presentation of material. Be sure your thesis is truly an argumentative one, and then argue it as you would any idea you believe in and can support with ample evidence. Take time to review both your sources and your own attitude toward what you have learned in your research. Compare, evaluate, define, make concessions, analyze, and comment just as you would in any thorough discussion.

12. I find little information that needs to be cited in my ten-page paper. Are three or four citations enough for a paper this long?

Probably not. A lack of citations results from inadequate use of your research data or weak support of your own arguments. Very likely, too, you have not always given credit to your sources as you should. Review the paper's contents to be sure that you have offered supportive evidence from your research and that you have properly cited the sources of that evidence.

13. I remember hearing something about using abbreviations like *ibid.*, *loc. cit.*, and *op. cit.* for subsequent references. What are they for?

These abbreviations formerly were used for specific kinds of subsequent references. Scholarly groups and universities, however, have generally abandoned them in favor of the simplified method described in this chapter.

14. One major work I read disagrees with several others on an issue important to my paper. How do I handle this situation?

Give careful consideration to the authority and evidence of all sources, and base your discussion on what you feel is a fair representation of the case. Provide an explanatory note to inform your readers of the differing opinion and to explain briefly the rationale for your presentation in the paper.

15. I have a magazine title with no capital letters. Do I write the title that way in my paper?

Capitalize according to standard practices. Commercial, popular writing often emphasizes visual impact over traditional uses of punctuation. Unless you know that such variations are part of the author's purpose, capitalize and punctuate all titles in accordance with standard rules.

16. Where can I find sources other than those in my library?

Go to public agencies, departments within your school, businesses, local museums, and special-interest groups or societies. Such groups usually have pamphlets or other material available for the public as well as special libraries devoted to their particular activities.

17. I heard a lecture in one of my classes and took notes on it. Is that a good primary source?

Yes. Be sure your notes are accurate. For your paper, cite the lecturer, place, and date, and identify it as a lecture.

18. After writing the first draft, I can tell that my paper is shorter than the length required by my instructor. What should I do?

Check to see that you have supplied ample support for your thesis and that you have discussed all relevant aspects of the topic. Is the issue you are writing about really as simple as you have made it sound? Is your thesis too narrow or obvious to allow much discussion and presentation of evidence? Perhaps you need to broaden your subject. If time allows, ask your instructor to look over the draft with you to see what parts might need fuller treatment.

19. I have cited six works in my paper, but I want to include in my list of works cited all twelve sources I listed in my working bibliography. Is that right?

No. Only the works cited in the text of your paper should appear in your Works Cited. Distinctions are sometimes made between works *cited* and works *consulted*, but if you have not used a source for other than common background information, it should not be cited.

20. How should I refer to an author? Should I use the full name or Dr., Mr., Mrs., Miss, or Ms.?

Simply use the full name without titles the first time you refer to an author. Then use only the last name through the rest of the paper. If, however, you have more than one author in your Works Cited with the same last name, use the first and last name throughout the paper.

Examining a Sample Research Paper

Leslie Webster's research paper, which follows, illustrates the advice given in this chapter. She followed the style for citations and list of works cited given in the *MLA Handbook*. The comments accompanying the paper identify specific points about the research paper format as well as some of the decisions Leslie made while writing.

1. Title page format: Leslie centered all the lines in the width of the title page. She began by typing the title of her paper a third of the way down from the top. About ten lines below the title, she typed *By*, skipped two lines, and typed her name. Ten lines below her name, she typed information her instructor requested: course title, instructor's name, and the date, all double-spaced.

1.

Credit Cards: A Popular Blessing or Curse?

By

Leslie Webster

English 100

Ms. Jeanette McGlynn

March 18, 1980

2. Outline format: Leslie placed her final outline, which many instructors ask students to include with the research paper, on the page after the title page. You can leave the outline pages unnumbered or number them with small roman numerals. If you number the outline pages, omit the number on the first page and number the second page *ii*. Type your last name before the page numbers. Center the heading *Outline* an inch below the top of the page.

3. Two lines below the heading *Outline*, type the final thesis statement, as Leslie did, so that the instructor can see how the parts relate to the thesis.

4. Although some instructors request topic outlines, which are written in phrases without periods following them, Leslie's instructor requested a sentence outline.

5. The main divisions of the outline (indicated by large roman numerals) refer to the main divisions of the paper, and all subdivisions refer back to their respective main divisions. Leslie's outline reflects the logical development of the thesis statement — that is, the movement from the past to the present and the future.

2.

3.

Outline

Thesis: The availability and convenience of credit cards
are both a blessing and a curse for consumers, but
the cards will continue to grow in popularity.

  I. The credit card's brief history demonstrates its
enormous impact on consumer buying habits.

    A. Prior to 1950 credit card purchasing was limited
to gasoline and department store items.

    B. In the 1950s and 1960s banks, retail chains, and
other corporations issued millions of credit
cards.

4.

    C. By the 1980s, more than half of all American fami-
lies were regularly using credit cards.

  II. The rapid success of credit cards is easily understandable.

    A. For most Americans, even those marginally quali-
fied, credit cards were readily available.

5.

      1. In the 1960s hundreds of banks mailed out thou-
sands of unsolicited cards to customers.

      2. Department stores issued credit cards to teen-
agers.

    B. Many card holders receive tangible as well as in-
tangible benefits from credit cards.

Sample Research Paper **353**

       1. Credit cards offer a convenient way to buy al-
          most anything in our society.

       2. Credit cards offer some card holders a sense of
          prestige.

III. The wide use of credit cards creates some economic
    disadvantages.

    A. The extra costs added to goods and services be-
       cause of wide use of credit cards are unfair to
       cash customers.

    B. Inflation is partly fueled by credit cards.

    C. Uncontrolled spending leads many card holders into
       bankruptcy.

 IV. In the future, the use of credit cards will continue
    to spread.

    A. Debit cards will be the next evolutionary stage.

    B. We may be heading toward a cashless society.

Sample Research Paper **355**

6. To begin, Leslie attracts her reader's attention by using a vivid example from a television commercial. The example introduces the paper's topic — credit cards — and some of the issues with which the paper is concerned.

7. Parenthetical citation acknowledges the source for the specific figure of 500 million plastic charge cards.

8. Once again Leslie adapts part of a quotation to her own sentence structure and content, identifying the quoted words as representing a particular point of view other than her own. Notice how she adapted the quotation as it appeared on her note card.

Credit card impact
Galanoy 35
The bank card, today, "is still the
agent of debt, of spending addiction,
of inflation, of loss of both privacy
and freedom."

9. Quotation marks identify these familiar phrases. Notice that Leslie does not include source citations for such common words and phrases.

6. A recent television commercial shows a wrecking crane smashing a giant gas credit card into a shower of frag-ments, as a background voice announces, "Arco is smashing credit cards to bring you lower prices on gasoline!" The voice then goes on to explain, "Arco's decision to stop taking all types of credit cards will mean lower gasoline prices because it eliminates the cost of processing credit purchases" ("Arco"). Meanwhile, other major gasoline com-panies try to lure more consumers to their pumps by offer-ing to redeem Arco cards with new competitor-brand cards. Thus the war for customers and profits goes on, with the same sure-fire bait: the much-loved credit card.

7. Today, in their wallets and purses, Americans carry over 500 million plastic credit cards, which they use to buy everything from groceries to blue-chip stocks (Small 76). Once limited to business executives or wealthy patrons, buying with credit cards has become a familiar part of life in this country. Although welcomed and used by almost everyone, the credit card is also becoming for many people

8. a symbol of costly affluence, "the agent of debt, of spending addiction, of inflation, of loss of both privacy and freedom," as one opponent of the bank credit card has described the situation (Galanoy 35). At a time when the

9. phrase "Charge it!" has become a part of Americans' vocab-ulary, so the phrases "credit limit," "minimum monthly

10. Having used the first paragraph as an introduction, Leslie continues her general introductory comments on the impact of credit cards, leading the reader into the final sentence of the second paragraph, which states the paper's thesis.

11. Leslie follows the topic sentence with a discussion and examples of the history of the credit card. Note 1 is an explanatory note in which Leslie defines what she means in her paper by *credit card*.

12. Since Leslie found the history of the credit card in a variety of sources, she did not feel obliged to indicate the sources for the preceding comments because her instructor did not expect a citation for commonly accepted information. Some instructors, however, require citations of representative sources for such common facts. Be sure to check with your instructor to determine whether you should identify your sources for information like this.

13. Leslie credits the source that gave her the specific, not commonly known or reported facts about the Diners Club beginnings.

payment," and "past—due amount" have added to their worries.

10. Indeed, the availability and convenience of credit cards are both a blessing and a curse for consumers, but the cards will continue to grow in popularity.

11. While buying on credit has a long tradition in society, the credit card itself is a child of the twentieth century.[1] The first mass—marketed charge card appeared in 1914 when the Texaco Corporation first offered its customers a gasoline charge card. The convenience of charging gasoline purchases caught on, and gasoline credit cards were soon familiar to drivers all over America. Local department stores began following the lead of the gas companies, and by the 1930s the idea of buying on credit appealed to consumers everywhere, from the corner grocery store to Wall Street. The 1929 stock market crash and the depression that followed slowed the popularity of credit buying for a while in the United States; then World War II restrictions on spending and on the production of goods held down any regrowth in purchasing without cash.

12. The proven success of the credit card led to a credit card boom in the next two decades. First, in 1950, came the Diners Club card, originally honored at only twenty-

13. two restaurants and one hotel in New York City (Galanoy 62). A year later came the first multipurpose retail card,

14. Leslie cites sources for the figures on credit card use, which are not generally known.

15. The topic sentence organizes Leslie's two-part discussion: credit card availability and advantages.

issued by New York's Franklin National Bank. In the years following, other banks, including the huge Bank of America, also began issuing cards. Despite some early problems and losses, by the mid–1960s the bank credit card business in the United States was going strong. American Express and Carte Blanche also joined the competition; BankAmericard and Master Charge were launched and well on their way toward dominating the entire card industry; and retail chains like Sears were issuing their own cards to millions of their customers. By 1970 the great success of BankAmericard's slogan "Think of it as money" had helped

14.   convince most people that saying "Charge it" was the same as paying immediate cash. By the end of 1979, there were 125 million credit cards in circulation, and plastic money had purchased $179 billion worth of goods and services in that year alone (Galanoy 56). In the 1980s more than five billion credit card transactions take place every year, with over half of American families using two or more credit cards to make purchases (Bequai 9).

15.   The great success of the credit card is easy to understand given its availability and its numerous advantages. During the biggest boom in the bank and retail card business in the 1960s, hundreds of banks simply mailed out thousands of unrequested, valid cards to potential customers across the United States. A 1971 federal law makes

16. Leslie develops an extreme example to illustrate her claim that credit cards are easy to acquire once a person has met minimum criteria and supports her claim with note 2. She supports her next claim with an example from a different source. In both cases, she felt the examples needed to be given although they were not an essential part of the immediate discussion; therefore, she placed them in notes.

17. The broadening of the discussion to include children and teen-agers reflects Leslie's thoroughness in investigating the extent to which credit card use has penetrated our buying habits.

that practice illegal, and it also forbids a card-offering company from refusing to issue a credit card on the basis of sex or marital status, race, color, religion, national origin, or income from public assistance. Virtually everyone with a bank account, regular employment, and a good

16. credit history can receive a credit card,[2] and in many cases even these criteria do not have to be met fully.[3] In fact, once a person is established in a community, cards are easy to attain, even hard to avoid. Retail stores routinely mail applications to newlyweds, parents of new babies, and new homeowners; meanwhile, banks send "preapproved" or "prescreened" Visa and MasterCard applications to people whose economic data show them to be credit-worthy.

This does not mean, however, that only affluent

17. adults use credit cards. Children and teen-agers may be the future's big users of credit cards. Already, studies show that about one in thirty-five teen-agers uses credit cards, and the number is growing ("Credit Cards"). Though they do not like to, many major department stores such as Macy's, Bloomingdale's, and I. Magnin allow minors to make purchases on their parents' charge cards if one parent has given authorization. In some stores, teen-agers can have their own credit cards. Mervyn's, a West Coast retail chain, for example, offers high school juniors and seniors

18. After a series of commonly known credit card purchase items, Leslie cites the sources for the less-known facts about using credit cards for bail and for purchases up to the established equity of a card holder's home.

who hold part-time jobs a "Merv Account." The teen-agers
are allowed a sixty-dollar credit limit and are required
to make minimum payments of five dollars a month on any
outstanding balances. So far, the program has proved successful with both teens and parents. Mervyn's believes it
is improving its general customer relations with the Merv
Accounts as well as educating young people in buying and
budgeting with what will no doubt be the economic currency
of their future, the credit card ("Teenagers" 346-48).

These teen-agers are learning exactly what their parents have learned: Credit cards offer a number of tangible
and intangible benefits. Most obvious is the fact that
credit cards make buying and paying convenient. Virtually
everything in our society is already available or soon
will be available through credit cards, from the usual
luxury expenses like buying golf clubs or splurging on an
expensive dinner to paying one's taxes or posting bail in
Ohio (Griffin 2). Also, most bank cards grant their holders a $1500 or $2000 cash advance almost automatically at
any bank in the country; some cards, like Merrill Lynch's
Equity Access card, grant to their bearers a $10,000 <u>mini-</u>
<u>mum</u> credit line, with the maximum based on the appraised
value of the card owner's home ("Prestige Plastic"). For
others, the credit card is safer to carry around than cash

18.

19. Notice the use of a colon to introduce the list of examples.

20. Leslie uses double quotation marks for a direct quotation from her source. "Charge it," a quotation within a quotation, requires single quotation marks.

and certainly accepted in more places around the country
and the world than a personal check.

In addition, bank credit cards and most travel and
entertainment cards offer their holders a number of other
extras: travel insurance, business newsletters, wholesale
catalogues of gift merchandise, health club memberships,
car insurance, interest–earning savings accounts, and special investment plans for card owners and their families.
Such extras are not free, of course, but their easy availability makes the cards that provide them all the more
valuable. It is not unusual for one person to have several
of the same kinds of cards--two gasoline cards, four department store cards, one travel card and one entertainment card, and three bank cards, for example.

Besides these tangible benefits to having a credit
card, there is one other: prestige. Part of the credit
card's appeal in America has always been its suggestion of
wealth and respectability. As one woman explained, "I use
credit cards . . . because when I say 'Charge it,' it
gives me a charge. You know, you feel great. Important"
(Meyer and Hunter 9–10). In today's prestige–conscious,
credit–wielding society, however, sporting a credit card,
or even several, matters less than what kind of card you
keep. A hierarchy of prestige exists within each category
of credit cards--store cards, gasoline cards, bank cards,

Sample Research Paper **367**

21. Leslie alludes to events mentioned in the paper's opening, thus helping to unify the overall discussion. She combines paraphrase, ellipsis, and quotation to reduce the length of the original quotation, which she had recorded on a note card.

Cost of credit card buying
"No More Credit at the Pump" 56
"Those paying cash were, in effect, subsidizing those buying on credit since the cost of maintaining the credit system had to be added to the pump prices," said a spokesman.

22. Leslie uses an ellipsis mark to prevent the appearance that the quoted material in her paper was a complete sentence in the original.

23. Leslie adds a minor but relevant explanation in parentheses.

travel and entertainment cards. A card from J. C. Penney does not get the same respect as an I. Magnin card. Visa and MasterCard rank equally, but the snob appeal depends on which particular bank issues the card--the local one-branch savings and loan, a public giant like Bank of America, or a small elite bank like Banker's Fidelity Trust.

Do Americans really understand how much they are paying for all the convenience and prestige the credit card has made so accessible? When Arco abolished credit card accounts for gasoline, it eliminated a $73 million expense that it had passed along invisibly to its consumers in the form of higher gasoline prices. A spokesperson for Arco admitted that the customers who had been "paying cash were, in effect, subsidizing those buying on credit . . ." ("No More Credit"). Unfortunately, what was happening at Arco stations is just a small example of what is occurring every day across America. Because of the wide use and acceptance of credit cards, almost all types of goods and services cost more, and those who pay cash are paying the added cost for those who charge. This seems blatantly unfair, of course, but there is really little the cash customer can do about it. Although 1978 legislation finally allowed merchants to give up to a 5 percent discount on cash purchases (the practice had earlier been illegal, to prevent a surcharge from being added on to charge pur-

Sample Research Paper **369**

24. Leslie created the example to illustrate what a merchant might earn on a $5 credit card purchase, another way of maintaining the role of commenting writer amid all her research information.

25. Leslie inserts a word in brackets to keep the meaning of the quotation clear. She also uses ellipsis marks to transform the original quotation for easier use in her own sentence structure. Her note card appeared as follows:

Cost of credit card buying
Meyer and Hunter 21
"Anyone engaged in consumer [price]
protection is a hypocrite if he has a
credit card," Ralph Nader told the
National Commission on Consumer Finance.
"I won't have a credit card," he added
heatedly, "because it increases the cost of
things to everyone."

chases), most merchants do not or will not give the discount ("Posting New Reward" 58).

    The cost of credit might be a lot higher than most
people think. For bank cards, the most widely used of all
types, merchants have to pay between 1 and 5 percent for
24. each dollar charged. Thus, a $5 item, for example, may
bring the merchant only $4.75. Last year merchants in this
country paid $3 billion in credit card fees to bank card
issuers ("Posting New Reward" 59). These fees, like the
Arco fee mentioned earlier, were included in the prices of
everything merchants sold. Whether you used a credit card
last year or not, if you bought anything, you undoubtedly
paid part of that $3 billion.

    Are credit cards, then, contributing to inflation? It
certainly seems so. According to Ralph Nader, in an address to the National Commission on Consumer Finance,
25. "Anyone engaged in consumer [price] protection is a hypocrite if he has a credit card. . . . I won't have a credit
card . . . because it increases the cost of things to
everyone" (Meyer and Hunter 91). Worries about credit
spending being the cause of inflation may be the reason
the federal government moved to impose lower credit limits
on card issuers in 1980, for in the opinion of one money
expert:

        The more money people have, the more they are

Sample Research Paper **371**

26. Leslie uses a long, indented quotation introduced by a colon. Notice that the parenthetical citation is placed at the conclusion of the quotation, after the period.

27. This sentence represents the final form of the information from Leslie's quotation note card reproduced on page 326.

28. This paragraph offers an extended example, summarized from the single source Leslie cites. Leslie uses the dash for emphasis.

26.   going to spend. Credit cards are the easiest, quickest, and most unconscious way mankind has ever invented for spending money. Inflation is a natural fact in most world economies, but credit card inflation is an unmeasurable, invisible creature that can't be seen until it has grown beyond control. ("Credit Causes Inflation")

27. The $55 billion used to purchase goods with credit cards in 1979 was created money, about two-thirds of which was never backed by actual cash and so did not really circulate in the economy (Galanoy 42). As any economist would point out, too much money leads to higher spending, higher wages, and higher costs, all of which generate higher demands for money and credit.

      Some people, however, know how expensive the cards

28. really are because they found out the hard way. Steve Brinkley and his wife, Jane, for example, earned $40,000 a year between their two jobs; besides the mortgage on their new home and car payments to make every month, they also ran up staggering amounts of debts on their credit cards—all fourteen of them. For instance, their Sears credit card paid for the extra new fixtures they wanted in their kitchen, and until those were installed they ate at restaurants. In less than two months they rolled up a $2000 bill on Visa and MasterCard, all just for meals out. They

Sample Research Paper **373**

29. In this brief paragraph, Leslie shows that the specific example of the Brinkley's plight is not an isolated case. To make the point, Leslie combines information from the following paraphrase note cards recorded from two separate sources. Note that she revises the original wording of the paraphrase notes to blend with her finished sentences while accurately relating the facts from her sources (see p. 376).

were soon broke, paying monthly installments on one card
by borrowing on another ("American Way of Debt" 46).

Luckily, the Brinkleys finally sought credit counseling and began a slow climb out of debt. But quitting the
credit card habit was not easy. Besides their own addiction to credit, there were other temptations. Stores where
they had not charged anything for months sent cards saying
"We miss you" and offering them more credit. The Brinkleys
resisted these temptations, but they wondered if other
people were able to do so. "We know doctors, lawyers, ac-
countants, FBI agents," said Steve, "and they're all kit-
ing credit—getting $2,000 from American Express to pay
off Visa. We used to think that was what all young couples
do. They still think that way, and we can't help wonder-
ing—aren't some of them in the same mess we were in?"
("American Way of Debt" 47).

29. The answer is that many, in fact hundreds of thousands, are in the same position as the Brinkleys. At the
end of June 1982, consumer installment debt already totaled $331.85 billion, up more than 4 percent from the
year before ("Consumer Debt Increased"). An ever-increasing number of Americans, half a million of them in 1978—
more than twice the number in 1981—are daily slipping
into and declaring bankruptcy, with credit card bills a
major portion of their debts ("American Way of Debt" 47).

Sample Research Paper **375**

Personal cost of credit cards

"Consumer Debt Increased in June by $1.35 Billion" sec. 1: 3

Thousands are in debt beyond their means to recover. At end of June 1982, consumer installment debt totaled $331.35 billion. It was 4 percent higher than the year before.

Personal cost of credit cards

"The American Way of Debt" 47

Personal debt is reaching frightening levels. Half a million Americans in 1978 and more than twice that in 1981 are walking through the doors of bankruptcy courts. Credit card bills are a major part of their debts.

30. The topic sentence signals another shift in the paper's direction — that is, to the idea that credit cards are here to stay.

With so many Americans in debt, it ought to be clear that a profit is being made somewhere, and it is. Studies show that credit card buyers purchase an average of 23 percent more than cash shoppers ("Teenagers" 354), reason enough why most retail stores are so eager to give out charge cards to everyone they can. Other cards are proving so lucrative that they have become a major source of profits for the issuers. Two million people last year paid fifty dollars apiece for the privilege of carrying an American Express gold card, and more than half of the standard MasterCard and Visa cards, about 120 million altogether, carry fees of ten to twelve dollars per year, most of which is clear profit for the card-issuing companies ("Prestige Plastic"). When these figures are added to the fact that the $331.85 billion that consumers owe on installment paying nets 14 to 24 percent annual interest, it is not difficult to see why credit cards are not only a big business but also such a significant factor in the way Americans live.

30. Yet despite all the problems that may be attributed to them, credit cards are clearly destined to remain an influential and basic part of our economic future. Major cards like Visa, MasterCard, and American Express are already used worldwide, while in Europe, the Middle East, Africa, and the Orient, both international and domestic

31. The double quotation marks around *money* indicate that Leslie does not mean to use the word literally.

32. Leslie writes an effective conclusion by summarizing the major ideas in her paper and by adding her final remarks or analyses. Notice that Leslie ends with her own words. She could have used a quotation in the conclusion, of course, but as a commenting writer she wished to have the final word herself. Also notice that Leslie reworded her thesis statement for the final effect in the last few sentences of the paper.

credit cards are fast becoming as common as their United
States cousins. One new development in the cards, the debit card, will undoubtedly have widespread growth and influence in the next decade. A debit card, according to
MasterCard's president Hogg, "looks like a credit card but
works like a check ("Now It's No-Credit"). Such cards are
seen as the next giant step toward what has been called
"the cashless society": a debit-card-carrying culture in
which every exchange now made with cash or checks will be
made with a computer-oriented transfer of credit from the
buyer's account to the seller's, all by means of the buy-

31.   er's debit card. Complex computers will keep track of
everyone's "money," crediting and debiting records as each
person earns credit from another's account or spends it
from his or her own.[4]

     The instant payment that debit cards offer, however,

32.   does not mean the end of credit card buying. The debit
card will, if nothing else, simply allow us the same kind
of credit buying with one basic card instead of the half
dozen or so that many people carry around today. In that
way, too, credit can perhaps be better controlled, on both
the personal and the national level. The cost of credit or
debit buying will also be greatly reduced, thereby lower-
ing prices and inflation; and perhaps people might finally
mature in their use of "card money," avoiding the problems

generated by overspending with the credit card of today.
Until then, many of us will have all the woes that accompany the use of credit cards. But whether we see them as a
blessing or a curse, credit cards will continue to be
available and convenient, and the phrase "Charge it" is
not likely to disappear from the language any more than is
the little card that makes charging it possible.

33. Leslie begins the commentary notes on a new page and centers the title *Notes* one inch from the top.

34. Note 1 defines how Leslie will use the phrase *credit card* throughout the paper.

35. Notes 2 and 3 give further information relevant to the topic and refer the reader to the sources of their contents.

36. Note 4 refers the reader to a source that discusses the subject of debit cards more fully. Such references, when appropriate, reinforce the writer's authority by showing that he or she has done broad research on the topic.

33.

34.

Notes

[1] Credit cards are not all the same, of course.
Basically, four major types are now in use: travel and entertainment cards, bank cards, retail store cards, and
gasoline cards. In this paper, I use the term "credit
card" to mean all of these, or any card that allows for
purchases of goods or services on credit.

35.

[2] That is how the current credit card record holder,
Walter Cavanagh (who is also known as "Mr. Plastic Fantastic"), got his 1003 valid, all different cards, worth more
than $1,250,000 in credit (*Guinness* 354).

[3] For example, in 1974 New York welfare recipients
successfully demonstrated at Sears and at Korvette (a discount chain) to demand that they be given credit cards and
the right to make purchases on them (Goldman, Franklin,
and Pepper xiii).

36.

[4] For a discussion of the major concerns and implications of debit cards and the "cashless society," see Colton and Kraemer.

37. Leslie begins her list of works cited on a new page and centers the title *Works Cited* one inch down from the top.

38. Entries are listed alphabetically, and each begins at the left margin. Indent the second and all succeeding lines of an entry five spaces.

39. List unsigned articles or references alphabetically by their titles. Since the second item is a television commercial, the opening words of the commercial serve as a title. An ellipsis mark shows the omission of words.

40. Include subtitles and use a colon to separate them from the main titles.

41. Reverse only the first author's name for an entry with two or more authors. Place the abbreviation *eds.* for "editors" after the comma following the names.

37.

Works Cited

38. "The American Way of Debt." Time 31 May 1982: 46–49.

39. "Arco Is Smashing Credit Cards. . . ." Commercial.

CBS. 23 Sept. 1982.

40. Bequai, August. The Cashless Society: EPTS at the Cross-

roads. New York: Wiley, 1981.

41. Colton, Kent W., and Kenneth L. Kraemer, eds. Computers

and Banking: Electronic Funds Transfer Systems and

Public Policy. New York: Plenum, 1980.

"Consumer Debt Increased in June by $1.35 Billion." Wall

Street Journal 10 Aug. 1982, sec. 1: 3.

"Credit Cards." Changing Times July 1982: 56.

"Credit Causes Inflation." Forbes 10 May 1981: 65.

Galanoy, Terry. Charge It! Inside the Credit Card Conspir-

acy. New York: Putnam's, 1980.

Goldman, Bruce, Robert Franklin, and Kenneth Pepper. Your

Check Is in the Mail: How to Stay Legally and Profit-

ably in Debt. New York: Workman, 1974.

Griffin, Al. The Credit Jungle. Chicago: Regnery, 1971.

Guinness Book of World Records. New York: Sterling, 1981.

Meyer, Martin J., and Mark Hunter. How to Turn Plastic

into Gold: A Revolutionary New Way to Make Money and

42. For articles that are not printed on consecutive pages, use a plus sign to indicate that there are additional pages. (This article appeared on pages 141, 346–48, and 354.)

Save Money Every Time You Buy Anything--with Credit Cards. 2nd ed. New York: Farnsworth, 1974.

"No More Credit at the Pump." Newsweek 15 Mar. 1982: 56.

"Now It's the No-Credit Card." Time 29 Sept. 1980: 67.

"Posting a New Reward for the Cash Customer." Business Week 29 June 1981: 58-59.

"Prestige Plastic." Time 21 June 1982: 51.

Small, Linda Lee. "Credit Cards: What You Should Know Now." McCall's Mar. 1981: 76+.

"Teenagers and Credit Cards." Good Housekeeping Nov. 1981: 141+.

42

Manuscript Form, Business Letter, and Résumé

49 Manuscript Form

50 Business Letter Forms

51 Résumé Form

49 Manuscript Form   *ms*

Following standard manuscript form is a courtesy to the reader. Manuscript form is merely a convention that defies logical explanation, but to ignore proper form is to risk annoying a reader — one who might be grading a college essay you have submitted.

Materials

For handwritten papers use 8½-by-11-inch lined white paper with neat edges, not torn from a spiral notebook. Use black or blue ink — not green or red — and write on one side only. Skip every other line to make reading and correcting easier.

For typewritten papers use 8½-by-11-inch white typing paper. Do not use onionskin because it is flimsy; do not use erasable bond because it smudges. You may use correction fluid ("white out") to cover any typing errors you have made. Double-space between lines and type on one side only. Be sure that you have a fresh ribbon in the typewriter and that the keys are clean.

Computer printed manuscripts should be formatted to resemble typewritten pages. Use a letter-quality printer or a dot matrix printer in a letter-quality mode.

Unless otherwise directed, use a paper clip to hold the pages together. Many instructors do not like pages stapled together, and no instructor likes the upper-left-hand corner to have been dog-eared to hold the pages in place.

Margins

Leave margins of about an inch on all sides of the paper to avoid a crowded appearance. On lined white paper the vertical line indicates a proper left-hand margin. On most personal computers, justification of the right margin creates awkwardly spaced lines. Turn the right justification control off while formatting your paper on a computer.

Indentations

Indent the first line of every paragraph uniformly — one inch in a handwritten manuscript, five spaces in a typewritten one.

Paging

Place the proper arabic numeral (*2*, not *II*), without a period or parentheses, in the upper-right-hand corner of each page. You may omit the number on the first page, but if you choose to include it, center it at the bottom.

Identification

Include your name, instructor's name, course title and number, the date, and any other information your instructor requests. Place that information in separate double-spaced lines, beginning in the upper-left-hand corner of the first page. (See also the sample research paper, p. 351.)

Title

In handwritten papers on lined paper, place the title in the center of the first line and begin the first sentence three lines below it. In typed papers, double space below the date and center your title on the page. Begin the first sentence four lines below it. Capitalize the first and last words, any word that follows a colon, and all other words except articles, conjunctions, and prepositions of fewer than five letters. Do not underline the title or place quotation marks around it. If, however, the title of another work or a quotation is part of your title, underline or use quotation marks as appropriate. (See quotation marks, p. 155; italics, p. 186; capitals, p. 172.)

Bill Pozzi
Professor Dees
English 147
May 12, 1986

Creative Speculation in Science

Scientists and space engineers are engaged in a universe-wide search for "life as we know it" on other planets. No one can predict what such life forms will look like, but science fiction writers have speculated. They have created imaginary worlds populated by intelligent and mobile plants, giant andro-phagous (people-eating) insects, and other life forms lower or higher on the evolutionary scale than humans. Such worlds are fun to read about, but the serious work of science fiction, the creative exploration of human problems and possibilities, is done by writers who create humanlike beings--that is, humanoids, robots, and androids.

A humanoid has some recognizable human characteristics: in-telligence, mobility, and the ability to communicate complex messages. A humanoid may have more body parts than we have--two hearts, twelve eyes, several heads; it may be more beastly-- scaly skin, a furry body, a reptilian face; or it may not breathe oxygen or use water as its principal body fluid. These details do not matter. What is important is that a humanoid ex-

periences humanlike situations. L. Sprague de Camp's imaginary
planet Osiris, for example, is inhabited by highly emotional di-
nosaur people who have developed a capitalist economy.

1

---

50 Business Letter Forms

In a business letter, come to the point quickly and tell the reader exactly what you want. Be courteous but firm if the reason for writing warrants firmness. As in all writing, observe the conventions of grammar, usage, and punctuation, for faltering in these skills can damage not only the clarity of your letter but also your credibility.

Format

Type a letter on unlined paper. Use one side only, single-space between lines, double-space between paragraphs, and allow one-inch margins on the left-hand and right-hand sides.

Return Address Heading

Include your address (unless you are using stationery with your address printed on the top, which is called letterhead) and the date. Do not include your name. Put the return address heading in the upper-right-hand corner, allowing enough space above it so that the whole letter can be centered vertically.

Inside Address

Include the name, title, and complete address of the person to whom you are writing. Begin the inside address a few lines below the return address heading but on the left-hand side of the page.

Salutation

Place the salutation two lines below the inside address and two lines above the body of the letter. If you are not addressing a particular person, use a general salutation such as *Dear Sir, Dear Madam*, or *Dear Sir or Madam*. You may use the person's position — *Dear Dean of Instruction* — or the name of the company — *Dear IBM*. Use *Ms.* if you do not know the marital or professional status of a woman or if you know she prefers to be addressed as *Ms.* End the salutation with a colon.

Body

Begin the body of the letter at the left margin. Double-space between paragraphs to set them off.

Close

Start the close two lines below the last line of the body. Except for full block form (see next page), align the close with the return address heading. Typical closes include *Sincerely yours, Yours truly*, and *Sincerely*. Capitalize the first letter only. Follow the close with a comma.

Your Name

Type your name four lines below the close. (Any title you might have if it is appropriate, such as *Julie Crane, Senior class president,* may follow your name.) Write your signature in the space between the close and your typed name.

Further Information

Below your name at the left margin you may want to indicate additional information, such as *Enc.,* which means something is enclosed, or *cc: Tom Jenkins,* which means a copy of your letter is being sent to the person named.

Formats

Business letters follow one of three formats: full block, block, and semiblock. Full block is the most formal and is used with letterhead stationery. All parts of the letter, including the date and the first line of every paragraph, are flush with the left margin. In block format, illustrated by the sample letter on page 396, the return address heading and the close are moved to the right. In semiblock, the least formal format, the heading and the close are also moved to the right and the paragraphs are indented.

FULL BLOCK   **BLOCK**   **SEMIBLOCK**

SAMPLE BUSINESS LETTER IN BLOCK FORMAT

2701 Fairview Road
Costa Mesa, CA 92626
March 16, 1986

Patricia R. Webber
Educational Consultant
TechTron Learning Systems
4345 Sandburg Way
Irvine, CA 92715

Dear Ms. Webber:

I still have not received a schedule of the training seminars
TechTron will be offering during the summer. After our telephone
conversation last month, I decided that a week's training in the
uses of microcomputers will help round off the program in business that I will complete this June.

I am particularly interested in the Apple system and the software the Apple company offers. Will your staff cover the Apple
and its software—especially software that applies to accounting
procedures? I am also interested in learning about the word-
processing capability of microcomputers. Are they as reliable as
systems specifically designed for word processing? These are
just a few of the areas I hope a week's training will cover.

Right now I have no plans for the summer, but in the next three
weeks I must develop a schedule. In order to help me do that,
please send me a list of your courses as soon as possible.

Sincerely yours,

Robert K. Stouts

Robert K. Stouts

Envelope

Use an envelope that is the same width as your stationery and about one-third its height. In the upper-left-hand corner type your name and address. To the right of center type the addressee's name, title, and address, just as you did for the inside address. Fold the letter horizontally into thirds to fit it into the envelope.

```
Robert K. Stouts
2701 Fairview Road
Costa Mesa, CA 92626


                        Patricia R. Webber
                        Educational Consultant
                        TechTron Learning Systems
                        4345 Sandburg Way
                        Irvine, CA 92715
```

51 Résumé Form

A résumé should organize your qualifications for employment in an easy-to-read format. When you send a résumé to a prospective employer, be sure to include a cover letter to introduce yourself and to identify the position for which you are applying.

Although no standard form will cover all résumé writing, some general principles are useful to know. For instance, your résumé should be brief, no more than one or two typed pages, and to the point, giving only the information an employer needs to decide whether you are a viable job applicant. Remember that a well-written résumé will not necessarily get you a job, but it may get you a job interview.

Personal Data

In the upper right-hand corner, type your name, address, and a telephone number where you can be reached during working hours. Do not include information such as your age, marital status, race, religion, height, or weight.

Education

List all the schools you have attended since high school. Begin with the most recent and work backward. Include the years you attended, the degrees you received, and your area of study. If you did not receive a degree, type the number of credits you accrued. If courses you completed specifically relate to the job, mention them in your cover letter, but do not list them on the résumé.

Experience

List the jobs you have held. Include the company's name and address and identify the position you held. Follow with a brief description of your responsibilities, which can be written in fragments that begin with action verbs, such as "met," "conducted," "supervised," "directed." Arrange the positions you have held with the most recent first.

References

If your school has a placement office, keep all your letters of reference on file there. If it does not have a placement office, you have two options: (1) You may list three or four former teachers, community leaders, and employers who can vouch for your skills and character. Provide their names, addresses, and phone numbers. (2) You may type "Available upon request" under references and then provide a list of them if the prospective employer asks for them.

Additional Information

You might want to include additional information about activities or awards that relate to your career goals. Have you worked as a volunteer? Have you been a leader in campus activities? Have you received awards or academic honors? You may list these under the headings "Activities" or "Academic Honors," whichever title is appropriate.

>

Pamela Richards
22 Meadow Sweet Way
Irvine, CA 92715
(714) 786-7389

Education: University of California, Irvine
1986 to present, B.A. expected in June 1987
Major: Psychology with emphasis in group dynamics
Minor: Business Administration with emphasis in corporate decision-making processes

Saddleback College
1984-1986, 60 units
Major: General Education

Experience: July 1986-present
Freidenrich and Associates, 3 Upper Newport Plaza,
Newport Beach, CA 92648. Administrative Assistant.
Draft fundraising proposals, solicit investors and
donors, create and coordinate campaign strategies.

February-June 1986
Friends of Larry Agran, 7 Mann Street, Irvine, CA
92715. Campaign Coordinator. Organized volunteers,
supervised fundraising efforts, recorded contributions, created campaign materials.

Summer 1985
Kenny the Printer, 17931 Skypark Circle, Irvine, CA
92714. Production Assistant. Coordinated printing
schedules with advertising campaigns, designed bro-
chures and pamphlets, served in customer relations.

References: Placement Office
University of California, Irvine
Irvine, CA 92715

Glossaries

Glossary of Usage

Glossary of Grammatical Terms

Glossary of Usage

The entries in this glossary are words and phrases that frequently cause problems for inexperienced writers. Based on recent editions of dictionaries and usage guides, the suggestions for standard written English included in this glossary represent current practice among experienced writers. You should avoid using words and phrases labeled *nonstandard* and use entries labeled *colloquial* sparingly and with care. They are used primarily in informal speech and writing and, therefore, are usually inappropriate in college and business writing.

"Diction and Logic" offers guidelines for selecting appropriate words and phrases in your writing, and this glossary makes specific recommendations. It is necessarily brief, so you should keep a good dictionary by your side when writing and refer to it when you question the appropriateness of a word or phrase you wish to use.

a, an Use *a* before a consonant sound, *an* before a vowel sound.

| a history | a university | a one o'clock meeting | a C |
| an hour | an undertow | an orphan | an F |

aggravate *Aggravate* means "make worse." In writing it should not be used in its colloquial meaning of "irritate" or "annoy."

agree to, agree with *Agree to* means "consent to" a plan or proposal. *Agree with* means "be in accord with" a person or group.

ain't Nonstandard for *am not* or *aren't*.

all right *All right* is always two words. *Alright* is a misspelling.

all together, altogether *All together* means "in a group," "gathered in one place," or "in unison." *Altogether* means "wholly" or "completely." *They made the jungle trek all together rather than in small groups. I did not altogether approve of the plan.*

allusion, illusion An *allusion* is a reference to something. An *illusion* is a deceptive appearance. *Dr. Conn fills his lectures with classical allusions. Despite the hard facts, she clings to her illusion of true love.*

a lot   *A lot* is always written as two words. *Alot* is a common misspelling.

among, between   *Among* is used to refer to three or more people or things. *Between* is used with two people or things. *Half the treasure was divided between the captain and the ship's owner; the other half, among the crew.* Sometimes *between* is used with more than two if the relationship concerns individual members of the group with each other. *The treaty between the five countries guarantees access to deep water ports.*

amount, number   *Amount* refers to a quantity of something that cannot be counted. *Number* refers to things that can be counted. *A large number of saltwater fish requires an aquarium that holds a tremendous amount of water.*

an   See *a.*

and etc.   *Et cetera* (etc.) means "and so forth"; *and etc.*, therefore, is redundant.

and/or   A legalism that many people consider awkward in college and business writing.

anxious, eager   *Anxious* means "nervous" or "worried." *Eager* means "enthusiastically anticipating something." *I am eager to start the trip across the desert but anxious about the weather.*

anyone, any one   *Anyone* means "any person at all." *Any one* refers to a particular person or thing in a group. Similar definitions apply to *everyone, every one, someone, some one. Anyone with the price of the membership can join. Any one of the seniors might have started the brawl.*

anyplace   Colloquial for *anywhere.*

anyways, anywheres   Nonstandard for *anyway* and *anywhere.*

as   Avoid using *as* for *because, since, while, whether,* and *who. Because [not as] the firm is almost bankrupt, buying a computer is out of the question. We doubt whether [not as] they can continue.*

as, like   See *like.*

awful   An overused word for *bad, shocking, ugly.* Colloquially substitutes for intensifiers meaning "very" or "extremely."

awhile, a while   *Awhile* is an adverb. *A while* is an article and a noun. *Awhile,* therefore, can modify a verb but cannot serve as an object of a

Glossary of Usage   **403**

preposition. *After six hours on the road, they rested awhile. After six hours on the road, they rested for a while.*

bad, badly   *Bad* is an adjective and should be used in formal writing to modify nouns and as a predicate adjective after linking verbs. *Badly* should be used only as an adverb. *The doctor felt bad. The tenor sang badly.*

being as, being that   Colloquial for *because. Because* [*not Being that*] *the sun has risen each morning of your life, you may expect it to rise tomorrow.*

beside, besides   *Beside* means "next to." *Besides* means "except" and "in addition." *The older sister stood beside her father. Besides one stranger, only relatives were on the bus.*

between   See *among.*

bring, take   Use *bring* to carry something from a farther place to a nearer one. Use *take* to carry something from a nearer place to a farther one. *Take these pages to the printer and bring me yesterday's batch.*

bunch   *Bunch* should not be used to refer to a crowd or group of people or things. Reserve it to refer to things that grow fastened together, such as grapes and bananas.

burst, bursted, bust, busted   The verb *burst* means "fly apart," and its principal parts are *burst, burst, burst.* The past tense *bursted* is nonstandard. *Bust* and *busted* are considered slang; therefore, they are inappropriate in college or business writing.

can, may   *Can* indicates ability, and *may* indicates permission. Colloquially, *can* is used in both senses. *If I may use the car, I believe I can reach the store before it closes.*

center around   *Center on* is more accurate than *center around.*

climactic, climatic   *Climactic* refers to a climax. *Climatic* refers to climate.

compare to, compare with   *Compare to* means "regard as similar." *Compare with* means "examine for similarities or differences." *The boy compared his father's bald head to an egg. The investigator compared the facts of the Rineman case with the facts of the Billings incident.*

continual, continuous   *Continual* means "often repeated." *Continuous* means "unceasing" or "without a break." *My afternoons are continually interrupted by telephone calls. The waves lap continuously at the shore.*

404   *Glossary of Usage*

convince, persuade   Careful writers use *convince* when someone changes his or her opinion. They use *persuade* when someone is moved to take action. *The attorney convinced several students that capital punishment is immoral. The attorney persuaded several students to demonstrate against capital punishment.*

could of   Nonstandard for *could have.*

couple of   Colloquial for *a few* or *several.*

credible, creditable, credulous   *Credible* means "believable." *Creditable* means "praiseworthy." *Credulous* means "inclined to believe just about anything." *Hitchcock's fantastic stories are hardly credible; nevertheless, as a director he gets creditable performances from his actors regardless of whether the audience is credulous.*

criteria, data, phenomena   *Criteria* is the plural form; the singular form *criterion* is seldom used. *Criteria* is often used as a singular noun, but careful writers use it only in the plural sense. *The criteria were so ill phrased that they were hard to apply.* Both *data* and *phenomena* are plurals of the same kind for the singular *datum* and *phenomenon.* They should be treated in the same fashion. *New data suggest the drug is harmful. Today's unexplainable phenomena are tomorrow's scientific explanations.*

data   See *criteria.*

deal   Colloquial and overused for *bargain, transaction,* or *business transaction.*

differ from, differ with   *Differ from* means "be unlike." *Differ with* means "disagree."

different from, different than   *Different from* is idiomatic and widely accepted. *Different than* is acceptable when it precedes a clause. *An elephant is different from a mastodon. Paris was different than I had expected.*

disinterested, uninterested   *Disinterested* means "impartial." *Uninterested* means "bored" or "indifferent."

don't   *Don't* is a contraction of *do not* and should not be used for *does not,* whose contraction is *doesn't. Although the performance doesn't begin for an hour, I still don't think Bernice will be ready.*

due to   Many people object to the use of *due to* as a preposition that means "because of" or "owing to." *The class was canceled because of* [*not due to*] *low enrollment. Due to* is acceptable when used as a subject complement. In this position it usually follows a form of *be. His unpredictable behavior is due to alcohol.*

eager See *anxious.*

enthused Colloquial for "showing enthusiasm." The preferred adjective is *enthusiastic.*

etc. See *and etc.*

every which way Colloquial for *in every direction* or *in disorder.*

everyone, every one See *anyone.*

everywheres Nonstandard for *everywhere.*

exam Informal for *examination.*

expect Colloquial when used to mean "suppose" or "believe." *I suppose* [*not expect*] *the Reynolds clan is still squabbling about the settlement of the will.*

explicit, implicit *Explicit* means "expressed directly or precisely." *Implicit* means "expressed indirectly or suggested." *The threat was explicit —* "*I'll break your nose!*" *Although his voice was gentle, his body carried an implicit threat.*

farther, further *Farther* refers to actual distance. *Further* refers to additional time, amount, or other abstract matters. *I cannot walk any farther. Further encouragement is useless.*

fewer, less *Fewer* refers to items that can be counted. *Less* refers to a collective quantity that cannot be counted. *The marsh has fewer ducks living in it, but it also has less water to support them.*

finalize Avoid using *finalize* for the verb *complete.*

fine A weak substitute for *very well.*

flunk Colloquial for *fail.*

folks Colloquial for *parents, relatives,* or *people.*

former, latter *Former* refers to the first named of two things or people. *Latter* refers to the second of two named. *First* and *last* are used to refer to items in a series of three or more. *John and Bill are very successful; the former is a dentist, the latter a poet. Jogging, biking, and swimming require tremendous endurance; the last requires the most.*

further   See *farther.*

get   A common verb used in many colloquial and slang expressions: *Get hip, get wise to yourself, her prattling gets me,* and the like. Using *get* in such ways is inappropriate in college and business writing.

goes   Nonstandard when used instead of *says* or *said* to introduce a quotation. It should not be used to indicate speech. *He said [not goes] "Leave me alone."*

good, well   *Good* is an adjective; *well* is an adverb. *Dr. Hodge is a good golfer. He strokes the ball well. Well* should be used to refer to health. *You look well [not good]. Are you feeling well [not good]?*

had ought, hadn't ought   Nonstandard for *ought* and *ought not.*

half   *Half a* or *a half* is appropriate, but *a half a* is redundant. *We drank half a [not a half a] gallon of moonshine.*

herself, himself   See *myself.*

hisself   Nonstandard for *himself.*

hopefully   *Hopefully* means "with hope." *They prayed hopefully for the blizzard to stop. Hopefully* is used colloquially to mean "it is hoped" in place of *I hope;* however, *I hope* is preferred in college and business writing. *I hope [rather than hopefully] the blizzard will stop.*

illusion   See *allusion.*

implicit   See *explicit.*

imply, infer   *Imply* means "suggest." *Infer* means "conclude." *Irving implied that he had studied for the quiz, but I inferred that he was unprepared.*

in, into   *In* indicates a location or position. *Into* indicates movement or change. *Barbara is in the study with a clairvoyant, who is in a trance. I must go into Murkwood, but I don't want to fall into danger. Into* has also come to mean "interested in" or "involved in" something, which is an inappropriate use in college and business writing. *My brother is interested in [not into] restoring Victorian houses.*

individual, party, person   *Individual* should be used to refer to a single human being when expressing that person's unique qualities. *Each individual has a right to pursue his or her interests within the law.* When not stressing unique qualities, use *person*. *A romantic person will love the Austrian countryside.* Except in legal documents, use *party* to refer to a group. *Who is the missing person [not party]?*

in regards to   Nonstandard for *in regard to* or *as regards.*

infer   See *imply.*

into   See *in.*

irregardless   Nonstandard for *regardless.*

is because   See *reason is because.*

is when, is where   A common predication error in sentences that define. *"Bandwagon" is a propaganda device by which [not is when or is where] advertisers urge consumers to become one of the millions buying their products.*

kind, sort, type   These are singular words and take singular modifiers and verbs. *This kind of butterfly is rare in North America.* When referring to more than one thing, *kind, sort,* and *type* must be made plural and then take plural modifiers and verbs. *These kinds of butterflies are rare in North America.*

kind of, sort of   Colloquial when used to mean *somewhat* or *rather.* *The picnic was rather [not sort of] dull.*

lay   See *lie.*

learn, teach   *Learn* means "acquire knowledge." *Teach* means "dispense knowledge." *I must teach [not learn] the children better manners.*

leave, let   *Leave* means "go away." *Let* means "allow" or "permit." *Let [not leave] me finish the job. The firm should have let [not left] her resign.*

less   See *fewer.*

let   See *leave.*

liable   See *likely.*

lie, lay   These verbs are often confused. *Lie* means "recline," and *lay* means "place." In part, they seem to be confusing because the past tense of *lie* is the same as the present tense of *lay*.

lie ("recline")	*lay* ("place")
lie	lay
lay	laid
lain	laid
lying	laying

Lay (meaning "place") is also a transitive verb and as such takes an object. *Don't forget to lay the book on my desk. Today I laid the tile, and tomorrow I'll be laying the carpet. Lie* (meaning "recline") is intransitive and as such never takes an object. *The book lay on my desk for weeks. I can't waste time lying in bed; I've lain there long enough.*

like, as, as if, as though   *Like* is a preposition and introduces a prepositional phrase. *As, as if,* and *as though* usually function as subordinating conjunctions and introduce dependent clauses. In college and business writing do not use *like* as a subordinating conjunction. *The sky looks as if* [*not like*] *the end of the world is near.*

like, such as   When introducing a representative series, use *such as*. To make a direct comparison with an example, use *like. This decade has produced some powerful hitters in tennis, such as Borg, Connors, and McEnroe, but I want to play a game of strategy like Vilas.*

likely, liable   *Likely* is used to express probability. *Liable* is used to express responsibility or obligation. *She is likely to finish the project before the weekend. Mr. Wert is liable for his son's destructive behavior.*

lots, lots of   Colloquial for *a great deal, much,* or *plenty.*

may   See *can.*

may be, maybe   *May be* is a verb phrase, and *maybe* is an adverb meaning "perhaps."

may of   Nonstandard for *may have.*

media, medium   *Media* is the plural form of *medium*. Be sure to use plural modifiers and plural verbs with *media. These kinds of mass media — television, radio, newspapers — influence our emotional attitudes.*

might of   Nonstandard for *might have.*

most   Colloquial when used for *almost*.

must of   Nonstandard for *must have*.

myself, herself, himself, itself, yourself   These and other *-self* pronouns are reflexive or intensive — that is, they refer to or intensify a noun or another pronoun in a sentence. *The family members disagree among themselves, but I myself know how the inheritance should be divided.* Colloquially these pronouns often are used in place of personal pronouns in prepositional phrases. This use is inappropriate in college and business writing. *None of the team except you [not yourself] has learned to rappel.*

no way   Nonstandard for *no*.

nowhere near   Colloquial for *not nearly. Brytan's game is not nearly [not nowhere near] as good as Schrup's.*

nowheres   Nonstandard for *nowhere*.

number   See *amount*.

OK, O.K., okay   All are acceptable spellings, but avoid using them in college and business writing.

party   See *individual*.

people, persons   *People* refers to a collective mass and emphasizes faceless anonymity. *Persons* refers to individuals who make up the group and emphasizes separate identity. *People surged into the convention hall. Several persons angrily denounced the membership's reluctance to act.*

per   An English equivalent is usually preferable to the Latin *per. The firm pays $10 an [not per] hour. The plans were carried out according to [not per] Mary's instructions.*

percent (per cent), percentage   Both *percent* (often spelled *per cent*) and *percentage* refer to numbers and should only be used in actual references to statistics. Avoid using them to replace the word *part. The major part [not percent] of my trouble is caused by mismanagement. Percent* is always preceded by a number *(sixty percent; 45 percent)*, and *percentage* follows an adjective *(a major percentage)*. In formal writing *percent* should always be written out (not %).

person   See *individual*.

persons   See *people*.

persuade See *convince.*

phenomena, phenomenon See *criteria.*

plus Nonstandard for *moreover. Bancroft Enterprises has a fine economic future; moreover [not plus], it offers young executives many tax-free perquisites.*

quote, quotation *Quote* is a verb. *Quotation* is a noun. Do not use *quote* when you mean *quotation. The quotation [not quote] was inaccurately reported.*

raise, rise Two commonly confused verbs. *Raise (raising, raised, raised),* meaning "force something to move upward," is a transitive verb and takes a direct object. *Rise (rising, rose, risen),* meaning "go up," is an intransitive verb. When the subject of the verb acts on something to force it upward, use a form of *raise. Increasing the interest rate will raise monthly mortgage payments.* When the subject of a verb is itself moving upward, use a form of *rise. Unsteadily, the ailing man rose from the chair.*

real, really *Real* is an adjective; *really* is an adverb. *The linebacker was really [not real] tough to block.*

reason is because Use *that* instead of *because* in the phrase *reason is because,* or rewrite the sentence. *The reason the MG stalled is that [not is because] the oil had leaked from the crankcase.*

respectfully, respectively *Respectfully* means "with respect" or "showing respect." *Respectively* means "each in the order given." *He respectfully expressed his opposition to the plan.* The Collector, The Optimist's Daughter, *and* The Human Comedy *were written by John Fowles, Eudora Welty, and William Saroyan, respectively.*

rise See *raise.*

said See *goes.*

says See *goes.*

sensual, sensuous *Sensual* refers to pleasures of the body, especially sexual pleasures. *Sensuous* refers to pleasures perceived by the senses. *The poet's sensual desires led him to create the sensuous images readers find in his work.*

set, sit Two commonly confused verbs. *Set (setting, set, set),* meaning

Glossary of Usage **411**

"put or place," is a transitive verb and takes a direct object. *Sit (sitting, sat, sat)*, meaning "be seated," is an intransitive verb. When you mean "put something down," use a form of *set*. *Ralph set the paint beyond the child's reach*. When you refer to being seated, use a form of *sit*. *Don't sit in the wet paint*.

shall, will   *Shall*, which was once used to form the simple future tense in the first person, has been replaced by *will*. *I will deal with him later*. In first-person questions that request an opinion, *shall* is the correct form to use. *Shall I march? Shall we strike?*

should, would   Use *should* when expressing a condition or obligation. Use *would* when expressing a wish or customary action. *If they should appear, you must be prepared to battle. He would nap each afternoon when he was on vacation.*

should of   Nonstandard for *should have*.

sit   See *set*.

someone   See *anyone*.

such as   See *like, such as*.

sort   See *kind*.

sort of   See *kind of*.

sure   Colloquial when used as an adverb for *surely* or *certainly*. *Barnett surely [not sure] was correct in his cost estimate.*

sure and, sure to, try and, try to   *Sure to* and *try to* are the preferred forms. *Try to [not try and] attend.*

than, then,   *Than* functions as a conjunction used in comparisons, *then* as an adverb indicating time. *I would rather be in class than [not then] at work.*

that, which   *That* always introduces a restrictive clause. *Which* may introduce a restrictive clause or a nonrestrictive clause. Many writers prefer to use *which* only to introduce nonrestrictive clauses. *This is the class that requires six outside reports. This class, which requires six outside reports, meets once a week.*

theirselves   Nonstandard for *themselves*.

then   See *than*.

try and, try to   See *sure and*.

uninterested   See *disinterested*.

use to, suppose to   Sometimes carelessly written for *used to* and *supposed to*.

wait for, wait on   *Wait for* means "await." *Wait on* means "serve."

ways   Use *way* when referring to distance. *The trout stream is only a little way* [*not ways*] *from here.*

well   See *good*.

which   See *that*.

which, who   Never use *which* to refer to people. Use *who* or *that* to refer to people and *which* or *that* to refer to things.

will   See *shall*.

would   See *should*.

yourself   See *myself*.

Glossary of Grammatical Terms

absolute phrase   A phrase that modifies a whole clause or sentence rather than a single word and is not joined to the rest of the sentence by a connector. It consists of a noun and a participle: *Hands trembling, she opened the envelope. Our original plan looks best, all things considered.* See phrase; also 3f, 23h.

abstract noun   See noun.

active voice   See voice.

adjective   A word used to modify a noun or pronoun. It tells what kind, how many, or which one: *Careless drivers must attend seven hours of that class.* A **predicate adjective** follows a linking verb and describes the subject of the sentence: *The speaker was nervous.* See also 2i.

adjective clause   A dependent clause that modifies a noun or a pronoun. See clause.

adjective phrase   Any phrase that modifies a noun or pronoun. See phrase.

adverb   A word used to modify a verb, an adjective, another adverb, or a whole phrase, clause, or sentence. Adverbs tell how, when, where, or to what extent. *He speaks hurriedly.* [*Hurriedly* modifies *speaks* by telling how.] *She was never ambitious.* [*Never* modifies *ambitious* by telling when.] *Our dog wanders everywhere.* [*Everywhere* modifies *wanders* by telling where.] *He is quite easily confused.* [*Quite* modifies *easily* by telling to what extent.] See also 1e.

adverb clause   A dependent clause that modifies a verb, an adjective, another adverb, or a whole clause. See clause.

adverb phrase   Any phrase used as an adverb. See phrase.

adverbial conjunction   See conjunctive adverb.

agreement   The correspondence in person, number, and gender between two words. A verb must agree with its subject in person and number. A pronoun must agree with its antecedent in person, number, and gender. A demonstrative adjective (this, that, these, those) must agree with its noun in number. See also gender, person, number; also 8, 9.

antecedent The word or group of words to which a pronoun refers. *When Stacy graduated, she immediately took a job in New York.* [*Stacy* is the antecedent of the pronoun *she*.] See also 9.

appositive A noun or group of words used as a noun, placed next to a noun or pronoun to explain, describe, or identify it: *The lawyer, a Harvard graduate, easily won her first case.* Most appositives are nonrestrictive and are set off with commas. See also 3b, 23c.

article *The* is a definite article. *A* and *an* are indefinite articles. Articles are classed as adjectives. See also 1d.

auxiliary verb See helping verb.

case The form of nouns and pronouns classified according to how they function in a sentence. English has three cases: the **subjective** to indicate the subject of a verb or a subject complement; the **objective** to indicate the object of a verb, verbal, or preposition; and the **possessive** to indicate ownership. Nouns and most pronouns change form only in the possessive case *(cathedral's, everyone's)*. All other uses require only the plain form *(cathedral, everyone)*. The personal pronouns *I, we, he, she,* and *they* and the relative or interrogative pronoun *who* have three case forms. The personal pronouns *you* and *it* have a separate possessive form. See also 10, especially p. 59.

clause A group of words that has a subject and a predicate. A **main (independent) clause** forms a grammatically complete sentence: *He ran all the way to the station.* Main clauses can be joined to other main clauses with coordinating conjunctions, conjunctive adverbs, or semicolons. (See 1g, 16a.) **Dependent (subordinate) clauses** are not sentences and must be joined to a main clause to form a grammatically complete sentence: *Although he was tired, he ran all the way to the station.* Dependent clauses function as adjectives, adverbs, and nouns. See also 4.

collective noun See noun.

comma splice An error occurring when main clauses are joined by a comma alone: *Last summer we went camping, everyone laughed at my inability to pitch a tent.* See also 4a and 7.

common noun See noun.

comparative degree See comparison.

comparison Adjectives and adverbs have three forms: the **positive degree**, which only describes [*large*]; the **comparative degree**, which compares two things [*larger*]; and the **superlative degree**, which compares three or more things [*largest*]. See also 15e.

complement A word or group of words that completes the meaning of a subject, an object, or a verb. Complements function as **direct objects, indirect objects, predicate adjectives**, and **predicate nominatives**: *The manager opened the door* [direct object]. *Please send me a letter* [indirect object]. *The sea was calm* [predicate adjective]. *Her father is an accountant* [predicate nominative]. See also 2g, 2h, 2i, 2j.

complete predicate See predicate.

complete sentence See sentence.

complete subject See subject.

compound Words or groups of words of two or more parts functioning as a unit. **Compound words:** *brother-in-law, lifeguard*. **Compound constructions:** *Betty and Joe* [compound subject] *flew to Chicago. The children giggled and blushed* [compound predicate]. See also 2e, 2f.

compound-complex sentence See sentence.

compound predicate See compound.

compound sentence See sentence.

compound subject See compound.

concrete noun See noun.

conjunction A word that connects and shows the relation between words, phrases, and clauses. **Coordinating conjunctions** *(and, but, or, nor, yet, for,* and *so)* connect items of equal grammatical rank: *The beauty of the scenery and the friendliness of the people make British Columbia an attractive tourist area.* **Correlative conjunctions** *(either . . . or, not only . . . but also,* and so on) are used in pairs: *You may choose either the vase or the picture.* **Subordinating conjunctions** *(when, while, if, although, because,* and so on) introduce dependent clauses and connect them to main clauses: *The carnival activity began when the sun went down.* See also 1g.

conjunctive adverb An adverb used to connect two main clauses: *Susan practiced faithfully; therefore, she improved rapidly.* See also 1g.

coordinating conjunction   See conjunction.

correlative conjunction   See conjunction.

dangling modifier   A modifying phrase or clause that does not sensibly connect to any word in a sentence. See also 17h.

degree   See comparison.

demonstrative pronoun   See pronoun.

dependent clause   See clause.

direct address   A noun or pronoun used parenthetically to indicate the person or group spoken to: *I believe, friends, that we will win this election.*

direct discourse   The presentation of the exact words, spoken or written, of another: *Steven asked, "Where have you been?"* **Indirect discourse** reports the words of another in paraphrase or summary form: *Steven wanted to know where we had been.* See also 19e.

direct object   See object.

double negative   Two negative words used in the same construction: *I didn't have no reason to stay home.* Double negatives are nonstandard English. The sentence must be revised: *I didn't have any reason to stay home* or *I had no reason to stay home.*

elliptical construction   A construction in which one or more words are omitted but understood. *Bob types faster than Margaret [types].* See also 10e, 20.

expletive   The word *there, here,* or *it* followed by a form of the verb *be* and used to begin a construction in which the subject follows the verb: *It is easy to spend money foolishly.* [*To spend money foolishly* is the subject of *is.*] See also 8h.

finite verb   A verb that makes an assertion about a subject. A finite verb can function as the main (or only) verb in a sentence: *On weekends, I work in the garden.* Gerunds, infinitives, and participles are nonfinite verbs and cannot function as main verbs in a sentence. See verbal.

fragment   See sentence fragment.

fused sentence   An error occurring when main clauses are joined without a coordinating conjunction or any mark of punctuation: *We traveled to Georgia it was a good trip.* See also 7.

future perfect tense   See tense.

future tense   See tense.

gender   The classification of nouns and pronouns as masculine *(man, he)*, feminine *(woman, she)*, or neuter *(house, it)*. See also agreement; 9.

genitive case   Same as possessive case. See case.

gerund   A verbal ending in *-ing* that functions as a noun. The form of the gerund is the same as that of the present participle. Gerunds may have objects, complements, or modifiers. *Cigarette smoking is dangerous to your health.* [The gerund *smoking* is the subject of the sentence. *Cigarette* modifies the gerund. *Dangerous* is a predicate adjective complementing the gerund.] See also verbal; 3e.

gerund phrase   See phrase.

helping verb   A verb used with a main verb to form a verb phrase: *Sarah was living in San Francisco at that time.* See also 1c, 11.

imperative   See mood.

indefinite pronoun   See pronoun.

independent clause   Same as main clause. See clause.

indicative   See mood.

indirect discourse   See direct discourse.

indirect object   See object.

infinitive   The form of a verb listed in the dictionary, it usually appears in combination with *to* to form a verbal that functions as a noun, an adjective, or an adverb. Infinitives may have objects, complements, or modifiers. *He promised to mow the lawn.* [The infinitive phrase *to mow the lawn* functions as a noun, the direct object of the verb *promised. Lawn* is the direct object of the infinitive *to mow.*] See also verbal; 3c.

infinitive phrase   See phrase.

intensive pronoun   See pronoun.

interjection   A word expressing surprise or strong emotion: *Oh, here he comes!* See also 1h.

interrogative pronoun   See pronoun.

intransitive verb See verb.

irregular verb A verb that does not form its past and past participle by adding *-d* or *-ed* to the infinitive form: *fly, flew, flown; sink, sank, sunk.* See also 11.

linking verb See verb.

main clause See clause.

misplaced modifier A modifier positioned incorrectly in a sentence. See also 17.

modifier An adjective, an adverb, or a word, phrase, or clause used as an adjective or adverb to limit or qualify another word or group of words.

mood The form of a verb indicating a writer's (or speaker's) intent in a sentence. The **indicative mood** is used for questions and statements of fact or opinion: *John is a good student.* The **imperative mood** indicates a command or direction: *Be a good student.* The **subjunctive mood** expresses doubt, a condition contrary to fact, or a wish: *I wish I were a good student.* See also 13.

nominative case Same as subjective case. See case.

nonrestrictive element A modifier that is not essential to the meaning of a main clause. Nonrestrictive elements are set off by commas; *Mr. Perkins, who retired from the grocery business last summer, is a noted rose grower.* See also 23c.

noun A word that names a person, place, thing, or idea. **Proper nouns** name particular people, places, or things: *James Joyce, Chicago, Fenway Park.* **Common nouns** name general classes: *athlete, singer, hotel.* **Abstract nouns** name intangible qualities: *loyalty, grace, devotion.* **Concrete nouns** name tangible things: *desk, snow, glasses.* **Collective nouns** name groups: *team, squad, committee.* See also 1a.

noun clause A dependent clause that functions as a subject, an object, or a complement. See clause.

number The indication of singular or plural in the forms of nouns *(toy, toys)*, pronouns *(I, we)*, demonstrative adjectives *(this, these)*, and verbs *(eats, eat)*. See also agreement; 8, 9.

object A word, phrase, or clause that receives the action of or is affected by a transitive verb, a verbal, or a preposition. A **direct object** receives the action of a transitive verb or verbal and answers the question What? or Whom?: *Stan made money tutoring neighborhood children.* [*Money* is the direct object of the transitive verb *make*, answering the question What? *Children* is the direct object of the verbal *tutoring*, answering the question Whom?] An **indirect object** indicates to whom or for whom an action is done: *I gave David five dollars.* [*David* is the indirect object of the verb *gave*. *Dollars* is the direct object.] An **object of a preposition** is the noun that a preposition relates to the rest of a sentence: *Joan sat by the door of the church.* [*Door* is the object of the preposition *by; church* is the object of the preposition *of.*] See also 2g, 2h, 3a.

objective case   See case.

parenthetical expression   A word, phrase, or clause that interrupts the thought of a sentence. See also 23d, 27a, 30a.

participial phrase   See phrase.

participle   A verbal that functions as an adjective, an adverb, or a part of a verb phrase. **Present participles** end in *-ing.* **Past participles** of regular verbs end in *-d* or *-ed: The light from the floating candles created grotesque shapes on the dark walls.* [The present participle *floating* is used as an adjective modifying *candles.*] *He ran screaming down the street.* [The present participle *screaming* is used as an adverb modifying *ran.*] *The thief had taken her favorite bracelet.* [The past participle *taken* is used as part of the verb phrase *had taken.*] See also verbal; 3d.

parts of speech   The classification of words on the basis of their use in a sentence. The parts of speech are nouns, pronouns, verbs, adjectives, adverbs, prepositions, conjunctions, and interjections. Each part of speech is defined in a separate entry in the glossary. See also 1.

passive voice   See voice.

past participle   See participle.

past perfect tense   See tense.

past tense   See tense.

perfect tenses   See tense.

person   The form of pronouns and verbs used to indicate the speaker (first person — *I am*), the one spoken to (second person — *you are*), or the one spoken about (third person — *she is*). See also agreement; 8, 9.

personal pronoun   See pronoun.

phrase   A group of words lacking a subject or a predicate or both and used as a single part of speech. A **verb phrase** consists of more than one verb: *had been talking, was swimming.* It functions as a predicate for clauses and sentences: *The professor has been lecturing for more than an hour.* A **prepositional phrase** consists of a preposition, its object, and any modifiers: *under the house, after the party.* It functions as an adjective, adverb, or noun: *She wandered to the elm grove beyond the fence.* [*To the elm grove* is used as an adverb modifying *wandered; beyond the fence* is used as an adjective modifying *grove.*] An **infinitive phrase** consists of an infinitive, its object, and any modifiers: *to hear the peaceful music, to learn I had been selected.* It functions as a noun, adjective, or adverb: *To see her again was a pleasure.* [*To see her again* is used as a noun, the subject of the sentence.] A **participial phrase** consists of a participle, its object, and any modifiers: *studying all night, glancing through the album.* It functions as an adjective or adverb: *The man jogging around the track is my brother.* [*Jogging around the track* is used as an adjective modifying *man.*] A **gerund phrase** consists of a gerund, its object, and any modifiers. Like participial phrases, gerund phrases use the *-ing* ending on the verb: *watching the birds, hoping for rain.* Therefore, they can be distinguished from participial phrases only in the context of a sentence. Gerund phrases function as nouns. *Jogging around the track is good exercise.* [*Jogging around the track* is used as a noun, the subject of the sentence.] An **absolute phrase** consists of a noun and usually a participle. It modifies a whole clause or sentence. *The election being over, the loser pledged support to the winner.* See also 3.

positive degree   See comparison.

possessive case   See case.

predicate   The part of a sentence that tells what the subject did or how it was acted upon. A predicate must have a finite verb. The **simple predicate** is the verb and its helping verb(s). The **complete predicate** is the simple predicate plus any modifiers, objects, and complements. *This play should set an attendance record in New York.* [*Should set* is the simple predicate. *Should set an attendance record in New York* is the complete predicate.] See finite verb; also 2b, 2d.

predicate adjective   See adjective, complement.

predicate nominative   See complement.

preposition   A word that shows the relation of a noun or a pronoun (the object of the preposition) to some other word in the sentence. See also object, phrase; 1f.

prepositional phrase   See phrase.

present participle   See participle.

present perfect tense   See tense.

present tense   See tense.

principal parts   The present, present participle, past, and past participle of a verb: *look, looking, looked, looked.* See also 11.

progressive tense   See tense.

pronoun   A word that takes the place of a noun. Words that function as pronouns are classified as follows. **Personal pronouns:** *I, you, he, she, it, we, they,* and their possessive forms, *my, mine, your, yours, his, her, hers, its, our, ours, their, theirs.* **Reflexive pronouns:** *myself, yourself, himself, herself, itself, ourselves, yourselves, themselves,* which are also sometimes used as **intensive pronouns,** as in *I myself saw it.* **Relative pronouns:** *who, whom, that, which, whose.* **Interrogative pronouns:** *who, which, whom, whose, what.* **Demonstrative pronouns:** *this, that, these, those.* **Indefinite pronouns:** *all, both, few, several, nobody,* and so on. See also 1b.

proper adjective   An adjective derived from a proper noun: *French perfume, Orwellian nightmare.* See also 34f.

proper noun   See noun.

quotation   See direct quotation.

reflexive pronoun   See pronoun.

regular verb   A verb that forms its past and past participle by adding *-d* or *-ed* to the infinitive form: *wander, wandered, wandered; scheme, schemed, schemed.* See also 11.

relative pronoun   See pronoun.

restrictive element   A modifier that defines or identifies the noun it modifies and is therefore essential to the meaning of the main clause. Restrictive elements are not set off by commas. *All students who have* *successfully completed sixty units may apply for upper-division standing.* See also 23c and 24f.

run-on sentence   See fused sentence.

sentence   A group of words that contains a subject and a predicate and is not introduced by a subordinating conjunction. Sentences are classified according to their structure. A **simple sentence** has one main clause: *Maria fell asleep.* A **compound sentence** has two or more main clauses: *Maria tried to stay awake, but she fell asleep.* A **complex sentence** has one main clause and at least one dependent clause: *When Maria lay down to rest, she fell asleep.* A **compound-complex sentence** has two or more main clauses and at least one dependent clause: *Maria tried to stay awake because she wanted to study, but she fell asleep.* Sentences may also be classified according to their purpose. A **declarative sentence** makes a statement: *I am going home.* An **imperative sentence** gives a command or makes a request: *Go home now.* An **interrogative sentence** asks a question: *Are you going home?* An **exclamatory sentence** expresses strong feeling: *We're going home!* See also 5.

sentence fragment   A portion of a sentence punctuated as though it were a sentence: *Suddenly appearing on the horizon.* See also 6.

simple predicate   See predicate.

simple sentence   See sentence.

simple subject   See subject.

simple tenses   See tense.

squinting modifier   A modifier placed so it may refer to either a word preceding it or a word following it. See also 17b.

subject   The part of a sentence that acts, is acted upon, or is described. The **simple subject** is the essential word or group of words of the complete subject. The **complete subject** is the simple subject plus its modifiers. *A tall, stately gentleman appeared at the door.* [*Gentleman* is the simple subject. *A tall, stately gentleman* is the complete subject.] See also 2a, 2c.

subject complement   See complement.

subjective case   See case.

subjunctive   See mood.

Glossary of Grammatical Terms   **423**

subordinate clause   Same as dependent clause. See clause.

subordinating conjunction   See conjunction.

superlative degree   See comparison.

tense   The form of a verb and its helping verbs that expresses the verb's relation to time. The **simple tenses** are **present** *(I laugh, you choose)*, **past** *(I laughed, you chose)*, and **future** *(I will laugh, you will choose)*. The **perfect tenses** indicate completed action: **present perfect** *(I have laughed, you have chosen)*, **past perfect** *(I had laughed, you had chosen)*, and **future perfect** *(I will have laughed, you will have chosen)*. The **progressive tense** indicates continuing action *(I am laughing, you are choosing)*. See also 12.

transitive verb   See verb.

verb   A word or group of words expressing action or a state of being. A **transitive verb** expresses action that has an object: *She painted a picture.* An **intransitive verb** expresses action that does not have an object: *The artist failed.* A **linking verb** expresses a state of being or a condition. It links the subject of a sentence with a complement that identifies or describes the subject: *Their laughter was maddening.* A verb may be transitive in one sentence and intransitive in another: *She paints pictures* [transitive]; *She paints well* [intransitive]. See also tense, mood, voice; 1c, 11, 12, 13, 14.

verb phrase   See phrase.

verbal   Also called *nonfinite verb.* A form of a verb used as a noun, an adjective, or an adverb. Gerunds, infinitives, and participles are verbals. Verbals may take objects, complements, and modifiers. A verbal cannot function as the main verb of a sentence. See also gerund, infinitive, participle, phrase; 3.

voice   The form of a transitive verb that indicates whether the subject acts **(active voice)** or is acted upon **(passive voice).** Active voice: *Debbie wrote a fine research paper.* Passive voice: *A fine research paper was written by Debbie.* See also 14.

(*continued from page ii*)

Rachel Carson, from *Silent Spring* by Rachel Carson. Copyright © 1962 by Rachel
L. Carson. Reprinted by permission of Houghton Mifflin Company and Frances
Collin, Literary Executor.

Victor B. Cline, from "How TV Violence Damages Your Children," © 1975 by
Family Media, Inc. Reprinted with permission of *Ladies' Home Journal.*

John F. Cuber, from *Sociology: A Synopsis of Principles*, Sixth Edition, © 1968, p.
34. Reprinted by permission of Prentice-Hall, Inc., Englewood Cliffs, N.J.

Lester Del Rey, from "The Mysterious Sky," 1964. Reprinted by permission of the
author and the author's agents, Scott Meredith Literary Agency Inc., 845 Third
Avenue, New York, New York 10022.

J. William Fulbright, from "The Two Americas," in *The Arrogance of Power.*
Copyright © 1966. Reprinted by permission of Random House, Inc.

Dick Gregory. From *Nigger: An Autobiography* by Dick Gregory with Robert
Lipsyte. Copyright © 1964 by Dick Gregory Enterprises, Inc. Reprinted by
permission of the publisher, E. P. Dutton, Inc., a division of New American
Library, and International Creative Management.

Helen Keller, from "Days of Discovery," in *The Story of My Life.* New York,
Doubleday.

N. Scott Momaday, from *The Way to Rainy Mountain* by N. Scott Momaday. ©
1969. The University of New Mexico Press.

Lael Morgan, from "Let the Eskimos Hunt," by Lael Morgan. © 1979 by
Newsweek, Inc. All rights reserved. Reprinted by permission.

The New York Times Index. Copyright © 1981 by The New York Times Company.
Reprinted by permission.

George Orwell, excerpt from "A Hanging," in *Shooting an Elephant and Other
Essays* by George Orwell, copyright 1950 by Sonia Brownell Orwell; renewed
1978 by Sonia Pitt-Rivers. Reprinted by permission of Harcourt Brace
Jovanovich, Inc. and the estate of the late Sonia Brownell Orwell and Martin
Secker & Warburg Ltd.

Roberta Ostroff, from "Big Red and Sweet Drifter," *Geo*, August 1982. Reprinted
by permission.

Readers' Guide to Periodical Literature. Copyright © 1982 by The H. W. Wilson
Company. Material reproduced by permission of the publisher.

Paul Roberts from *Understanding English* by Paul Roberts. Copyright © 1958 by
Paul Roberts. Reprinted by permission of Harper & Row, Publishers, Inc.

Murray Ross. "Football Red and Baseball Green" by Murray Ross first appeared
in *Chicago Review* Vol. 22, Nos. 2 & 3, copyright 1971 by Chicago Review.

Mark Schorer from *Sinclair Lewis: An American Life*. Reprinted by permission of the University of Minnesota Press.

Susan Sontag, from "Camus' Notebooks," in *Against Interpretation* by Susan Sontag. Copyright © 1963, 1966 by Susan Sontag. Reprinted by permission of Farrar, Straus and Giroux, Inc.

Caroline Sutton, from "How do they get the stripes onto Stripe toothpaste?" in *How Do They Do That?* by Caroline Sutton with Duncan M. Anderson. Copyright © 1981 by Hilltown Press Inc. By permission of William Morrow & Company, Inc.

Judy Syfers. "Why I Want a Wife" from Ms., Vol 1 (December 31, 1971). Reprinted by permission of the author.

Deems Taylor, from *Of Men and Music*. Copyright © 1937, 1965 by Deems Taylor. Permission granted by Curtis Brown Associates Ltd.

Robert I. Tilling, from "A Volcanologist's Perspective," *Geo*, August 1980.

Mark Twain from *Mark Twain's Autobiography*, Volume I, by Mark Twain. Copyright, 1924 by Clara Gabrilowitsch; renewed, 1952 by Clara Clemens Samossoud. Reprinted by permission of Harper & Row, Publishers, Inc.

John F. Wilson and Carroll C. Arnold, from *Public Speaking as a Liberal Art*. Allyn & Bacon, Inc., 1964, 1974.

INDEX

Abbreviations
in bibliographies, 189, 348
capitalization of, 181
for dates and numbers, 189
for days, months, holidays, 189
for educational courses, 189
in footnotes and comments, 189
for geographical names, 190
with names, 181, 187–88, 189, 349
for organizations, 188
for parts of books, 189
periods with, 171
for units of measurement, 190
abide by, 224
Absolute phrases, 24, 140
Abstract nouns, 2
Abstract words, 222–23
Academic words, 180, 181, 188
accept, except, 206
according to, 224
Action verbs, 5–6
Active voice, 78–81
Addresses, 142, 197
Ad hominem argument, 240
Adjective clauses, 26
Adjectives, 8–9, 82–86
and adverbs, 82–84
comparative form, 85–86
coordinate, 138
cumulative, 138
after direct objects, 83
after linking verbs, 82–83
positive form, 85
predicate, 8, 18
and pronouns, 9, 82

proper, 179
superlative form, 85–86
Adverb clauses, 27
Adverbs, 9–10
and adjectives, 82–84
comparative form, 85–86
after direct objects, 83
after linking verbs, 82–83
positive form, 85
superlative form, 85–86
See also Conjunctive adverbs
advice, advise, 206
affect, effect, 206
Agreement of pronoun and antecedent, 53–57
with antecedents joined by *or* or *nor*, 53–54
with collective nouns, 55
with compound antecedents, 53
with indefinite pronouns, 55–56
and problem of generalized *he*, 56
with relative pronouns, 56–57
Agreement of subject and verb, 44–50
with collective nouns, 47
with compound subjects, 45, 48
with *every* or *many a*, 49
with expressions of time, money, measurement, 49
with indefinite pronouns, 46
with intervening words, 44–45
with inverted order, 48
linking verbs and, 48
with nouns of plural

form and singular meaning, 47
with relative pronouns, 48–49
with subjects joined by *or* or *nor*, 45–46
with titles of works, 50
word expressing amount, 49
agree with, to, on, 224–25
all, 46
all ready, already, 207
along with, 44
already, all ready, 207
Analogies, 263
false, 239–40
angry with, 225
Antecedents, 3
agreement of pronouns and, 53–57, 104–06
collective nouns as, 55
indefinite pronouns as, 55–56
relative pronouns as, 56–57
any, 46
APA citation style, 340–43
Apostrophe
to form contractions, 186
misuse of, 186
to form plurals, 186
to form possessives, 184
Appositives, 19–20
case of pronouns with, 61
colon to introduce final, 156
dashes for, 158
Archaic words, avoiding, 216
Argumentative essay, 270
Articles (*a, an, the*), 9
as, 61
as follows, 156
Association fallacy, 240–41

as well as, 44
Audience, for essays, 282–83, 299
Auxiliary verbs, 7

bad, badly, 83–84
Balanced sentence, 121
Biblical citations, 157
Bibliographies, 315–23, 345, 346
  abbreviations in, 189
  form for, 316
  punctuation in, 157
Block form for quotations, 160–61
Books, bibliography form, 157, 317–20, 346
both . . . and, 117
Brackets, 170, 344
break, brake, 207
Business letters
  body of, 394
  closing of, 394
  envelope for, 397
  format of, 393, 395
  inside address on, 394
  return address on, 393
  salutations in, 394
  sample, 396
  signatures on, 395
by, buy, 207

capital, capitol, 207
Capitalization, 176–82
  of abbreviations, 181
  of academic words, 180, 181
  avoiding mistakes in, 181–82
  of celestial bodies, 180
  after colons, 176, 177
  of days of week and months, 179
  in dialogue, 178
  of directions, 182
  of educational institutions, 180
  of family relations, 182
  of geographical names, 179

  of government departments, 179
  of historical events, 179
  of holidays, 179
  of *I* and *O*, 177
  of organizations, 179
  in poetry, 178
  of political parties, 179
  of proper nouns and adjectives, 179
  of question fragments, 176
  in quotations, 178
  of races, nationalities, and languages, 180
  of religious terms, 180
  of titles of persons, 181
  of titles of works, 177
  of trade names, 180
capitol, capital, 207
Card catalogue, 310–11
Case, 58–64
  in appositives, 61
  after *as* or *than*, 61
  before gerunds, 62–63
  with infinitives, 62
  objective, 59, 60, 62
  possessive, 59–60, 62, 184–85
  in subject complements, 59–60
  subjective, 59
  who or *whom*, 63–64
Cause and effect, 264–65
Character, 296
Characterization, 296
charge for, with, 225
cite, sight, site, 207
Classification, 263–64
Clauses, 25–27
  adjective, 26
  adverb, 27
  coordinate, 90–92
  noun, 27
  subordinate, *see* Dependent clauses
  See also Dependent clauses; Main clauses
Clichés, common, 228
Climax, order of, 254–55

Clincher, 249
Clustering, 281–82
coarse, course, 207
Coherence, 253–60, 270–71
Collective nouns, 2
  agreement of pronouns, 55
  agreement of verbs, 47
Colloquial writing, 213–14
Colons, 155–57
  with appositives, 156
  in biblical citations, 157
  in bibliography, 157
  capitalization after, 176, 177
  to introduce series, 155
  with main clauses, 156
  misuse of, 157
  with quotations, 156, 163
  in salutations, 157
  in subdivisions of time, 157
  before subtitles, 157
  after *the following* or *as follows*, 156
Command, *see* Imperative sentence
Commas, 126–48
  with absolute phrases, 140
  in addresses, 142
  with contrasting expressions, 140
  between coordinate adjectives, 138
  in dates, 142
  in direct address, 136
  in friendly letters, 142–43
  with interrogative elements, 140–41
  with introductory phrases and clauses, 127–28
  between main clauses, 126
  with mild interjections, 136

misunderstanding, to prevent, 143
misuse of, *see* Unnecessary commas
with nonrestrictive elements, 129–32
in numbers, 142
with parenthetical expressions, 135–36, 168
in place names, 142
with quotation marks, 162
with quotations, 140
between series items, 137
to show omission, 144
with *yes* and *no*, 136
See also Unnecessary commas
Comma splices, 40–41
Common nouns, 2
Comparative degree, 85–86
compare to, with, 225
Comparison and contrast, 262
Comparison of modifiers, 85–86
Comparisons, faulty, 114
complement, compliment, 207
Complements, 17–18
Complete predicates, 15
Complete subjects, 15
Complex sentences, 29
compliment, complement, 207
comply with, 225
Compound antecedents, 53
Compound-complex sentences, 29–30
Compound nouns, 3
Compound numbers, 195
Compound predicates, 16
as sentence fragments, 37
Compound sentences, 29
Compound subjects, 15

agreement of verb with, 45, 48
Compound words, 185, 194–95
Computer data bases, 314–15
Conciseness, 229–35
empty phrases and, 230–31
euphemism and, 233–35
redundancy and, 232
repetition and, 232
Conclusions, 271, 293, 302
Concrete nouns, 2
Concrete words, 223
concur with, in, 225
confide in, to, 225
Conflict, 296–97
Conjunctions, 11–12
conjunctive adverbs, 12, 90–91, 152
coordinating, 11–12, 41, 90–91
correlative, 12
subordinating, 12, 93
Conjunctive adverbs, 12, 90–91
semicolons with, 152
Connotation, 220–21
conscious, conscience, 207
Consistency, 107–13, 214
Contractions, 186, 214
Contrast, 262
Contrasting phrases, 140
Coordinate adjectives, 138
Coordinate clauses, 90–92
Coordinating conjunctions, 11–12, 90–91
to correct comma splices and fused sentences, 41
semicolon before, 152
Coordination
for equal emphasis, 90–91
faulty or excessive, 91–92
Correlative conjunctions, 12, 90–91
course, coarse, 207

Critical review, 298
Cumulative adjectives, 138

Dangling modifiers, 102–03
Dashes, 158–59
for appositives, 158
for break in thought, 159
for clarity, 158
comma unnecessary with, 148
for emphasis, 158
for introductory series, 158
for parenthetical elements, 158, 168
for quotations, 159
with quotation marks, 163
typed, 344
Data bases, 314–15
Dates, 142, 189, 197
Days of week, 179
decent, descent, dissent, 207
Decimals, 197–98
Declarative sentence, 30
Definition, 265–67
Definitions, italics or quotation marks for, 193
Degree, *see* Comparative degree; Positive degree, Superlative degree
Demonstrative pronouns, 4
Denotation, 220–21
Dependent (subordinate) clauses, 26, 90, 93–96, 98
as sentence fragments, 34–35
verb tenses in, 72
descent, decent, dissent, 207
Descriptive essay, 270
desert, dessert, 207
Details, 261
Dialogue, 161, 167, 178
Diction, *see* Conciseness;

Diction [*cont.*]
    Exactness; Language,
      appropriate
die of, from, 225
different from, than, 225
differ with, from, about,
    over, 225
Direct address, 136
Direct discourse, 110
Directions, 182
Direct objects, 17, 83
Direct quotations, *see*
    Quotations
Discourse, direct and indi-
    rect, 110
Discussion, in essay, 271,
    291, 300–02
dissent, decent, descent,
    207
Double comparatives and
    superlatives, 86
Drafts, of essays and pa-
    pers, 290–91, 294–95,
    333, 343

each, 45
effect, affect, 206
ei, ie, 201
either . . . or, 117
Either/or fallacy, 238
Ellipses, 166–67
Ellipsis, faulty, 114–15
Elliptical constructions,
    114
Emphasis
  dashes for, 158
  exclamation point for,
    172
  repetition for, 259
Emphatic form of verb
  tense, 70
Empty phrases, 230–31
Encyclopedias, bibliog-
  raphy form, 321
Endnotes, 334; *see also*
  Notes
English, standard vs. non-
  standard, 213
Essays, 268–95
  audience for, 282–83

coherence, in 270–71
conclusion of, 271, 293
development of, 271
discussion in, 291–92
final draft of, 294–95
first draft of, 290–91
ideas for, 278–82
introduction to, 271, 291
outline for, 287–89
planning for, 278–90
revision of, 294–95
sample, 271–77
thesis statement of,
    285–87, 291
title of, 293
tone of, 290
topic of, 278–79
types of, 270
unity in, 270
See also Literature, ana-
    lytical essay about
Euphemism, 233–35
every, 45, 49
Exactness, 220–28
  denotation and connota-
    tion, 220–21
  figurative language,
    226–27
  general vs. specific lan-
    guage, 222–23
  idioms, 224–26
  trite expressions, 228
Examples, 261
except, accept, 206
Exclamation point, 172–
  73
  comma unnecessary
    with, 148
  with quotation marks,
    163
  after title of work, 173
Exclamatory sentence, 30
Expletives, 48
Explication, 298
Expository essay, 270
External conflict, 296

Fallacies, 236–41
  ad hominem argument,
    240

association fallacy, 240–
    41
either-or argument, 238
false analogy, 239–40
non sequitur, 239
overgeneralization, 236–
    37
oversimplification, 237
post hoc argument, 238–
    39
False analogy, 239–40
Family relations, 182
Faulty comparisons, 114
Faulty ellipsis, 114–15
Faulty predication, 112
Faulty shifts, 110, 112
Figurative language, 226–
    27
Flat character, 296
Footnotes, 189, 334; *see
    also* Notes
Foreign words, 192
Formal letter, 157; *see also*
    Business letter
Formal standard Ameri-
    can English, 213–14
formerly, formally, 207
forth, fourth, 207
Fractions, 195, 197–98
Fragments, 34–39
Friendly letters, 142–43
Fused sentences, 40–41
Future perfect tense, 71
Future tense, 70–71

General-to-specific order,
    255
General words, 223
Genitive case, *see* Posses-
    sive case
Gerund phrases, 23–24,
    62–63
Gerunds, 23–24
good, well, 83–84

he, she, 56
hear, here, 207
heard, herd, 207
Helping verbs, 7
herd, heard, 207

here, 48
here, hear, 207
his, her, 56
Holidays, 179, 189
Hyperbole, 227
Hyphens
  to avoid confusion, 196
  for compound numbers, 195
  for compound words, 194–95
  in fractions, 195
  to join letters to words, 195
  for prefixes and suffixes, 195
  suspended, 196
  in word division, 194

I, 177
identical to, with, 225
Idioms, 224–26
ie, ei, 201
if, 77
ignorant of, 225
Imperative mood, 76–77
Imperative sentence, 30, 171, 172–73
in addition to, 44
Indefinite pronouns, 4
  agreement with antecedent, 55–56
  agreement of verb with, 46
Independent clauses, *see* Main clauses
Indicative mood, 76
Indirect discourse, 110
Indirect objects, 17–18
Indirect quotations, 147, 161
inferior to, 225
Infinitive phrases, 21
Infinitives, 21, 65–68, 72, 73
  case with, 62
  split, 101
  to form subjunctive, 77
Informal (colloquial) standard American

English, 213–14
instance, instants, 207
Interjections, 13
  commas with, 136
  exclamation points with, 172
Internal conflict, 296
Interrogative elements, 140
Interrogative pronouns, 4
Interrogative sentences, 30
Intransitive verbs, 6
Introductions, in essays, 271, 291
Introductory elements, 127–28
Irregular verbs, 66–68
Italics
  for definitions, 193
  for emphasis, 193
  for foreign words, 192
  in titles, 190–92, 193
  underlining to indicate, 190–93
  for vehicle names, 192
  for words as words, 186, 193
its, it's, 208

Jargon, avoiding, 216

Key words and phrases, 259

Language, appropriate, 213–20
  jargon, 216
  neologisms, 216
  obsolete or archaic words, 216
  pretentious language, 218
  regionalisms, 215
  sexist language, 56, 219–20
  slang, 214–15
  standard American English, 213
  technical terms, 216
lessen, lesson, 208

Letters, forming plurals of, 186
Letter writing, 142–43, 157, 391–95
Library sources, 308–15, 346
like, such as, 146
Limiting modifiers, 99
Linking verbs, 6, 48, 82–83
Literature, analytical essay about, 296–305
  conclusion of, 302
  discussion in, 300–02
  introduction to, 299–300
  quotations and references in, 303
  selecting subject for, 296–98
  thesis statement of, 298
  title for, 303
  use of verb tense in, 304
Loaded words, 221
loose, lose, 208
Loose sentence, 121

Main (independent) clauses, 25–26
  colons with, 156
  commas with, 126
  semicolons with, 151–52
Manuscripts
  handwritten, 390
  identification on, 391
  indentations in, 391
  margins for, 390
  materials for, 390
  pagination, 391
  sample, 392–93
  titles of, 391
  typewritten or computer-printed, 343–45
many a, 49
Metaphor, 226
Misplaced modifiers, 100–01
Mixed metaphor, 227
MLA citation style, 334–40
Modifiers
  dangling, 102–03

Modifiers [*cont.*]
limiting, 99
misplaced, 100–01
placement of, 97–103
squinting, 98–99
verbal, 128
Months of the year, 179, 189
Mood, 76, 109

Narrative essay, 270
Neologisms, 216
no, 136
Nominative case, *see* Subjective case
none, 46
Nonfinite verbs, *see* Verbals
Nonrestrictive elements, 129–32
non sequiturs, 239
Nonstandard English, 213
nor
and agreement of pronouns, 53–54
and agreement of verbs, 45–46
Notes, 333–43, 344–45
APA style, 340–43
MLA style, 334–40
numbering of, 340
parenthetical citations, 334–40, 341–42
Note taking, 325–31
direct quotation in, 327–29
paraphrasing in, 328, 330–31
summarizing in, 326–27
not only . . . but also, 117
Noun clauses, 27
Nouns
abstract, 2
case of, 58, 62–63, 184–185
collective, 2–3, 47, 55
common, 2
compound, 3
concrete, 2
plurals of, 204–05

possessive forms of, 184–85
proper, 2, 179
Number
consistency in, 107–08
pronoun-antecedent agreement in, 53–57
subject-verb agreement in, 44–50
Numbers
commas in, 142
figures or words for, 196–98
plurals of, 186

O, capitalization of, 177
Objective case, 59, 60, 62
Objects
direct, 17, 83
indirect, 17–18
of prepositions, 10–11
Obsolete words, avoiding, 216
occupied by, in, with, 225
Omissions, 144
or
and agreement of pronouns, 53–54
and agreement of verbs, 45–46
Outlines, 287–89, 323–25, 331–32, 344
Overgeneralization, 236–37
Oversimplification, 237

Pagination, 391
Paragraphs, 244–67
closing of, 244
coherence of, 253–60
development of, 261–67
opening of, 244–45
topic sentence in, 245, 246–50
unity of, 251–52
Parallelism
for comparison or contrast, 116–17
for coordinate elements, 115–16

for correlative elements, 117
Parallel structure, 260
Paraphrasing, 328, 330–31
Parentheses, 168–69, 188
Parenthetical citations, 334–40, 341–42
Parenthetical expressions
commas with, 135–36, 168
dashes with, 158, 168
parentheses with, 168, 169
Participial phrases, 22
Participles, 21, 65–68, 73; *see also* names of participles
Parts of speech, 2–13
passed, past, 208
Passive voice, 78–81
Past participles, 21, 73
of irregular verbs, 66–68
Past perfect tense, 71
Past tense, 66–68, 70
peace, piece, 208
Percentages, 197–98
Perfect tenses, 71
Period, 171–72
with abbreviations, 171
comma unnecessary with, 148
with ellipsis mark, 167
with quotation marks, 162
Periodicals
bibliography form, 320–21
guides to, 311–14
Periodic sentence, 121
Person, 53, 297
consistency in, 107–08
Personal pronouns, 3
Personification, 226
Phrase fragments, 36
Phrases, 19–24
absolute, 24, 140
contrasting, 140
gerund, 23–24
infinitive, 21
participial, 21–22

prepositional, 19, 98
as sentence fragment, 36
verb, 7
verbal, 21–24
piece, peace, 208
Place names, 142
Plagiarism, 333
plain, plane, 208
Plan for essays, 278–90
Plot, 296–97
Plurals of nouns, 204–05
Poetry, quoting, 160–61, 178
Point of view, 297
Positive degree, 85
Possessive case, 59–60, 62, 184–86
Possessive pronouns, 3, 186
post hoc argument, 238–39
Predicate adjectives, 8, 18
Predicate nominatives, 18
Predicates
  complete, 15
  compound, 16, 37
  simple, 15
  See also Complements; Objects; Verbs
Predication, faulty, 112
Prefixes, 195
Prepositional phrase, 10–11, 19, 98
Prepositions, 10–11
Present infinitive, 73
Present participle, 21, 73
  formation of, 21, 65
  gerunds and, 23–24
Present perfect infinitive, 73
Present perfect participle, 73
Present perfect tense, 71
Present tense, 69–70, 304
Pretentious language, 218
principal, principle, 208
Principal parts of verbs, 65–68
prior to, 226
Process, 267
Progressive form of tense, 72

Pronoun reference, 104–06
Pronouns
  and adjectives, 9, 82
  agreement with antecedents, 53–57
  antecedents of, 3
  case of, 58–64
  demonstrative, 4
  indefinite, 4, 46, 55–56, 184
  interrogative, 4
  personal, 3
  possessive, 3, 186
  reflexive, 4
  relative, 4, 48–49, 56–57, 93
Proper adjectives, 179
Proper nouns, 2, 179

Question fragments in series, 176
Question marks, 172
  comma unnecessary with, 148
  within parentheses, 172
  and quotation marks, 163
  after title of work, 173
Quotation marks
  for definitions, 193
  in dialogue, 161
  double, 159–62
  with other punctuation, 162–63
  for poetry, 160–61, 162
  single, 163
  for special sense, 162
  for titles, 162
Quotations
  capitalization in, 178
  colons in, 156
  commas in, 140–41
  dashes in, 159
  ellipses in, 166–67
  identifying, 303
  indirect, 147, 161
  in note taking, 327–29
  in research paper, 344
  within quotations, 163

Redundancy, 232
Reference, pronoun, 104–06
Reference books, 308–15
Reflexive pronouns, 4
Regionalisms, 215–16
Regular verbs, 66
Relative pronouns, 4
  agreement with antecedent, 56–57
  agreement of verb with, 48–49
  list of, 94
  as subjects, 48–49
Repetition
  avoiding, 232
  for emphasis, 259
Research papers, 305–87
  avoiding plagiarism, 333
  bibliographies for, 315–23
  citing sources in, 333–42
  drafts of, 333, 343
  gathering information for, 315
  guidelines for typing, 343–45
  library sources, 308–15
  notes for, 333–43
  questions and answers about, 345–49
  sample, 349–85
  taking notes for, 325–31
  thesis and outline for, 323–25, 331–32
  topics for, 306–08
Restrictive elements, 129–32
Résumé form, 397–400
Revision, 294–95, 331–32
right, rite, write, 208
road, rode, 208
Round character, 296
Run-on sentences, 40–41

Seasons, 181
-self, -selves, 106
Semicolons, 151–53
  before coordinating conjunctions, 152

Semicolons [*cont.*]
  to correct comma
    splices and fused sen-
    tences, 40–41
  misuse of, 153
  with quotation marks,
    163
  to separate main
    clauses, 151–52
  in series, 152
Sentence fragments, 34–39
Sentence(s)
  balanced, 121
  beginnings, 119–20
  completeness, 113–15
  complex, 29
  compound, 29
  compound-complex, 29–
    30
  declarative, 30
  exclamatory, 30
  forms, varying, 121
  fused or run-on, 40–41
  imperative, 30
  incomplete, 34–39, 113–
    14
  interrogative, 30
  kinds of, 28–30
  loose, 121
  parts, 14–18
  periodic, 121
  purposes, 30
  simple, 29
  structures, 29–30, 120
  variety, 119–21
Sequence of tenses, 71–74
Series
  colon to introduce, 155
  commas in, 137
  dashes with, 158
  parentheses and, 169
  semicolons in, 152
Setting, 297
Sexist language, avoiding,
    56, 219–20
she, 56
Shifts, faulty, 110, 112
sic, 170
sight, site, cite, 207
Simile, 226

Simple predicates, 15
Simple sentences, 29
Simple subjects, 14–15
site, sight, cite, 207
Slang, 214–15
Slashes, 160, 170
some, 46
Sources, 308–15, 348–49
  in bibliographies, 322–
    23
  citing, 333–43
  primary and secondary,
    315
Space order, 254
Specific-to-general order,
    255–56
Specific words, 223
Spelling, 199–209
  commonly misspelled
    words, 206–09
  plurals, 204–05
  suffixes, 202–03
Split infinitives, 101
Squinting modifiers, 98–
    99
Standard American Eng-
    lish, 213–14
States, abbreviations for,
    171
stationary, stationery, 208
Stock phrases, 228
Subjective case, 59
Subjects
  agreement of verbs
    with, 44–50
  complete, 15
  compound, 15, 45, 48
  consistency in, 109–10
  simple, 14–15
Subjunctive mood, 76–78
Subordinate clauses, *see*
    Dependent clauses
Subordinating conjunc-
    tions, 12, 93
  to correct comma
    splices or fused sen-
    tences, 41
Subordination, 93–94
  faulty or excessive, 94–
    95

Subtitles, 157
such as, like, 146
Suffixes, 195, 202–03
Summarizing, 326–27
superior to, 226
Superlative degree, 85–86
Suspended hyphens, 196
Syllable division, 194
Symbols, 297
Synonyms, 221

Technical terms, 216
Tenses 69–72, 108–09; *see
    also* names of tenses
than, 61, 147
that
  agreement with anteced-
    ent, 48–49, 57
  and subjunctive, 78
that, which, 130
the following, 156
their, there, they're, 208
Theme, 297–98
there, 48
Thesis statement of essays,
    285–87, 291, 298, 324,
    331
Time, 157, 181, 189, 197
Time order, 253
Titles
  of essays, 193, 293, 303
  of manuscripts, 344, 391
  of persons, 181, 187–88,
    304, 349
  of works
    capitalization in, 177
    italics for, 190–92
    quotation marks for,
      162
    singular verb with, 50
to, too, two, 208
together with, 44
Tone, 290
too, to, two, 208
Topic, of essay, 278–79
Topic sentences, 245, 246–
    50
Transitional words and
    phrases, 257–59
Transitive verbs. 6

Trite expressions, 228
two, to, too, 208

Underlining (italics), *see*
    Italics
Unity, 251–52, 270
Unnecessary commas,
    144–48, 304
  between compound
    words and phrases,
    145–46
  before items in series,
    147
  with indirect quota-
    tions, 147
  between modifier and
    word modified, 138,
    145
  with other punctuation
    marks, 148
  between preposition and
    its object, 145
  to separate restrictive

elements, 129–32, 146
between subject and
    verb, 144
after *such as* and *like*
    146
before *than* in compari-
    sons, 147
between verb and com-
    plement, 144

Variety, sentence, 119–21
Verbal modifiers, 128
Verbal phrases, 21–24
Verbals, 21–23
Verb phrases, 7, 21–24
Verbs, 5–7
  action, 5–6
  agreement with sub-
    jects, 44–50
  auxiliary, 7
  forms of, 65–68
  helping, 7
  intransitive, 6

irregular, 66–68
linking, 6, 48, 82–83
mood of, 76, 109
regular, 66
tenses of, 69–71, 304
transitive, 6
Voice, 78–81, 109–10

weak, week, 208
weather, whether, 208
well, good, 83–84
whether, weather, 208
which, that, 130
who, whom, 63–64
whoever, whomever, 64
whose, 57
whose, who's, 208
Word division, 194
write, right, rite, 208

yes, 136
you, 105
your, you're, 209

i. Contrasting phrases, interrogative elements
j. Expressions such as *he said*
k. Numbers, etc.
l. To avoid misreading

g. Faulty predication

20 Sentence Completeness *inc* 113
a. Comparisons
b. Omitted words

21 Parallelism // 115
a. Coordinate elements
b. Compared and contrasted ideas
c. Correlative constructions

22 Sentence Variety *var* 118
a. Beginnings
b. Structures
c. Forms

Punctuation 125

23 The Comma ⌃ 126
a. Main clauses
b. Introductory elements
c. Nonrestrictive elements
d. Parenthetical expressions
e. Interjections, direct address, *yes*, *no*
f. In a series
g. Coordinate adjectives
h. Absolute phrases

24 Unnecessary Commas *no* , 144
a. Between subject and verb
b. Between verb and object
c. Between preposition and object
d. Between adjective and word it modifies
e. With compound elements
f. With restrictive elements
g. After *such as* and *like*
h. Before and after a series
i. Indirect quotations
j. Before *than*
k. With periods, etc.

25 The Semicolon ; 151
a. Main clauses without conjunctions
b. Main clauses with conjunctive adverbs
c. Long main clauses
d. In a series
e. Misuses

26 The Colon : 155
a. Introducing a series
b. With *the following* and *as follows*
c. Separating main clauses

d. Preceding final appositives
e. Introducing long quotations
f. With subtitles, etc.
g. With formal salutations
h. Misuses

27 The Dash — 158
a. For parenthetical elements
b. Preceding a series
c. For emphasis and clarity
d. For breaks in tone
e. Preceding an author's name

28 Quotation Marks " " 159
a. Direct quotations
b. Titles
c. Words used in a special sense
d. With other punctuation
e. Single quotation marks

29 The Ellipsis Mark . . . 166
a. Omissions in quotations
b. Omissions in prose and poetry
c. Unfinished statements

30 Parentheses ( ) 168
a. Enclosing parenthetical elements
b. Labeling a series

31 Brackets [ ] 170

32 The Slash / 170

33 End Punctuation . ? ! 171

a. Periods in statements, etc.
b. Periods with abbreviations
c. Question mark
d. Question mark within parentheses
e. Exclamation Point

Mechanics 175

34 Capitals *cap/lc* 176
a. First word of sentence
b. *O*, *I*, *I've*, and *I'm*
c. Titles of works
d. Direct quotations and dialogue
e. Poetry
f. Proper nouns and adjectives
g. Titles and degrees
h. Abbreviations
i. Common mistakes

35 The Apostrophe ⌄ 184
a. Possessive case
b. Possessive pronouns
c. Contractions
d. Plurals of letters, etc.

36 Abbreviations *ab* 187
a. Titles before proper names
b. Titles following proper names
c. Corporations, etc.
d. Common abbreviations
e. Footnotes, etc.
f. Common mistakes

37 Italics *ital* 190
a. Titles of works
b. Spacecraft, etc.
c. Foreign words and phrases